The Design of
TEILHARD DE CHARDIN

The Design of
TEILHARD
DE CHARDIN

An Essay in Theological Reflection

by PIET SMULDERS, S.J.

Introduction by CHRISTIAN D'ARMAGNAC, S.J.
Translated by ARTHUR GIBSON

The Newman Press NP Westminster, Maryland, 1967

The English translation has been made from *La Vision de Teilhard de Chardin,* published by Desclée de Brouwer, Bruges, in 1964. The French edition was a translation and adaptation of the 3rd Dutch edition (Desclée de Brouwer, Bruges, 1963) by Augustin Kerkvoorde, O.S.B., and Christian d'Armagnac, S.J. Copyright © 1964 by Desclée de Brouwer.

INTRODUCTION TO THE FRENCH TRANSLATION

It would be a mistake for any reader to allow himself to be checked by an initial feeling of surfeit at the prospect of "another book on Teilhard." The work here presented in translation can be compared in depth and thoroughness only with that of Georges Crespy and that of P. Henri de Lubac. It is the work of a theologian. Father Smulders is professor of theology in the Maastricht (Holland) Jesuit scholasticate. And he has taken a different approach from that of previous books on Teilhard. Not content with a simple global analysis of the thought of Father Teilhard nor with a positioning of the problems raised by that thought, Father Smulders has chosen a limited number of questions, important at once in the thought of Teilhard and in present-day theologizing. Smulders treats Teilhard as a witness of his age but goes beyond the terms in which Teilhard poses these questions for us and treats the questions for their own sake, offering us theological reflections which are most interesting, especially to anyone not a specialist in this area; the matter is treated in depth but the style and terminology are not forbidding nor overly technical. The problems broached are thus clarified from a deeper, broader, and more detached point of view.

The reader is thus introduced into present-day thinking on religion, on points as important as the theological sense of the first chapters of Genesis (Chapter 3), the nature of the soul and the body (Chapter 4), the hope of the human race (Chapters 5 to 7), original sin and monogenism (Appendixes III and IV), Teilhard's spirituality (Chapters 8 to 11), and the cosmic role of Christ and the Eucharist (Chapter 11). On some of these points, Smulders himself admits that his analysis of Teilhard's writings is not exhaustive; thus some of Smulders' judgments are open to modification, for example, those relative to Teilhard's statistically grounded optimism concerning the success of the future evolution of humanity (Chapter 7): we feel that this optimism in Teilhard is a "phenomenological" computation rather than a final "solution" or doctrine of salvation; the salvation of the individual human being is really of infinite importance for Teilhard and *it comes only from Christ*, as Teilhard repeats even in the writings of his last years.

In any case, Father Smulders' work is a step forward in the intellectual pioneering which Teilhard himself hoped to set in motion.

This translation includes some small additions and refinements of the Dutch text, made in cooperation with the author, to take account of recently published writings by and about Teilhard.

C. D'ARMAGNAC, S.J.

PREFACE

Teilhard's whole thinking aims at a confrontation and a synthesis of the Christian faith and evolutionist cosmology; his ultimate aim was a new motivation of the Christian orientation, based on this synthesis. Since theology is scientific reflection on the faith, it is bound to take cognizance of Teilhard's theorizing and spirituality, to test their value, to examine the degree to which they can contribute to a Christian way of thinking and intellectual posture keyed to our present age.

The present work thus has three objectives: first, to provide a brief theological outline and preliminary evaluation, as detached and objective as possible, of the cosmology and salvation theology proper to Teilhard; secondly, to institute a comparison of this design with the traditional Catholic teaching; finally, to sketch the tentative outline of a possible integration of the two. In our essay, consequently, certain elements of the Teilhardian design must be accorded an emphasis somewhat different from that which he gave them, while others (few in number and obviously subsidiary) can scarcely be built in at all; nevertheless, the over-all picture here presented can constitute an important fertilization and enrichment of theological thought.

Nor can this study limit itself strictly to Teilhard's ideas; it must take account of other problems involved in the confrontation of evolutionism and Christianity. Many Christians will indeed discover in Teilhard's writings the cogency and import of the theory of evolution and be compelled to initiate a critical evaluation of certain notions intimately bound up with their own faith and, at the same time, with a vision of the world differing from ours and of disputed value.

vii

On the other hand, it is not the office of the theologian to discuss the scientific value of Teilhard's evolutionist views nor yet to formulate any judgment on the appropriateness or efficacy of his phenomenological method. In this area, we can present only a brief summary of what is indispensable to an accurate understanding of his ideas. The author must ask indulgence in these areas where he is not a specialist.

The author asks the same indulgence for the theological area. This work is an *essay in theological reflection* and the word *essay* must be taken literally. It would be pointless and even foolhardy to aim at giving a definitive solution to the many and varied problems posed for the theologian by Teilhard's ideas, on points on which there are as yet few competent works. For the same reason, these problems have necessarily been treated with varying degrees of thoroughness. Some of them it has been possible to study fairly adequately in a rather brief exposition. Others would require a whole volume to themselves. The author hopes he has given a sufficient idea and evaluation of the problems posed for theological thought by Teilhard's views and indicated the general line along which a reciprocal integration can and should be sought.

This can be no more than a preliminary essay because Teilhard's works are not yet known in their entirety. Even his published writings do not always clearly reveal their exact intention: were they intended for publication or were they private jottings in which the author was trying to clarify his own thought or to submit it to a small number of specialists? Often the published works do not tell us. So it seems still premature to attempt any history of the crystallization of the Teilhardian system, a history of which may be of capital importance for the definitive interpretation and evaluation of this system. We have, however, indicated the dates of our quotations, with the exception of those from the great works whose dates are well known to the reader.[1] Thus, a distinction can be made between the writings dating from the stage of exciting discoveries, those of the stage of development, and those emanating from a maturity of which the author was himself aware.

Although this study can be no more than a preliminary essay, it cannot be postponed. The very wide circulation of Teilhard's works and the considerable echo they have evoked make it necessary that some elements of reflection be afforded readers, in view of the confrontation between partially new conceptions and the old notions in the area of religion. This work is not intended exclusively for those who have had the benefit of a formal theological training; it is directed to wider circles. Reflection on the faith is no longer the monopoly of the priests; the laity also feel the need and the duty of possessing and justifying to themselves and the world an exact notion of their faith.[2] It is precisely the layman, whose mind is being moulded daily by science and technology in the world in which he lives, who recognizes his own problems in the problematic of Teilhard and who ought to be helped to transform Teilhard's conceptions by critical personal reflection upon them. In order to enable our readers to form for themselves a broader idea of Teilhard's notions, we have taken our quotations with preferences from his other writings rather than from the best-seller *The Phenomenon of Man*. Matters of a more technical nature, not essential for an understanding of the grand design of Teilhard, have been relegated to footnotes and appendices.

Two groups of readers will perhaps think that our study has a tendency to warp Teilhard's ideas to the bias of traditional theology. One of these groups will suspect an attempt to save Teilhard's orthodoxy; the other group will suspect an effort to stifle his revolutionary flame. Thus it will not be out of place to say a few words here in self-justification.

The author of this work is a professor of dogmatic theology, his special areas of interest being Patristics and the history of dogma. For twenty years, he has been endeavoring to reveal the continuity between the thought of the Fathers of the ancient Church, the thinking of the great masters of Scholasticism in the Middle Ages, and contemporary theological thought. His daily task and favorite occupation has been to take an interest in remote and unaccustomed notions, to probe for and discover common thought beneath surface divergences, to build bridges between antiquity and modern times. He has been steadily strengthened in his conviction that all the great Catholic thinkers have been animated by the same intuitions and that there is room in Christian thought for a living evolution, though not for a violent revolution. Perhaps this bias of mind has enabled him to navigate better than others in the world of Teilhardian thought which certainly makes an initial impression of strange newness on one trained in the school of Scholastic philosophy; perhaps it has enabled him to recognize, under outward forms sometimes deceptive, the authentic Catholic intuition.

The author has always endeavored to enrich modern Catholic thinking by dipping sympathetically into the world of faith of antiquity and of the Middle Ages, a world with a bias often quite different from our own; he believes just as firmly that present-day theology can be enriched by dipping, with sympathy and equanimity, into the thought of Teilhard. This thought demands a critical examination just as does the thought of antiquity. This critique will be pertinent only if it is based on a sincere and receptive understanding which succeeds in revealing the Spirit rather than trammeling it.

PIET SMULDERS

FROM THE PREFACE TO THE
SECOND EDITION

. . . On 30 June 1962, a *Monitum* concerning Teilhard was issued by the Supreme Congregation of the Holy Office. Bishops, religious superiors, and rectors of clerical training institutions were urged by this *Monitum* "to protect minds, especially young minds, against the dangers of the works of Father Teilhard de Chardin and of his supporters." Reference was made to the "inaccuracies and even serious errors" in philosophical and theological matters with which these works "teem." Several of the expressions used indicate that the Holy Office wishes primarily to warn against the blind and infatuated Teilhardianism of which symptoms can be observed in several parts of the world.

But the author is confident that no serious reader of his study will be numbered among the "blind partisans" of Teilhard, against whom the *Monitum* warns: that is the real meaning of the Latin word *asseclae* used in this document. He hopes on the contrary that he has, in his own way, contributed to forewarn the readers and admirers of Teilhard against the dangers of Teilhard's works. . . . Without concealing his high regard and deep admiration for Teilhard's thought, the author has attempted to aid the reader in maintaining this critical attitude which renders this thought genuinely fruitful. In the words of St. Paul: "Do not stifle the utterances of the Spirit, do not hold prophecy in low esteem; and yet you must scrutinize it all carefully, retaining only what is good . . ." (I Thess. 5: 19 ff.).

P. S.

CONTENTS

CONTENTS

The Design of

TEILHARD DE CHARDIN

THE MAN AND HIS WORK

In the course of my life, through my whole life, the world has kindled by degrees, taken fire before my eyes, until permeated all about me with an interior radiance. . . . Purple glimmers of matter changing imperceptibly to the gold of Spirit, mounting the spectrum to the ultimate incandescence of the Cosmo-Personal. . . . The diaphany of the Divine in the heart of a universe aflame, of the Divine radiating from the depths of a Matter on fire: that is what I am going to try to reveal momentarily and communicate here.[1]

CHAPTER I

We are already in possession of excellent biographies of Teilhard. No figure of modern times can have been the object of a more careful and warily sympathetic study than that on Teilhard by Claude Cuénot.[2] Yet it seems useful to present at first Teilhard the man to the reader of this work, the rest of which is exclusively devoted to his ideas. For few men have been so entirely absorbed in their ideas and rarely have ideas spilled so directly from the intimate personal life of a man. A familiarity with the man is essential for a good grasp of his teaching.

Pierre Teilhard de Chardin was born on May 1, 1881, in Sarcenat, seven kilometers west of Clermont-Ferrand, in those mountains of Auvergne which have been called the paradise of the geologists. From his father, a true country gentleman who cultivated his lands and devoted himself to amateur scientific researches, Pierre inherited a love for nature. But curiously enough, the boy was less interested in the living plants and animals, so fragile and so perishable, than he was in the stones and rocks of his native region. He was later to link this preference with the almost religious veneration which he accorded, while still a child, to certain objects which were for him a symbol of solidity and durability: an old ploughshare, a stone. Was this a precocious nostalgia for elementary and intangible realities?

He attended high school at the college of Mongré, where Henri Bremond was one of his teachers. Bremond later recalled this "pupil from Auvergne, very intelligent, first in every subject, but disconcertingly sophisticated. Even the most restive or dull-witted boys sometimes took a real interest in their work. . . . Not so this boy and it was only long afterwards that I learnt the secret of his seeming indifference. Transporting his mind far away from us was a jealous and absorbing passion—rocks."[3]

After his graduation from the college, he entered the novitiate of the Jesuits in Aix-en-Provence on March 20, 1899. He followed the normal course: three years of philosophy, several years of college teaching, four years of theology, culminating in his ordination to the priesthood on August 24, 1911. An ordinary training but accomplished under extraordinary circumstances. In 1902, the religious were expelled from France. Teilhard took his philosophy on the island of Jersey, did his college teaching in Cairo, studied theology in Hastings (Sussex, England). Each of these regions served him as an occasion for geological researches: the geological structure of Jersey, the molluscs and insect fossils of Egypt. In England he was in touch with Dawson, discoverer and probably perpetrator of the hoax of the Piltdown Man, and with Smith Woodward, curator of the geological section of the British Museum: it was from these contacts that his interest for human paleontology derived.

In the early days of his priesthood he was sent to cultivate his taste for geology by technical studies, from 1912 to 1914, in Paris, notably under the direction of Marcellin Boule. But in December, 1914, he was called up for military service and a few weeks later joined a regiment of Moroccan infantry at the front as a stretcher-bearer. Even in the trenches he was gathering the initial material for a thesis on the mammals of the Later Eocene epoch, a thesis he was to defend in 1922 at the Sorbonne.

Surprisingly enough, these years spent at the front—Yser, Verdun, the Oise—were crucial for his development, not only because he there acquired the physical endurance and spiritual hardiness required by his later toil in the outposts of the civilized world, but chiefly because his thought and his personal religious practice there found their own mould. For the young man who had always lived in a sheltered environment, life at the front was "a baptism into reality."[4] There he discovered himself, there he discovered his fellows, the world, his God and the task assigned by God to his life for humanity. The many letters that he wrote to his cousin and confidante, Marguerite Teillard-Chambon,[5] helped him to a greater clarity in his understanding of himself, and convey the impression of his struggles with the problems that were to dominate his life, the dawning of the intuitions that were to develop later on.[6] It was an unremitting confrontation with the ultimate realities of existence: life and death; contact with the human animal in his weird mixture of pettiness, vulgarity and heroism; amazement at the unity that can be engendered by a common need or effort among men of different languages, cultures or nationalities; prayer and meditation to find God in everything, down to the harsh reality of every day; the constant effort and sometimes the deep personal happiness of being able to show Christ to men who did not know him or who had forgotten him.

In 1916, he began writing a series of religious and philosophical essays, in the hope that the light he had discovered might enlighten his friends. Some of these essays are more philosophical in tone, others have more the style of prayers and mystical considerations; all revolve around the problems posed by the relations between the material reality of this world and the divine, by the Christian interpretation of this-worldly activity, by the possibility of meeting and serving Christ in all things.[7]

After his demobilization in early 1919, he resumed his university studies. From 1920 he held the chair of geology in the

Institut Catholique in Paris. But he preferred field explorations. In 1923, he accepted an invitation by his confrere E. Licent to take part in a (subsidized) mission of the Paris Museum: an excavation in China. During the summer of 1923 and the spring of 1924, the two Jesuits worked in expeditions in the Ordos, a mass of mountains in Northwest China, bordering on the Gobi Desert. Teilhard succeeded in clarifying somewhat the geology of the eastern part of the continent of Asia. But his chief discovery was a rich stock of paleolithic tools, first proof of the presence of prehistoric man in the region south of the Yenisei.[8] Cases of documents were dispatched to Paris and Tientsin. It was during these months that Teilhard composed one of his most lyrical religious texts, *La Messe sur le monde*, dated symbolically Ordos, Easter, 1923[9] and developing a theme of past years at the front. A year and a half later, he returned to Paris.

There he set his discoveries in order, made study trips to Belgium and England. But a storm was brewing on his teachings. In his absence, some private notes on original sin and monogenism, written by Teilhard the geologist and displayed without his consent, brought on a denunciation.[10] Shortly after his return, he signed a declaration at the request of his superiors; but this did not suffice to dissipate the distrust directed against his teachings. Probably a contributing factor in the increase and intensification of this distrust was the zeal with which Teilhard preached evolutionism on every possible occasion. No doubt another complicating factor was his close ties with the philosopher Edouard Le Roy, who asserts his great debt to Teilhard in several of his works written in these years.[11] Now the orthodoxy of Le Roy's thinking on creation and evolution was keenly disputed. The whole controversy ended by Teilhard resigning his professorship, at the instance of his superiors, and leaving again for China in early 1925.

Peking was to remain his base of operations until the end of World War II. Teilhard himself felt this to be an exile, not in the sense of a punishment, but because the fact of not being able to reside in Paris is tantamount to an exile for any French scholar. He did spend a few months in Paris at intervals, to give lectures and renew his spiritual contacts. He also made study trips and lecture tours in Somalia, Burma, the Indies, Java and the United States. But China remained his main field of labor. He was attached, as scientific associate, to the Geological Survey of China. He took part in several expeditions in various regions of China and neighboring countries. During these years, he published many scientific studies on the paleontology and geology of East Asia. In this field, he ranked as one of the great specialists. He also took part, as a Survey expert and paleontologist, in the Chu-Ku-Tien excavations. After the discovery there in 1929 of the first skull of Homo Sinanthropos, Teilhard afforded proof of his geological age; he seems also to have been the first to give a precise interpretation of the traces of human culture recovered in Chu-Ku-Tien. On the sudden death of his friend Davidson Black, director of the excavations, Teilhard took personal charge of the excavations for several months.[12] These years put him in the vanguard of paleontology. In addition, by his correspondence and his personal contacts in Paris, New York and Peking, which became an extraordinary international meeting place, he wove that close web of friendly relations with the leading figures of geology and paleontology which was so typical a feature of his personality.

Even while engaged in this intensive and fruitful scientific endeavor, he found the time and energy to reflect on religious and spiritual questions. His correspondence attests this, notably his letters to Marguerite Teillard-Chambon which have been published in part.[13] He used his free time and the enforced leisure of his sea voyages to formlulate his ideas in a great number of essays, intended for his close associates and friends but often widely circulated, and in articles published in various reviews. This long Chinese period is framed primarily by his two principal works. During the winter of 1926–27, after completing the study of the scientific material accumulated during the preceding season, he composed *Le Milieu divin*, which he himself called "a little treatise on the spiritual life" and which is a synthesis of his spiritual experiences of the preceding twelve years.[14] But an untoward concatenation of circumstances prevented the publication of the manuscript. Any publication of a member of the Society of Jesus must be approved by two censors. The censors of *Le Milieu divin* were "very favorable" and Teilhard's friend, Pierre Charles, accepted the book for publication in the well-known collection *Museum Lessianum,* published by the Jesuits of Louvain. In July, 1929, they informed him that the manuscript had been put into the hands of the printer. But an anonymous reader who had laid hands on a mimeographed copy alerted the authorities in Rome and the publication was stopped.[15]

In the period from 1938 to 1940 Teilhard composed *Le Phénomène humain,* which he completed in June, 1940. Another conspiracy of circumstances prevented this work as well from appearing until after the death of the author.[16] When he returned to Europe after World War II and submitted the work to the censors, they made certain objections. Teilhard added some observations of which he himself said, "I think these retouchings have improved my original draft."[17] That was the state of the matter when in late 1948 there erupted in France and Rome the storm over what was called "the new theology": the multigraphed writings of Teilhard were one of the storm centers. His superiors, fearing to add fuel to the flames, did not give permission to publish. It is in this work, translated into several languages, that Teilhard's reputation was established outside of specialist circles and his vision of the world found at last its unique expression. More even than *Le Milieu divin* and the essays of the first period, this work is penetrated and sustained by scientific evolutionism. Starting from the data of his own science, Teilhard develops a vision of the world and of man designed to be acceptable to any impartial observer, Christian or no. It is a vision which bridges the span of evolution from the distant past to the future development of mankind but whose bias is explicitly Christian.

Teilhard made his headquarters during World War II in Peking where he was able to pursue his scientific work in the capital's laboratories and libraries as well as in the immediately adjacent countryside. Before a very limited colony of foreigners, Teilhard gave during these years several lectures, outstanding among his works of popularization for their concise and zestful exposition of his ideas. The lack of intellectual stimulation, resulting from the impossibility of exchanging ideas with the best minds of world science, was nonetheless a grievous deprivation as was the separation from France.

After Japan's surrender, passport delays prevented Teilhard's leaving China until March, 1946. Unaware that he would never see China again, he had left books and notes in Peking which have since been lost. In May, 1946, he arrived back in Paris, renewing old friendships and initiating new ones. He gave many lectures and engaged in varying degrees of controversy with Berdiaev on Marxism and Existentialism, with Gabriel Marcel on the spiritual value of human structures and institutions, with Lavelle on the meaning of matter, with Hippolyte on the future of man. The offer of a Chair in the Collège de France was a recognition of his status in the world of French science and thought. Teilhard referred this matter to his religious superior in Rome and spoke with him personally about the matter; after prolonged hesitation, permission was refused. Teilhard was, however, permitted to give a series of courses in the winter semester, 1949–50, in the Sorbonne; these were expanded into *Le Groupe zoologique humain*,[18] a sober and balanced synopsis of Teilhard's global vision of nature. In May, 1950, he was elected member of the Academy of Sciences.

A serious illness forced postponement of Teilhard's study trip to South Africa, where the excitement caused by the discovery of Australopithecus was at its height. In the spring of 1948, Teilhard undertook a visit of several months in the United States, where he met again with many of his old friends. In the United States, Teilhard was able to expound his ideas in various scientific circles and before a wider audience as well, propagating his ideal of a new anthropology that would include in its subject matter man as a spiritual being and would aim at indicating the direction of the future evolution of mankind and preparing the conditions necessary for this evolution. This American visit resulted in an invitation to Teilhard in 1951 from the Viking Fund (later to become the Wenner Gren Foundation); to this institute for the encouragement and support of anthropological studies, Teilhard was to remain attached as scientific associate until his death. His new headquarters was New York where he compiled a written

7

outline of a very extensive program of anthropological studies, to be pursued in collaboration by various specialists. He was entrusted by the Viking Fund with two study trips to South and Central Africa. His commission was twofold: he was to procure, for himself and his employers, a clear idea of the researches being conducted in Africa; and he was to use his extensive experience in China and his far-ranging international contacts to assist in coordinating the work of the various teams. In the summer of 1954, he had occasion to make a last trip to France.

During this period, Teilhard edited various religious and scientific essays. These were not intended for publication, for since 1947 his superiors had asked him not to deal with philosophical and theological problems. The new essays were intended for the circle of disciples and admirers which had formed around Teilhard, mainly in France. Some of these essays, such as *Comment je vois* (1948) and *Le Christique* (1955), are explicitly theological in subject matter. As we shall show later on in this study, Teilhard presents in these essays several valuable notions with a kind of blunt temerity reminiscent of his first essays. The essay *Le Coeur de la matière* (1950) is a kind of autobiographical sketch of the development of his ideas. These essays have not yet been published.

On his return from his French visit in the autumn of 1954, the now septuagenarian Teilhard was feeling the physical and psychological effects of these crowded months of unremitting effort. More than ever in the period since his war years at the front he was engrossed by the thought of death: "I am going to Him who is coming." On March 15, 1955, he told friends he hoped he would die on Easter Sunday, the feast of his own *Messe sur le monde*. On Holy Saturday he went to confession and on Easter Sunday, April 10, 1955, assisted at Mass in St. Patrick's Cathedral. In the afternoon, at the house of friends, he was felled by a heart seizure; regaining consciousness for a moment, he died a few minutes later, on this great day of the Resurrection of the Lord whom Teilhard had served and sought his whole life long.

* * *

What I should like is to construct a continuous series of phenomena, extending, under the action of a fundamentally unique evolutional process, from the spiritual to the material pole of experience. As you know, my "hobby" is showing that science is marking time and turning its back on religion, simply because science has never attempted to integrate its *thought* into their systems. It is towards history, then, that I am tending, rather than towards metaphysics.[19]

This brief outline of Teilhard's career may suffice to give the reader an idea of his personality and of the world in which he moved. He was one of the great names in paleontology who, during the last half century, threw such a vivid light on the origin of humanity and on the place of man in the world. Very highly esteemed, he maintained numerous and very amicable contacts with his fellow scientists and, indeed, with the representatives of all the natural sciences. He proved himself an excellent companion on long expeditions, a devoted collaborator, persevering and intelligent, in every team of which he made part in fieldwork or in laboratories, a lively and stimulating conversationalist. He was entirely at home in the fascinating world of men and ideas which constitutes the vanguard of modern science; he knew the thrill of the great discoveries of modern science and technology.

But in this environment, often so alien to religion, Teilhard always behaved as a believer, as a member of a religious order, as a priest, not as a man of science who was incidentally a priest nor yet like a priest who was incidentally a man of science. His faith as a priest inspired his scientific work and thought; his scientific thought assumed the aspect of a genuine creed. The following study will simply illustrate the harmony of this Christian faith and this scientific thought, with a final section being devoted to the essential outlines of the spirituality expressed and developed out of this integral unity. We limit ourselves here to a preliminary sketch of the scientific ideal which motivated Teilhard.

First, a word about his conflicts with his religious superiors. His faith and his loyalty to the Catholic Church were never shaken. He did indeed deplore the pusillanimous conservatism displayed by many of his fellow Catholics and even by some members of the hierarchy, for he felt that the Church could and should be in the vanguard of human progress.[20] Any failure of the Church to respond to this ideal caused him suffering and even at times aroused him to a holy indignation; but this was precisely because of his passionate belief in the Church and his sincere love for her. In his early years, he expressed this stand in a "Beatitude": "Blessed are they who suffer at not seeing the Church as fair as they would wish and who are only the more submissive and prayerful for it."[21]

At the end of his life, he declared: "In truth (and in virtue of the very structure of the whole of my thought), I feel myself today more irrevocably bound to the hierarchical Church than I have ever been at any point in my entire life."[22]

He was convinced that his membership in his own Order formed "my particular point of engagement and of activity in the universe" ordained for him by God.[23] The painful and restrictive decisions of superiors may be the way in which God realizes His plan for an individual. Sometimes God sends harsh trials to those who are his special instruments, while at the same time surprising them with encouraging consolations.[24] Father Teilhard felt the pain of exile in leaving Paris for China in 1926. But the part this transfer enabled him to play shortly afterward in several discoveries, notably that of Sinanthropus, was a compensation which seemed to Teilhard a providential confirmation of his personal mission. Teilhard's superiors repeatedly showed distrust of his ideas, thwarting their propagation and trammeling the very venture they had entrusted to him. These displays of distrust were for Teilhard bitter disappointments and very severe trials, requiring on his part great and stalwart trust in God in order to persevere in his mission and in his submission. He always comported himself as an exemplary priest and Jesuit. An American fellow Jesuit, himself an eminent scholar, who knew Teilhard from 1948, wrote recently: "He was a man of unalloyed holiness, manly personal integrity and deep human sympathy, and of an astonishing degree of childlike conscientiousness and humility . . . He kept the rules of the Society, not with ordinary correctness but with intense delicacy of childlike exactitude."[25] At the second climax of the difficulties caused by his ideas and his influence, he could write in all sincerity to the Jesuit General in Rome: "Despite certain appearances, I am resolved to remain a 'son of obedience.' "[26] His goal in his works and in his thinking was not personal prestige and vindication but rather the building up of the Kingdom of God and of the Body of Christ which is the Church: "My only ambition is to be cast into the foundations of the rising edifice of the future."[27] Teilhard believed firmly that any work accomplished in self-immolating love was bound to bear fruit in God's good time.

The clashes with his superiors certainly did not originate in the area of personal relations, where there was a perfect accord between the real esteem and solicitude of his superiors and Teilhard's own humility and obedience, an accord which can perhaps only be understood by those who have had personal experience of religious obedience and especially Ignatian obedience. Teilhard wrote from Rome: "I have had several conversations with the authorities in an atmosphere of complete confidence and friendship."[28] But there was a persistent and profound misunderstanding on the nature and goal of his scientific activity. His superiors had assigned him the study of paleontology. There is no doubt that they were disturbed by the zeal with which Teilhard propagated evolutionary theory. But they recognized his great competence in his own scientific field and valued his will to excell in the venture entrusted to him. Teilhard had no difficulty in obtaining their approbation, collaboration, and full support for his researches and his scientific journeys. He was never restricted in any way so far as his strictly technical and scientific publications were concerned. But this was for Teilhard only the less-important half of his scientific activity. He held that science could not content itself with studying the origins and primitive history of man nor could the scientific method be limited to the analysis and indexing of fossil finds; science must aim at a study of the human being in his past and in his future. He regarded it as his personal, apostolic, and sacerdotal vocation to start from technical specialization and forge a path to these vast horizons. He believed that his own personal experience had revealed to him that this cosmological area could form the nexus between modern science and religion, a channel of ingress into the Christian message. This divergence of opinion on the true office of science resulted in Teilhard's superiors' continually urging him to limit himself to science and not to venture into philosophy or theology, while Teilhard was always recurring to theses which were, in the eyes of his superiors, philosophical and theological.

Even as Teilhard, the trained paleontologist, was writing a continuing series of important articles on the development of life on earth, Teilhard the man was steadily losing interest in this aspect of his field of specialization. As early as 1916, he was questioning whether the history of life in the distant past still had any great number of new horizons to offer. This change in perspective, which caused him to search for a synthesis[29] as well as an analysis of the primordial elements, made him ask whether the history of life ought not to be able to reveal something about the future of the earth and of man.[30] Ten years later, his attitude on this matter had hardened:

> Intellectually I am still very interested in technical geological researches in a field and in a geographical area still full of things to be discovered. But I feel that I have been attracted, especially during the last two years, more and more to the study of present-day man rather than prehistoric man . . . I am discovering human extensions of geology.[31]

Certainly geology and paleontology would always continue to be for Teilhard subjects of passionate interest. But within geology, he was discovering an anthropological dimension: how could the science of the earth remain indifferent to the vast terrestrial phenomenon constituted by life and especially by the fact of man? The study of human evolution inevitably points to the future; if man is a child of evolution and has been evolving to the present time, it is inescapable that the problem should be posed of his future evolution. Teilhard's center of interest shifted from the past to the present and toward the future. He began to be interested in the past less for itself than for the light it could shed on the present state of man, for the law and message for the future that might be found in that past. In an article on the significance of the science of paleontology, published in 1935 in *Etudes*, he notes: "What more can be demanded of these inanimate remains than their confirmation of the opportunities still open for advances by the living?"[32]

There followed a series of essays during the thirties in which Teilhard's own thought was using the technical science of evolution as a mere point of departure for an examination of the future open to man and of the attitudes to be taken in the face of this evolution. In these writings, Teilhard's scientific speculations assumed such unexpected dimensions—he himself called some of his own speculations visionary to the point of the fantastic[33]— that the ecclesiastical authorities were put on their guard and the opposition of professional theologians was aroused. Teilhard does, indeed, seem to be crossing the frontiers of science and invading the realms of philosophy and theology. Never hitherto had man attempted to explore and chart his own future himself; the Christian world had borrowed exclusively from revelation the picture of that future. Teilhard went on to sketch certain principles, attitudes, and lines of conduct in function of this plan of the future, amounting to a kind of ethic, which had always been considered the purlieu of philosophy and theology. He seemed to be getting entirely out of his own field into that of the other disciplines. And his manner of speaking was disturbing and even alarming to others. He would speak in the same breath of the atom and man's longing for eternity, of the evolution of life and of the love of God and neighbor. In 1936, Teilhard wrote in the covering letter accompanying an essay he was submitting to a friend of his, a fellow Jesuit: "I am like a bull in the china shop of scholastic thought. Try to forget my clumsiness and understand what I am trying to say."[34]

These essays, of which the most fully developed specimen is *The Phenomenon of Man*, do not pretend to be philosophy or theology properly speaking; rather they aim at being a kind of "hyperscience." Other writings of Teilhard, like *The Divine Milieu*, are efforts to sketch a sprituality; they are a reflection on the reality of the life of faith and of Christian perfection. Teilhard is consciously theologizing in these writings, as also in the essays written during the war years and several writings of subsequent years that are exclusively philosophical or theological. We shall encounter in the course of our study several examples of the ideas Teilhard developed in these writings. His defective expression of a basic intuition that is sometimes superb and of sterling worth is probably due to his lack of familiarity with the apparatus of metaphysics and theology. The importance of this group of philosophical and theological writings lies in the light they shed upon the motivation dominating all his endeavors. But these writings are not typical of his personal style and method which can be better observed in the *Phenomenon of Man* and the many writings after 1930 in which he attempted a synthesis.

Teilhard sometimes calls this method a "hyperphysics" or a "hyperbiology,"[35] but his favorite designation for it is a "phenomenology," i.e., a science of phenomena. But he is not here using the terms *phenomena* and *phenomenology* in the fixed meaning they have acquired in the wake of the theories and conclusions of a Husserl or a Sartre. These thinkers use the term to designate the phenomenon as phenomenon, i.e., as it appears to man, enters into human knowledge, and there finds its meaning and value. Their phenomenology aims at a "description and clarification of the meaning of phenomena of *perception* or of operations of the *spirit*, the *vital principle*."[36] This phenomenology is thus closely allied to psychology and logic and could be called introspective and subjective. For Teilhard, on the contrary, the word *phenomenon* retains its primordial signification, its prephilosophic meaning: it includes everything presenting itself as an objective datum to human cognition and experience. Teilhard's phenomenology is thus "extroverted," turned toward the objective factual reality of things and of the world. It is intimately allied to the natural sciences. Even man and his subjectivity, his consciousness and his liberty are studied rather as objects. Man is just as much the center of reference for Teilhard as for the great phenomenologists but for a very different reason:[37] for the phenomenologists, man is the center of reference because it is the human mind in operation which confers divergent meanings on things and relations; for Teilhard, man is the center of reference because he constitutes objectively the crown and goal of evolution and thus its meaning.[38]

Teilhard describes his own phenomenology as "purely and simply *scientific* treatise," whose object is "man solely as a phenomenon" and "the whole phenomenon."[39] It is a reflection he wishes to present, not a simple analysis or description of phenomena, but this reflection remains on the level of science itself, not ascending into the realm of philosophy proper. Teilhard is not seeking, like the philosopher, for the ultimate principles and causes of being, but rather for the bond between things, and he is seeking this nexus as it appears at the level of science itself. It is on this level that he tries to discover and delineate "a coherent order between consequents and antecedents."[40] And so the principle according to which this order must be structured will be a principle of scientific validity: the principle of evolution, assigning to every terrestrial reality its proper place in the process of becoming, the law of "interiorizing complexification"[41] (Teilhard's own phrase, implying a simultaneous intensification of complexity of structure and interiority, i.e., internally motivated operation), which envelops the sum total of phenomena in a limpid unity. The ideal of such a phenomenology is: "a connected series of phenomena, extending from the spiritual pole of existence to the material pole, under the action of an evolutionary process which is fundamentally one and the same throughout."[42]

This phenomenology is not identical with science, although it does have as its object phenomena as they present themselves to science. Teilhard's phenomenology is rather a "hyperphysics" or a "hyperbiology" and Teilhard himself compares it to the φῠσική of the Greeks, which also strove to synthesize the sum total of contemporary scientific knowledge into a single homogeneous design.[43] Teilhard reproaches contemporary sciences with limiting themselves to a closed area of investigation: physics studies the laws of matter but excludes animate matter; biology studies life but excludes human life;[44] anthropology and the allied sciences dealing with man study the life and history of the human race but take little or no account of prehuman reality. Teilhard opposes to this fragmentation a scientific reflection that would envelop the *sum total* of phenomena, bringing to light their structure and unity. This new science would integrate the data of the specialized sciences and transcend their limitations to embrace the whole of terrestrial reality from primordial matter to immatered spirit, man. Its aim would be the blending of all the data and all the reaches of human experience into a single cosmic design extending from chemistry and physics to history and the science of religion. And its instrument would be a principle itself borrowed from experience and vindicated by experience.

The biological doctrine of evolution is the point of departure for this venture. Biology, the home ground of evolutionary teaching, occupies a privileged central position, inasmuch as its subject matter extends from the deepest material roots of life to its flowering in the loftiest spiritual specimens. Teilhard's scheme calls for a two-way bridge from biology to the sciences of inanimate nature on the one hand and to the sciences of consciousness up to its highest forms on the other. Even ethics and religion have their place in this scheme, a crucial and central place for the totality of the phenomena of life.[45] Thus did Teilhard conceive and record a vision of the world extending in a single homogeneous thrust from primordial matter to man and to the ultimate consummation of history, a cosmic evolutionary process marked by a gradual ascent toward ever-higher forms of existence and of life.

We do not intend to venture an estimate of the merits or the weaknesses of this ideal or of Teilhard's way of presenting it. Such an estimate is the business rather of the philosophers of nature and of science.[46] We shall limit ourselves in this introduction to a few remarks on the points at which Teilhard's thinking impinges upon philosophy and theology. The great design envisioned by Teilhard will leave more than one scientist sceptical; such a specialist will find it philosophical or even mystical. The philosopher and the theologian, for their part, are smitten with consternation at Teilhard's use of methods alien to their own field of specialization. Yet Rabut rightly draws attention to the profound impression that Teilhard's intuitive articulation is capable of producing on the "simple layman," the human individual whose reflection transcends the bounds of his own specialty and who surveys the global totality of available data with the eyes of a "generalist."[47] Modern man is suffering from the effects of a drastic specialization. Science has made astounding progress in every field; yet its insight into the global phenomena of the cosmos and of man is dimmer than ever. The peculiar fascination of Teilhard's thought is precisely that it transcends the limits of each and every specialized field and gravitates toward a global insight, an intuition of man as an integral whole. It imparts a genuinely human and even religious imprint to the most practical of the sciences, to those dealing most exclusively with material phenomena, to advances in technology and economics. Anyone following Teilhard's line of vision sees the whole of created nature directed toward man, and beyond man, toward the Son of God made man. Even at the level of scientific reflection, the material world is set toward man and man toward the edification of that humanity promised us by the revelation of the Mystical Body of Christ. Thus Teilhard's articulation provides a global interpretation of the world in its "entirety." This result may well be the best justification of the method employed. Is not every new science operative as an applied science before it has had its method buttressed by a reasoned justification?

Teilhard's meritorious global phenomenology would nevertheless profit from a critical analysis of the method employed in its articulation. He is continually insisting, in the essays we have cited, that he does not wish to philosophize; yet he inevitably uses principles that are, to a greater or lesser degree, precisely philosophical. He admits, in the preface to Le Phénomène humain, that his phenomenological articulation hinges on two propositions which he accepts as axioms: first, the primacy of spirit,[48] i.e., the ontologically superior value of the conscious over the unconscious or preconscious, and of conscious reflection over instinctive awareness; second, the "biological" value of the fact of society, i.e., the hypothesis that social consciousness is an enrichment of conscious reflection.[49] But he goes still further and, in the development of his thought, frequently appeals to principles that are strictly philosophical but which he himself does not always seem to have realized to be such; for example, the thesis, fundamental for Teilhard's evolutionism, that "there can be, in the Universe, no sudden terminal epiphany of anything . . . that has not first been obscurely primordial."[50] Another example is the principle "union differentiates,"[51] which Teilhard uses as the basis for his prophetic revelation of the evolution of mankind. The very aim of his phenomenology itself, namely, the blueprint for a coordinated interpolation of all phenomena into a single evolutionary process,[52] rests upon the conviction that the world is intelligible and that this intelligibility raised to act is always a knowing of unity. And finally, the way in which he deduces the existence and nature of the Omega Point, of the necessary conditions for human action,[53] is quite plainly in line with transcendental analysis, redolent of the most typically philosophical modes of thought. Teilhard's phenomenological articulation is thus much more philosophical in scope than he is willing to concede. Now philosophical principles require philosophical justification. The validity of the articulation can only profit from a thorough elucidation of these philosophical elements and a critical justification at the level of philosophy itself.

The global *Weltanschauung* of a convinced Christian like Teilhard obviously cannot but be intimately linked with his faith. Even apart from his specifically theological writings, the whole of his thought is obviously and undeniably animated by the Christian faith. The primacy of the spirit is for him a dogma of faith before it is a phenomenological datum; the Christian message was clearly instrumental to his discovery of the crucial role of love in the terminal evolution of man; his belief that the material world is a work bearing the signature of God is anterior to his demonstration that God is at the terminus and summit of evolution; he would probably have been unable to trace with such sure strokes the lineaments of Omega had he not already been acquainted with the mystery of the Body of Christ. Indeed he says as much in so many words.[54] Yet he is convinced that he has been led to these conclusions by a genuinely scientific phenomenology. Revelation does indeed provide him with a deeper and surer ground than could possibly be furnished by mere phenomenological reflection for defining the nature of the Omega as terminal point or fraternal love as the motive force of evolution. But Teilhard is convinced that an unbiased reflection on the sum total of phenomena would lead to conclusions gravitating, at least, toward the Christian doctrine and thus positively compatible with it.

We do not wish to enter at this point into the heart of this problem. The mutual relations between faith and the secular sciences such as psychology or the natural sciences constitute a point not yet sufficiently studied in depth and requiring a special study of its own. We prefer simply to trace the actual unfolding of Teilhard's thoughts and the objective development of his articulation. There is just one point we should like to deal with in some detail.

Both scientists and theologians were surprised at the fashion in which Teilhard deduced from his scientific phenomenology the set of the whole of created nature toward man and the set of man toward a union of love with God. After years of bedevilled controversy and discussion, a frontier had finally been established between faith and natural science. The demon of concordism had been finally exorcised, this devil which had been the cause of so many clashes between science and faith, by finding in the six days of the Genesis account of the creation the geological and paleontological periods, or by suggesting that the zero point of the matter of the universe, toward which science seems to be pointing, was the initial creation as described in the Bible.[55] The house seemed swept and garnished with science and faith, each amicably installed in their own floor. Would the devil return with companions worse than himself? An outstanding expert on the problems of the relation between science and faith believes himself justified in characterizing and condemning Teilhard's own conception as a new concordism.[56]

Teilhard was not so naïve. He knew that a distinction had to be made between the truth of revelation and that of science, inasmuch as these two truths are on different levels. But he was also convinced that there could be no complete divorce between the two. The elimination of concordism during the last fifty years has indeed put an end to the undignified scrimmage between science and faith. But it has also resulted in scientific thought breaking off all contact with religious persuasion and faith becoming a foreign body for the scientist. The resulting intellectual schizophrenia of the believing scientist became in turn a threat to faith. Teilhard was convinced that this divorce between science and faith could not be the last word. He was himself in the heartland of modern science and saw how this science was gravitating toward globalism, an all-embracing and comprehensive notion of the universe.[57] This tendency flows from the very nature of science itself, which has as its object "bedrock investigation,"[58] and which can be satisfied with nothing less than an integration of the entire sum total of phenomena into a single panorama. Since knowledge is the perception of unity, this tendency to seek a single all-embracing conception of the universe is in harmony with the nature of science and of man; therefore it cannot be bad,[59] even if it does involve a somewhat broadened notion of science. On the other hand, the believer is persuaded that the final reply to the vital questions of the universe can be given only by divine revelation proposed to faith. The Christian cannot therefore accept, in the final analysis, a state of affairs in which science and faith ignore each other completely; this can too easily develop into an implicit or explicit hostility between the two. There must be the possibility of a harmonization and positive synthesis of science and faith. If the mind of the scientist is motivated by the deep-seated desire to reach the contemplation of the one all-pervading truth which is God, then his science ought to contribute to the search for God, to the extent to which it wishes to be faithful to its own innermost nature. The Christian ought thus to gravitate to a goal where science has transcended itself to culminate in a view of the universe opening upon the vistas of faith, and where the revelation proposed to faith appears as the crown and consummation of man's search conducted with the resources of human science. This is not concordism but it is a firm interior concord.[60]

Teilhard gravitated toward this positive concord and realized it for himself in his own life as a Christian with a reasoned faith and as a man of science; as a Christian he sought his all in God, as a scientist he felt and lived the great forward thrust of knowledge which is modern science. In the bold perception of a global knowledge of the universe, his science flowered into adoration. His faith in God and in creation found its echo in the daily study of the humblest terrestrial reality. His own life bore out his contention that:

On the contrary neither [Science and Faith] can develop normally without the other. And the reason is simple: the same life animates both. Neither in its impetus nor its achievements can science go to its limits without becoming tinged with mysticism and charged with faith.[61]

He felt himself to have been entrusted by Providence with the proclamation of this conviction in Christian circles and in scientific circles alike. This conviction was one of Teilhard's great strong points and the limipidity and zeal with which he put it into practice in his life and work are the key to his salutary and emancipating influence on so many searchers and perplexed agnostics.

Yet anyone studying Teilhard's works may wonder if there are not in these works some overhasty efforts at harmonization. Sometimes his philosophical intuition seems to make contact too readily and facilely with the mystery of faith. On such occasions he seems to forget that the world of phenomena is not simply a transparent epiphany of the truth but also a veil obscuring the face of that truth.[62] Teilhard is indeed ready to admit a certain obscurity in the nexus between phenomenology and the faith,[63] an obscurity common to every commensuration of a human value and the Supreme Good.[64] But he feels that his radical vocation is that of demonstrating and proclaiming the positive harmony before warning against possible deviations.

The distinctive and drastic originality of Teilhard's scientific speculation necessarily entailed a radical incapacity on his part to limit himself to pure "science," as his superiors wished him to do. This powerful originality is likewise the explanation of the difficulty encountered in the interpretation of his thought. Teilhard simply cannot trace a precise boundary line between his conclusions as the end product of his scientific thought and his philosophy as the latent product of his Christian faith. The scientist, therefore, suspects Teilhard of dogmatism on seeing how closely his phenomenology approaches Christian dogma. The theologian questions Teilhard's orthodoxy on finding this approach nothing more than an asymptotic one, which leaves the essential elements in suspension. Until both scientist and theologian adopt Teilhard's own angle of vision, neither will be able to see why he feels he can go so far and no farther. And this angle of vision has not been sufficiently pinpointed and critically justified for the reader to be able to adopt it without reservation. The result has been that Teilhard's writings have inevitably given rise to misunderstandings.

The distinctive style of Teilhard's philosophical essays, a style which creates a further difficulty in interpretation, is probably also explained by his unusual point of vantage in the no man's land between the fronts of science and faith. Teilhard has been called a poet, and his letters and earliest essays do indeed show an extraordinary sensitivity and power of evocation. The fact that his first compositions were written "in the style of Benson" may indicate that he deliberately took as his model this English writer who had a unique gift for verbal expression of the mid-region between reality and creative imagination.[65] Teilhard is eminently capable of a closely reasoned exposition. But always the edges of his intellectual clarity are licked by the flames of that inner intensity which he hopes will touch the heart of his reader. Even in his phenomenological scientific writings, he brushes the boundary of spirituality. He has a message to transmit. He writes as a witness to that message, as a sort of prophet. He expects of his readers a kind of "conversion" which will enable them to "see" the universe in its powerful upward thrust toward man and man in his divinely assigned task of the edification of the human race into the Body of Christ. This inspiration and this vision compel him to forge new terms, to demolish the old stereotyped categories. For the same reason, he is forced to repeat himself. A hundred times he traces the same sketch but it is never absolutely identical. Nor is it ever entirely accomplished. Reality, that echo of the creative and redemptive word of God, is beyond the tether of all our human words.

Consequently, a special measure of sympathetic attention is essential for an understanding of Teilhard's works. The reader must be actively willing to listen to the message that the words attempt to mediate. He must retain his critical faculty in order to avoid being dazzled by the beauty of the form; but he must also pay attention to the authentically human and Christian content, the message. Above all, he must set his course, with Teilhard, toward a world where God will be found and served in all things in Christ. On the day when scientific reflection and Catholic thought have, by this effort, transcended the pioneering thrusts of Teilhard and corrected the flaws and shortcomings of this intellectual explorer, that hope may be fulfilled which Teilhard himself expressed in the final years of his life: "If I do have a mission to accomplish, the degree of my success in fulfilling that mission will only be able to be judged in terms of the extent to which I am surpassed."[66]

PART I

From Primordial Matter to Man

THE LAW OF COMPLEXIFICATION
AND INTERIORIZATION

We tend naturally to be overwhelmed most by the first shock of realization of the dizzying vastness of the Universe. The starry heavens could still be regarded with serene admiration in the old days when the Earth was thought to be the fixed center of a small number of spheres revolving around it in staid unfailing orbit. But this tidy system has been thrown out of focus for us by recent discoveries of science, which have stretched it to bursting and launched it explosively into space. Our units of measurement have been distended to thousands of light years and to staggering galaxies; and our instrument-sharpened vision has detected the Macrocosm reappearing, at the antipodes of the astronomical immensities, in the fathomless ferment of the Microcosm. This forcible dilation of our horizons has served but to heighten our awareness of our own absolute insignificance and to intensify our resultant disquiet. Pascal's two abysses [have been] more manifestly sounded and aggravated by two other abysses: the abyss of Number, a bewildering plethora of bodies and corpuscles all about us; and the abyss of Time, that endless axis around which Space coils and uncoils incessantly . . .

In the gulf of these vastnesses, in the swarm of these myriads, what is left of us, ourselves? How can we escape the feeling of simple annihilation, extinction? . . . The soul of modern man has suffered its first twinge of apprehension at the loping shadow of the sheer vastness of the Cosmos.[1]

CHAPTER 2

Although it is Teilhard's view of the future of mankind and the world which constitutes the chief theological interest of his thought, some knowledge of the evolutionary process leading to the origin of man is essential to a proper understanding of this view. In this very process lies the problematic confronting modern man, for it is precisely the accepted theory of evolution which has undermined and destroyed the time-honored picture of the world; and in this same process there appear to the keen and perceptive eye, contends Teilhard, the principles determining and controlling the future of the world and of man.

Evolution is, for Teilhard, an established fact. There may well be felt to be many peripheral uncertainties around this central fact. In the realm of inorganic matter, geology and astrophysics can, with the aid of atomic chemistry, form a fairly accurate idea of the origin and development of the Earth and even of the solar systems and galaxies. Yet these theories always remain partially hypothetical and could require drastic, even fundamental, modification in the light of new scientific discoveries. In the realm of organic matter, science is still groping after the initial origin of life out of inorganic matter. Modern chemistry has indeed managed to synthesize proteinic substances. But it is a long way, as we shall see, from these relatively simple compounds to the organic proteins of the living cell.

Even with regard to evolution within the animate world, present-day science is still faced with many question marks, despite the important information it has already amassed. Paleontology can chart a well-documented genealogical tree for some animal species. It notes the increasing convergence of these genealogical trees at ever earlier levels, a fact which seems to indicate a common origin. Similarly, the higher species of animals seem more recent in date than the lower ones. Remarkable coincidences of anatomical structure can be noted which are also indicative of a common origin, precisely because they are devoid of importance for survival.

Thus, all mammals, from the mouse to the giraffe, have the same number of cervical vertebrae. On a much larger scale, biology notes several phenomena common to all life, animal or vegetable: hemoglobin and chlorophyll always have the same composition wherever they occur and they are chemically allied; the same enzymes are operative at all levels of life; in the animate world, all the albumins are levogyrous and all the amines dextrogyrous. . . . In short, the evidence of the greatest variety of sciences conspires to show that all the forms of life on this earth are descended from a single common primitive ancestor.

Yet despite the success of synthetic Neo-Darwinism as a plausible explanation, we do not as yet have complete knowledge of the factors and forces determining evolution. Does the crux of the matter lie in abrupt mutations, transformations in the hereditary factors and the germ cell plasma under the action of chemical and radioactive factors, combined with the natural selection championed by Darwin and the interior predisposition to adaptation advanced by Lamarck?[2] Or are there other factors operative in evolution which have not as yet been discovered?

Teilhard knew as well as did his associates of these uncertainties in our science of evolution. Any reply to a question about the "how" of evolution will perforce be partly hypothetical.[3] They all agree. But the *fact* of evolution has, in their view, been established beyond all possible doubt: on the one hand, by the evidence of a broad mass of varied phenomena which indicate the truth of evolution and are susceptible of a corporate alignment within the framework of evolution; and on the other hand, by the inability of modern science, as Teilhard repeatedly insisted, to conceive of a single phenomenon outside of the evolutionary context.

We are the witnesses of a staggering inversion of the very picture of the universe. Until a century and a half ago, man regarded the macrocosmic structure of the universe at least as a solid and immutable datum. Change applied only to the individual and amounted to little more than ripples on the calm surface of an ocean. Set in their orbits at the beginning of time, the heavenly bodies held fast to their unchanging course, the seasons followed one another in orderly cycle, generations of animate beings succeeded one another within the fixed limits of their various species. But in our own days, the various sciences have acquired the capability of looking back millions of years and are discovering multi-dimensional vistas of change in what seemed immutable when considered over a briefer span. For science our solar system is no longer immutable; it is in process of gradual development. Not one of the phenomena of our own earth, not even that earth itself, can any longer be conceived, except as determined by the time in which it is situated. Life could not have appeared on the earth until the earth had cooled sufficiently. Higher animals could not have come into existence until a sufficient atmosphere of oxygen had been formed. All phenomena have their origin in time. In origin, nature and operation, they are linked with and dependent upon a whole complex chain, an infinite number of preceding phenomena. The origin of all things within the cosmos is determined by intracosmic forces. Teilhard likes to use, in this context, the image of an "organic" origin or a "birth" to signify that every single thing arises within the womb of the cosmos, that its existence and its life are linked, as by an umbilical cord, to this maternal womb. Our way of seeing any phenomenon is intrinsically determined by this new vision of a more unified world, a more cognate cosmos: "An organic universe in which no element and no event can appear except by birth, i.e., in association with the development of the whole. . . . The Universe has taken on a new dimension."[4]

In this general sense, evolution must be accepted as a solidly established and unassailable fact: "Considered at this level of generality (namely, that every empirical reality is part of a process, i.e., is born, in the Universe), Evolution has long since ceased to be a hypothesis and become a *general epistemological condition* (one more *dimension*), which must henceforth be satisfied by *every* hypothesis."[5]

This notion of evolution abstains from any judgment on the nature of the factors and forces producing a new form of being or of life. In this realm, the various sciences, including philosophy in its proper place, must look for a solution.[6]

This notion of evolution does in fact rest upon a philosophical postulate; but this postulate is so evident that it is embarrassing to have to state it in so many words. It is the presupposition that intracosmic phenomena ought to be explicable in terms of intracosmic causes. Yet only recently a critic of Teilhard presumed to write that the appearance of new species in the evolution of life and the geographic differences between animate forms might be explained in terms of the will of the Creator.[7] Science cannot admit such an "explanation." Her task is to seek for the natural causal nexus between phenomena. Science would be betraying her first and most sacred duty were she to content herself with admitting an intervention by the Creator as an "explanation" of a normal natural phenomenon (i.e., of one not clearly bearing the marks of a "miracle" in the strict sense of a sign of an extraordinary immediate operation of God).[8] For this duty consists in inspecting the intracosmic causal nexuses and showing the internal coherence of the universe: "a *positive* scientific problem . . . demands . . . a positive solution in the scientific order."[9]

This implies no reproach to earlier thinkers. Former generations could well believe that each living species had been fashioned directly by God, because the origin of a species was not, in their eyes, a phenomenon of nature; it was not an intracosmic event nor yet an intratemporal occurrence, but rather something pertaining to the original institution of the cosmos and the beginning of time. But in our days, when man has begun to discover that not only the origin of new species but even that of life itself and of the earth *are* in fact intratemporal and intracosmic events, science is under obligation to search for the natural causes of these phenomena. Even a decent respect for the Creator and for his creative operation obliges science in our days to abandon the hypothesis which has been given the highly unfortunate and deceptive title of "creationism" and which champions divine intervention in the constitution of the various species.[10] Despite all obscurities and uncertainties, science must admit and accept evolution as a fact.

Science has but one alternative to an admission of the unintelligibility of the universe, and that is to suppose that the universe with all its elements, large and small, past, present and future, forms a real unity whose laws must be sought out and discovered. This is nothing other than the transposition into present-day terms of the time-honored thesis of philosopher and theologian: "All things which issue from God are in relation with one another and with God. Therefore all things necessarily belong to a single universe."[11] Every phenomenon must have an internal nexus with the sum total of phenomena. It is simply and literally unthinkable that it should be otherwise. To know is to see unity:

> On pain of being irreducible to scientific thought, everything must plunge its empirical roots into an indefinite past and into the entire area of its own present. [For] the fundamental unity of the Universe and the inexorable interconnection and interaction of the cosmic elements . . . preclude any new being from emerging into our experience otherwise than in function of all the present and past states of the empirical world.[12]

It may seem astonishing that, despite the lacunae in our knowledge of the concrete factors determining evolution on this earth, or even indeed of the factors governing the transition from a lower to a higher form of life, Teilhard should deem it possible to formulate a general law for this entire evolutionary process, a law which would hold for inanimate matter, life and even, as will be shown in Part II, for human history. It may be that the study of the vast spans covered by geology and the history of life sharpened Teilhard's eye, for he is convinced that a simple scanning of the panorama of the history of the earth as described for us by the various sciences will suffice to render this law "apparent."[13] If we stand back far enough from the details in which each one of these sciences naturally and rightly becomes submerged, we shall perceive one great line, one general law expressive of the direction of evolution at all levels of material existence. This is the *law of complexification*.[14]

A great number of Teilhard's essays and a considerable portion of his great works of synthesis, such as *Le Phénomène humain* and *Le Groupe zoologique humain*, are aimed at making this law "apparent." It is not to our purpose here to present a detailed report of Teilhard's demonstration nor *a fortiori* to pass judgment upon it. But we must try to provide the reader with a synopsis of this insight, central to the whole of Teilhard's ideas but notably of those pertaining to the future. This law of complexification states that the fabric of the universe[15] evolves through a series of more and more complex structurings, proceeding toward a kind of concentration into organized unitary entities of ever-increasing magnitude and excellence, constituting as it were a "convolution" of the fabric about itself, each of which involves a more complex combination of forms than did the preceding one. It is a "centro-complexification" which Teilhard outlines as follows: "We will define the 'complexity' of a thing, if you allow, as the quality the thing possesses of being composed a) of a larger number of elements; which are b) more tightly organized among themselves."[16]

He develops this more explicitly as follows:

By the complexity of a whole I do not mean simply the number and variety of the elements comprising this whole. My chief focus of attention is on their arrangement. If simply lumped together *with no principle of order*, the 360 types of atomic nuclei known today to physics, from hydrogen to uranium, would form a *Heterogeneity* not a *Complexity*. As I am using it here, complexity is an *organized heterogeneity*; consequently it is centered. . . . Two different factors or terms are therefore required to convey the complexity of a system: the one expresses the number of elements and groups of elements contained in the system; the other, much more difficult to symbolize, expresses the number, variety, and compactness of the bonds (the density) existing between these elements in a minimal volume.[17]

The law of complexification, therefore, means that the more highly evolved beings comprise a larger number of constitutive elements of a greater variety and bound together by a more compact network of relations. Let us follow, with Teilhard, the progress of the fabric of the universe in accord with and under the influence of this law.

First in the quantitative order. Nuclear physics and astrophysics describe how, in the gigantic laboratories that are the stars, the tiniest particles (electrons, neutrons, and mesons) combine, unite to form atoms. Chemistry describes how these atoms constitute molecules, first simple ones, and then gradually more

33

and more complex. A simple count of the number of atoms of which these molecular combinations are composed reveals an ascendant line. The largest molecules of the inorganic world have about 100 atoms. Now when we come to living beings, the chief constituents revealed to us by organic chemistry—namely, the proteins—are molecules comprising a very great number of atoms. Insulin, one of the smallest protein molecules, has 791 atoms. On the threshold of animate nature we find the viruses which still hover in the no man's land between chemical giant molecules and living infra-bacteria: here the number of atoms per molecule rises to several millions.[18] Thoroughgoing animate beings make a forward leap in this regard which is almost impossible to imagine. The smallest unicellular being presently known presents a great complexity and an enormous number of protein molecules, so that the number of atoms it contains must be of the order of 10^{10}. And finally in the multicellular beings this number rises to astronomical proportions: for a plant as lowly as duckweed it has been calculated that it must be of the order of 4×10^{20}; and for man it must exceed 10^{25}.[19]

More important even than the quantitative curve of increasing complexity in the series of natural individual entities, is the curve of increasing density of the network of relations uniting and binding their constituent elements. The bodies of which Teilhard is speaking are not simple conglomerations or arbitrary unions of disordered particles, similar to a pile of sand or even a star; nor are they the result of an exclusively numerical and geometric repetition of identical unitary structures, like crystals. They constitute a combination in which a definite number of constituent elements differing in nature are amalgamated into a structured and closed unity, an individual entity possessing a certain autonomy and interior cohesion. This summary analysis of the series of natural bodies likewise reveals an increase in the cohesion of the individual entity, a stronger centering. Not only does the number of constitutive particles increase; so do the number, density, and wealth of relations binding the particles together. The example cited by Koningsberger well illustrates to what limits this complexity of living beings attains:

A segment of a hemoglobin chain, 300 amines long, has already been "decoded." . . . Evidence has been found that, in a human being, the replacement of one definite amine by another leads in one case to what is called anemia of the crescent-shaped cells, in another case to the hemoglobin C malady, both of them hereditary constitutional malformations provoked by one little "misprint" of a single letter.[20]

A natural unitary entity like a molecule, or a living being (in the realm either of the unicellular or multicellular organisms) is thus composed not only of constituent elements susceptible to chemical and physical analysis, but of links, bonds, relations between the elements, which make of the whole a coherent unity.

Teilhard calls this interior bond and unity of the natural body its *interior*. This *interior* Teilhard derives from the notions of modern chemistry and biology, but it must be understood analogically in function of the degrees of being; it seems to correspond to what Aristotle called the *entelechy* and medieval Scholastic philosophy the *forma substantialis*, the form understood not in the sense of the exterior appearance but rather as the interior constitutive principle, the factor of unity, the substantial form. To the notions of interiority and exteriority, Teilhard links another pair of concepts: "radial energy" and "tangential energy."[21] The terms *radial* and *tangential* must not be taken in a literal technical sense; rather they must be accepted in the symbolic sense of an image, a spatial symbolization, of which there are several to be found in Teilhard's writings: thus the *radial* energy would be that which binds every part of a being to its *center* (on analogy with the *radius* of a sphere), that is to say, to its unity. The *tangential* energy is, for its part, neutral with respect to this unity and this organization (the tangent being perpendicular to the radius and therefore neutral with respect to centering). The *tangential* energy is in fact the energy which is susceptible to measurement by the physicists and chemists. The *radial* energy is the degree of organization of a being and that being's resultant power of efficient operation.

Whatever may be the status of this terminology—and "radial energy" is a magnitude difficult to circumscribe—as soon as the inquirer has admitted that "centrocomplexity"[22] is a dimension of the fabric of the universe, the development of this fabric on earth seems to hold to a steady course toward an ever greater interior complexity and unity of natural bodies. The law of entropy is well known to mechanics. But there seems also to be operative in our world a law of interiorizing complexification, a "constant, perennial current of interiorizing complexification."[23] Seen in broad perspective in this light, our world appears as "a universe in process of convolution upon itself, in a solidary mass, from top to bottom, interiorizing itself into an ever-growing complexity."[24]

The history of the earth and of life on earth thus evinces a tendency to the formation of individual entities of ever-increasing magnitude, not necessarily in terms of their dimensions but in terms of their centrocomplexity. The smallest and simplest elements unite "organically" in the course of terrestrial history into more and more complex unitary entities: atoms into simple molecules, these latter into complex molecules, which unite in turn into micella; these micella become organized into cells, the cells into plants and animals.[25] In spite of the uncertainties surrounding the concrete causes of this development, the over-all trend seems clear and seems to culminate in man. Even as the galaxies represent an extreme in the order of magnitude, so does man in the order of centrocomplexity.[26]

The first phases of this process of combination seem to be completely governed by the laws of statistical probability, in such a way that the system of elements, for example, can be determined mathematically. But moderating temperatures render possible the emergence of more complicated molecular combinations. Giant molecules form, especially around the carbon chains; and these giant molecules begin to show a certain pliancy and capacity to absorb new elements, though they remain for all that essentially themselves, the proteins. Since we have as yet no real familiarity with proteins in the free state, we are unable to form a clear idea of their origin. But the present widespread distribution of organic carbon compounds over the surface of the earth cannot but suggest the hypothesis that a rather thick layer of protein-type molecules formed upon the surface of a zone favorably disposed because exposed to radiations and cooled to a moderate temperature. This hypothesis has moreover presently assumed a fairly precise scientific form, and has received further support from the remarkable experiments in synthesizing amino acids out of a mixture of natural gases imitating the primordial atmosphere of our planets.[27] It is therefore becoming possible to imagine what precise processes may have led to the emergence of life. Within this layer, the process of complexification would continue its course in such a way that the tension would increase and the whole arrive at a point of supersaturation. From this seething effervescent mass would burst forth life.[28]

The first living cells are structures of an extreme complexity, but they are sufficiently centered upon themselves to absorb new elements without their own unity being ruptured. They can nourish themselves and open themselves to an increasing complexity. At the same time they can multiply: the cell divides into two new cells, possessing the same properties as the mother cell. This brings gradually nearer and nearer the possibility of the formation of genera and species. The life of the cell always lies within a series of ancestors and descendants: succession in time, "phylogenesis," becomes one of the intrinsic factors of life.[29]

Was the birth of life a unique single occurrence at a specific point of the earth's crust or was it an event that was repeated every time the circumstances proved favorable? This question will probably never be definitively answered. The first origins of any new phenomenon are necessarily cloaked in obscurity. Some will say that a single origin and kinship of all life is indicated by the fact, mentioned above, that all the primordial elements of life are similar, even those which appear accidental or merely accessory. Others will maintain that these similarities are but the secondary result of selection and convergence. In any case, life seems to have established itself very rapidly over the whole surface of the earth, as if the entire proteinic mass had been in a state of supersaturation and the whole of the fabric capable of vivification had in fact been vitalized apace. Thus was the earth covered with a thin film of living matter which was to proliferate into a biosphere.[30]

From this mass of closely packed primordial life, probably concentrated in the oceans, there surged forth the kingdoms of plants, assimilating matter and energy by means of light and chlorophyll, and of animals, with their nourishment derived from plants; and within these kingdoms all the ramifications which divide the main trunk into an infinite diversity of species, described by systematics: a veritable virgin forest of primordial forms. Here a special difficulty arises. Can any sense of direction be distinguished in this forest of lines of evolution? Can the line of complexification be traced? Can it be measured by an objective parameter? Up to the level of the primordial proteins and the unicellular organisms, the degree of complexity could be measured by the number of atoms, of molecules and of bonds involved. But as soon as we penetrate into the realm of the higher forms of life, this standard can no longer be profitably utilized because this number reaches astronomical proportions. Is there any objective standard for comparing the complexity of the octopus and that of the ant, or the complexity of the giant reptile and that of the mammal? We are going to see that there is indeed such an objective standard. It must be remembered, notes Teilhard, that for every degree of complexity there is a corresponding degree of interiority, an "interior."

Now in the animal kingdom there appears a new form of complexity which makes it possible to measure the degree and rapidity of interiorization. The degree of interiority and of "consciousness" (which makes its first appearance, properly speaking, at this point) can be determined anatomically in function of the development of the central nervous system and especially of the brain in the case of the vertebrates, or of the cervical ganglion in the case of the insects. In brain or cervical ganglion we have, in fact, the central switchboard connecting all the organs constituting the living being and meshing them into a single vital activity. The main factor, once again, is not the material quantity of nerve cells (although this does provide a preliminary indication); it is rather the subtlety and density of their structure and their interconnections.[31]

The application of this parameter of increasing complexification immediately reveals a clearly channeled thrust in the evolutionary process. Large phyla, like the Annelida, the Coelenterata, the Echinodermata and the Porifera, are left behind as backwaters; so are the arthropods. The nervous system of the higher insects appears well developed but is quite inferior in degree and kind to that of the vertebrates. These vertebrates incontestably constitute the axis of evolution; there is a steady and drastic development and perfecting of the brain throughout the course of the history of this phylum, in which appear successively fishes, amphibians, reptiles and mammals. The cerebral development speeds up among the mammals and especially among the primates. These latter constitute a group of "cerebral" or "cerebro-manual" animals in which the central nervous system and particularly the brain show extreme refinement and capacity.[32]

During the Tertiary era, the primitive primates range initially over the immense continent then comprising present-day Asia, America and Europe; in Africa, we find no signs of primates as yet during the later Eocene age. As this biological development continues, the American group becomes isolated, while a group of highly developed anthropoids, in evolutionary ferment, begins to spread over an ideal evolutionary incubator of tropical and subtropical regions extending from West Africa to the east coast of China and what is now the Indonesian archipelago. There has gradually been forming in the biosphere a plethora of living beings of great complexity and interiorization, highly diversified and progressively richer in nervous structure and constitution. During the latter part of the Tertiary era, the most highly developed and most progressive branch becomes concentrated in a limited area of the earth, which is specially fertile and makes possible the formation of various centers of development, sufficiently mutually accessible to favor reciprocal communication. The result is that in this zone the intensity of animal consciousness attains a maximum and there begins to be evidence of a supersaturation similar to that prevailing on the threshold of life.[33]

At some definite site within this zone (Kenya? Southwest Asia? The problem will arise again in connection with monogenism) the explosion occurs. A further development of the nervous system and of the brain precipitates an overleaping of a

39

critical point of cephalization. And a totally new form of consciousness appears. Man is born. And man possesses, in respect of interiorizing complexification, a new degree of consciousness, consciousness to the second power. Not only does he know, he knows that he knows. The spontaneous and direct perception of the higher animals becomes reflexive perception, "reflected mental operation."[34]

"Upon arrival . . . at a critical point of arrangement (or, as we have been saying in this context, of convolution), life has become hypercentered upon itself, to the point of becoming capable of prevision and invention. It has become conscious 'to the second degree.' "[35]

"For the first time on earth, consciousness has become so folded back upon itself as to become Thought."[36]

Man is distinguished by a maximum of physico-chemical complexity, for in him matter attains its most synthetic stage; by a maximum of interior organization, for he is the most perfect and most thoroughly centered corpuscle in the cosmos; and finally by a maximum of psychic development, for he constitutes the high point of life. Man is the ultimate fruit of evolution.[37] In him, that development, which has been steadily progressing from the beginning, attains a higher level and will henceforth function, together with the law of interiorizing complexification proper to it, on a new plane, that of reflective consciousness and liberty.[38]

Teilhard's introduction of this parameter of interiorizing complexification has enabled him to express the unity of the whole process of evolution on our earth, from the primordial elementary fabric to man, and indeed even further, to the consummation of terrestrial history. He has at his disposal a formula capable of expressing the unity of all the sciences treating of man: physics, biology, and the sciences of the mind. This formula likewise enables him to maintain the distinction between inanimate matter, animate animal matter, and animate human matter. For the same law does indeed operate at the different levels of being, but this law of interiorizing complexification operates in a specifically different manner at each level. Anticipating the science of the future, Teilhard risks this paradoxical thesis that the history of man (even, indeed precisely, history in the classical sense) is the ideal terrain for a study of the development of life.[39]

Teilhard's crucial contribution to the genius of human thought may well be realized one day as having been precisely this discovery of the law of interiorizing complexification, which he found by studying the great over-all line of biological evolution, spotted later in the realm of inorganic matter thanks to the modern advances of physics and chemistry, and finally discovered operative again in the cultural history of man. This formula, so simple in itself, might well signify a revolution for all the sciences. Not only does it establish a bridge between the sciences of nature and the sciences of mind; pre-eminently it signifies for the sciences of nature an inversion of perspective which again places man in his true position. And this restoration of man to his true position is, in turn, of crucial importance for the reconciliation between the natural sciences and Christian thought.

Present-day science investigates with much zeal and perspicacity the whole area of the simplest and most elemental. It is in the main analytic, breaking down every whole into its smallest elements. It has already scored striking successes along this line. But at the same time, present-day science is incontestably caught in an impasse. Physics, which studies matter, always considers that prime material phenomenon which is life as a mere concomitant datum which it can neglect with impunity. Biology, in turn, studies life, but regards the peerless vital phenomenon which is the psychic life of man as an accidental epiphenomenon. For Teilhard, on the contrary, life becomes the supreme form of the fabric of the cosmos, in which a fundamental law of that fabric, to wit, the law of interiorizing complexification, manifests itself at its utmost pitch with unrivalled clarity. Consequently, biology, as a science of life, becomes an integral part and crown of physics, the "physics of the 'ultramacrocomplex.' "[40] And the psychic life of man becomes the supreme actualization and crown of all life, the long-awaited clarification of the nature of the living world: "Man is a part of Life; indeed . . . he is the very type, polestar and quintessence of Life."[41]

In consequence, neither biology nor even physics itself can

continue as in the past the disregard they have been evincing for the phenomenon man, even in his highest operations. On the contrary: "The true physics is that which will, one day, achieve the inclusion of man in his wholeness in a coherent picture of the world."[42]

For life, especially human life, tinged as it is with both the material and the spiritual, is not an anomaly in the fabric of the cosmos; it is rather the actualization and crown of a fundamental property of that whole fabric, namely, the tendency to interiorizing complexification.[43] We have not acquired a complete grasp of the nature of that fabric so unfortunately dubbed "matter," a term evocative of inertness, until we have penetrated the highest form of manifestation of that fabric.

To see in all this a materialist philosophy would be to misconstrue entirely Teilhard's meaning. In Chapter 4 we shall show that Teilhard's whole conception here is rooted in a belief in the primacy of spirit.[44] A few more remarks, now, on the inversion of perspective involved for the sciences in the Teilhardian view. It is not man who must be reduced somehow to the prevalent material and quantitative categories of physics; it is rather physics which must flex itself to the dimensions of man. If physics is desirous of comprehending the phenomenon of the material world in all its breadth and abundance, then physics must broaden its frame of reference to make room for the highest form of physical reality, which it would be justified in its own terms of reference in designating as living human matter, but which Teilhard would prefer radically to designate as the human living fabric of the cosmos. To this end, the natural sciences must cease to limit themselves exclusively to their present course of analytical investigation; they must also and to an equal degree essay the road of synthesis. They must not confine their course to a descent to the most elementary constituents; they must also undertake the ascent to more complex structures. To the unprejudiced observer, the history of the cosmic fabric on this earth provides clear evidence that the upward-and-inward thrust of evolution is an objective datum of the material world. The fabric of the cosmos on our earth (that reality which the natural scientists, properly enough in their erstwhile frame of reference, designated as "matter") is manifestly governed by laws, not all of which are reducible to the laws of entropy. Entropy does indeed entail the distribution of matter in function of the most probable structures. But there is also operative the contrary or complementary law of interiorizing complexification, which manifests itself in life: "Life, in its global acceptation, is manifestly a current running counter to entropy. . . . Life is the opposite of the leveling stroke of entropy; it is the methodical construction, on an ever-broader scale, of an ever more improbable edifice . . . an invariable ascent to the summit of consciousness."[45]

Teilhard describes the evolution of the fabric of the cosmos, from the primordial atom to man, in order to demonstrate that this thrust to synthesis is an objective datum of that fabric on our earth; and he indicates why the unilaterally analytic bent of the natural sciences in our day must necessarily be corrected.

This adjustment of perspective will restore to man his proper place in this world. Teilhard's law of interiorizing complexification imparts to the ancient tenet of faith a form acceptable to science; stated in this way, the contention that man is the crown and end of creation acquires scientific respectability. Man lost his pride when the old geocentric picture of the world went by the board, and there opened up before his dazzled eyes the fathomless abysses of the infinitely large and the infinitely small, the infinitely manifold and the infinitely old. Any notion that he himself had a value, and *a fortiori* a supreme value, appeared to him nothing but naive egocentricity. Every day new discoveries kept undermining the very foundations of his faith. He saw himself as a dwarf amid the gigantic cosmos of the stars and galaxies, as a puny chance spawn amid the composite of elementary forces dominating the universe, as an ephemeral blossom on the ancient tree of life. This crisis was occasioned by the unilateral direction of the gaze of modern man to the elementary and the quantitative. Man's mind, moulded and enthralled by his own science, was seeking the key of reality in a return to the most elementary and simple elements, ultimate and sometimes "evanescent" products of his own analysis. But for a comprehensive understanding of the world, there is need as well for a reversal of direction to follow the thrust of reality itself from this simple origin to ever more complicated and comprehensive forms of being. Only a partial knowledge of the oak tree is attained by a chemical analysis of the acorn; to complete that knowledge, there is need for inspection of the tree itself, with its mighty trunk and its well-proportioned crown of branches, blossom and fruit. If man traces the development of the earth in this direction, that of construction, of synthesis, of increasing complication and interiorization, he will discover that he is himself the crown of the world. For man then appears as the actualization and consummation of what the material world in its entirety has borne within it throughout the billions of years it has been in existence. However insignficant man may be in time and space, he assumes truly cosmic dimensions because the entire cosmos, with all its tremendous power of being and of life, has ultimately served to mould him. Then is there born in man, purged by the crisis and permeated with humility, a new and conscious pride.

The inversion of perspective and the new vision of man were in the first instance for Teilhard a kind of faith, a deliberate choice by which he wished to come out anew in favor of the primacy of consciousness, of thought, of freedom and of mind and spirit.[46] And this despite appearances to the contrary, despite the fact that the magnitude of the universe and the omnipresence of matter seemed to reduce man to nothingness. Man believes in his own worth because he must believe in it; in the final analysis he cannot but believe in that worth.[47] But the strong point in Teilhard's contribution is the demonstration that this faith is objectively justified even at the level of the natural sciences. The instant that science takes stock of the global phenomenon of the history of the earth and of life on earth, it discovers in that fabric which it calls "matter," and which it has subjected to radical analysis, the thrust toward synthesis. This movement, this thrust, commencing with the primordial fabric (science's "primordial matter"), leads to man. At first glance, it might seem that evolution diminishes man's status, reducing him to a product of the animal life and primordial forces of the earth. But a global inspection of evolution shows us man as "the very pinnacle of a universe in process, simultaneously, of material 'complexification' and psychic interiorization, at an ever-increasing velocity."[48]

CREATION AND EVOLUTION

Far from being incompatible with the existence of a First Cause, the transformist views as here expounded are the noblest and most consoling fashion of picturing to ourselves the influence of that First Cause. Christian transformism conceives the creative operation of God not as an intrusive thrusting of his products into the midst of preexisting beings, but rather as a bringing to birth *within the womb of things the successive goals of his workmanship. The operation is no less essential, no less universal, and preeminently no less intimate for this reason.*[1]

Evolution . . . is not itself "creative" as science managed for a moment to believe; but evolution is *the expression in our field of experience, in Space and Time, of creation.*[2]

CHAPTER 3

We shall have to follow the trail of interiorizing complexification until it leads us into the midst of human history and opens up to us a view of its final consummation. But first we must pause upon the significance that the evolutionist doctrine may have for the faith and for theology. The questions we pose here refer rather to evolution in general than to Teilhard's own vision. We must pause upon this point because the importance accorded to evolutionism by Teilhard and the conviction with which he expounds it will involve some of our readers for the first time in the grave confrontation between the new scientific view of the world and the familiar notions of their traditional faith. This confrontation may well be useful in promoting reflection on the data of faith. The questions we propose to treat comprise that of creation in general, that of the creation of the human soul, and that of the specifically spiritual nature of the human soul.

On October 1, 1859, appeared Darwin's *On the Origins of Species,* providing a solid scientific base and a first explication of the evolutionary teaching. In 1871, there followed *Descent of Man.* But as early as 1860, the Provincial Council of German Bishops of Cologne declared "contrary to Holy Scripture and to faith" the opinion holding that "man's body issued, by spontaneous mutation, from a less perfect nature into a more perfect nature and finally into human nature." This declaration unleashed a conflict between incipient natural science and the defenders of the traditional Christian view; this conflict was to last for dozens of years. These disputations compelled believers to a new reflection upon the data of faith and, especially, upon the sense of the biblical creation narrative. Everyone nowadays knows what this narrative does *not* intend to say; but does everyone know as well its positive meaning?[3]

The first chapter of Genesis,[4] which narrates the creative work of God within a framework of six days (whence the "work of six days," or the "hexaemeron"), remains one of the most fundamental texts of divine revelation. Towering in monumental mystery as the portal of entry to the entire Bible, it announces the fundamental message of the first and last religious reality: the relations between God, the universe, and man. It is the prologue to salvation history, the stage on which the drama is to be played out.

For centuries, the traditional believer reading this narrative believed he had found in it an almost historical account of the order in which God made things. This led to a conflict with natural science which was tracing a quite different picture of the origins of things terrestrial. The force of evidence has led us to a rediscovery of the incontestable principle that the Bible is not a manual of natural science; the writer of this account is utilizing a graphic portrayal (consciously naive, according to Renckens,[5] or skillfully adapted to his purpose, according to von Rad[6]) to express a truth infinitely transcending in importance this graphic portrayal of it. In rediscovering this principle, we have rediscovered a way of looking at things that was common in Jewish and Christian antiquity and persisted even to the end of the Middle Ages. Even the Hellenistic Jews and the Fathers of the Church grasped the fact that the picture of the six-days' creation was different from the "modern" picture of creation. The Greek and Latin versions of Ecclesiasticus wrote: "He who lives eternally and has created all things at once,"[7] expressing the conviction that God does not proceed slowly and gradually like man in his creative operation. On the basis of this conviction, Philo and a number of the greatest luminaries among the Fathers of the Church saw in the enumeration of the works mentioned in Genesis I not a chronological but rather a systematic order, reflecting the dignity of the things created.[8] For our modern minds, St. Athanasius' argument seems particularly telling: the light (First Day) could not have been created before the sun and moon (Fourth Day). St. Gregory of Nyssa and St. Augustine outlined a system involving the "implicit" creation of all things by God at the first moment of creation, in such a way that these things later attained actuality through the gradual unfolding of their latent powers, according to God's plan, indeed, but without his special intervention. These Fathers were certainly not evolutionists, as some have claimed them to be, but no more would they have opposed the Bible to the evolutionary teaching. St. Thomas, for his part, has this to say of these opinions: "The first explanation [the literal one] is more general and more in accord with the letter of Scripture, considered on the surface. The second is more reasonable; it better defends Scripture against the criticisms of the unbelievers, of which criticisms, as Augustine says, serious account must be taken; it pleases me more."[9] At the beginning of the sixteenth century, Cardinal Thomas de Vio, Cajetan, was still agreeing on this point with his master St. Thomas Aquinas. How did this freedom with regard to the letter of Scripture come to be lost? It would be an interesting subject for research. Possible contributing causes may have been the cult of the printed word, so typical of Humanism; the distrust for some of the occasionally strained and even fantastic patristic and post-patristic exegesis; perhaps also the new notions being bruited abroad by the natural sciences.

The misunderstanding about the first chapters of Genesis which engendered the conflict with the natural sciences had, nonetheless, its providential fruits. It compelled the believers to examine with greater attention the sense of these chapters. Since we too must take account of these first pages of the Bible for the doctrine of paradise and the fall, it will be useful for us to examine them a little more closely. The modern reader, accustomed since childhood to a biblical history which runs with no hiatus from the narrative of creation and paradise, via the flood, to the story of Abraham and the patriarchs, must rather drastically rechannel his thinking in order to grasp the meaning of primitive history writing. He must radically alter his angle of vision. He must cease looking from Adam toward Abraham, Moses and David, and begin looking backward from the Jewish religion of the age of the prophets toward Abraham and Adam. Only in this way will he succeed in grasping the context of the first eleven chapters of Genesis. For the first pages of the Bible were not the first to be written. On the contrary, as often happens with a preface, they were composed only after the completion of the great work of the six books, the Hexateuch. These books comprise the history of the establishment of Israel as the people of God: the calling of Abraham and the covenant between God and Abraham, the adventures of Abraham's offspring, the deliverance out of Egyptian bondage, the renewal of the covenant on Sinai, the settlement of Israel in the Promised Land. This imposing "Founding Fathers" narrative was given a prologue, linking the Abraham-history to the history of mankind and the very existence of our earth. Thus the prologue is written in the spirit of the religious mind of Israel looking back upon the lofty deeds and words of God upon Sinai, back still further to Abraham, and desirous of piercing still farther backward to the very dawn of the human race. It is only from this point of view that the situation of the people of God can be fully comprehended. "To speak adequately of Israel, to have an adequate understanding of Israel, it is mandatory to commence at the creation of the world, for Israel has its place in the mind of God, in his plan for the world."[10] There is no reason to suppose the creation and paradise narratives to have been founded upon any mysterious, original special revelation. These narratives were born of the reflections of a believing Israel upon the mystery of God and of the world. The doctrine of Genesis I developed out of the salvation doctrine that was contained in the stories of Moses and of Abraham. "Israel learned first to know God as its national God, Yahweh, as its *Savior*. It was by the intermediary of its experience of the salvific acts of Yahweh that Israel learned to know him also as *Creator*."[11]

After these two preliminary observations, we can now proceed to a brief exposition of the doctrine contained in the first chapter of Genesis. In the first place, this chapter aims at giving us a genuine cosmogony, such as was contained in the writings of the neighboring peoples as well. The writer does intend to establish the foundation of the world. This is shown by his initial phrase: "In the beginning." It is shown likewise by the learned and artificial enumeration of the works and their subdivisions forming the integral whole that is the world. The first three Days see the formation of the fixed elements, the "immovable goods" or "real estate": day and night, the two mysterious halves of all terrestrial existence; the vault of heaven, the firmament, conceived as a dome whose base rests upon the earth which in turn floats upon the vast reaches of the waters; finally the plants, wild and domesticated, and the trees, whose immobility ranks them likewise within the first series. The second series describes the "movable goods" or "chattels" of the terrestrial inventory: the sun, the moon and the stars in the firmament of heaven; the fishes, the birds, the terrestrial animals, wild and domesticated. Finally God makes man with special care, because man is to be the lord of the world and, so to speak, "God's viceroy upon earth."[12] There is a manifest intention to assert that everything without exception is the work of God. There is an equally manifest intention to state that all things have been made for the service of man: God builds him a house, furnishes and organizes that house, and then confides it to man. There is undoubtedly a polemical element in this narrative. The neighboring peoples were worshiping the sun and the stars, even animals, and the cult of these mysterious powers of nature was exercising a persistent magnetism upon the people of Israel.

"Be watchful, then, at the peril of your lives. When the Lord spoke to you from the heart of the flame on Mount Horeb, there was no outward shape you saw. And will you now be deluded into carving some outward image of likeness, of man or woman, of beasts that roam on the earth or birds that fly in the air, of creeping things on land or fish that dwell in the waters, down at the roots of the earth? Wilt thou be led astray as thou lookest up at the sky, at sun and moon and all the host of stars, into making gods of them, worshipping those creatures which the Lord thy God has made, to be the common drudges of every nation under heaven? Why else did the Lord choose you out, deliver you from Egypt's furnace of iron, but to make you a people all his own, as you are this day?"[13]

The prophet is teaching us that everything in the world has the function of rendering service, and lowly service at that! The God who revealed himself to Abraham and to Moses is a God whose special concern is mankind. Even those lofty, mysterious and enthralling beings, the sun and the moon, are ordained to light the earth for man and to govern the course of the seasons. Man must neither fear nor venerate these powers of nature. He is brought into immediate contact with the very Lord of heaven and earth. It is for him that God has made all things.

The second point the writer aims at expressing is that all things take their origin from the free initiative of God. "God said": such are the initial words of the narrative of each new day of creation. The Israelite was familiar with this word of God addressed in secret to Abraham and revealed to Moses and the people at the time of the exodus. By this word, God had presented himself as a real person with whom man could engage in conversation, but only because God had first spoken to man. This word of God had made of Abraham, of Moses and of the Chosen People what they were. And this word had declared itself efficacious: "So shall my word be, which shall go forth from my mouth; it shall not return to me void, but it shall do whatsoever I please, and shall prosper in the things for which I sent it."[14]

Now, the sacred writer teaches us, just as the word of God, the expression of his personal benevolent favor to his chosen ones, has been efficaciously actualized in the existence of the people of Israel, even so the whole world is nothing else but the echo of his word. Man may feel that his ultimate security in this life lies in the immobility of the earth upon which he has been set, or in the unfailing cycle of the heavenly bodies. In reality, it is quite otherwise: true security lies in the free will of God: "The Lord became my stay. And he brought me forth into a large place; he delivered me because I pleased him."[15]

For the keen, perceptive ear, this is an astonishing outburst of faith. What is more fleeting than the word, that tenuous exhalation of the mouth? Yet the word of God is a firm foundation for the world itself!

In the third place, the writer is instructing us that everything is good, because everything is as God has willed it: "God said: let there be light. And there was light. And God saw that the light was good."[16]

This insistent refrain of every work of creation likewise contains a polemical element. The thinking of Oriental antiquity, like that of the Greek and Hellenistic world, was radically dualistic: it recognized not one but two principles as basic to the world, namely, God and matter.[17] According to this way of thinking, the world was born when the Creator imposed order upon a primordial chaos which existed independently of him and which is regarded either as passive matter, or as a downright anti-God, a potentate of darkness and of evil. The world as "cosmos," as an ordered and harmonized whole, is the happy issue of a struggle between the good spirit of light and the somber dark power of chaos. And so this world, this "cosmos," has had a hard birth. And it never responds perfectly to the ordering will of the divinity. This divinity is not the "Almighty," for his might and power is limited by the sluggishness of matter and even by the opposition of the adversary. Dualism was a ready-made solution for the problem of evil; furthermore, it inclined its adherents to see in matter the source of evil and to seek perfection in terms of a deliverance from matter. Clothed in various myths, this dualist thinking dominated the advanced cultures adjacent to Israel. These myths were not entirely unknown even in Israel, where certain poetic biblical texts use imagery evocative of the heroic struggle of God with the waters of the great chaos.[18] But Israel steadfastly refused to see in this dualism the solution of the mystery of suffering and of evil. Even the Genesis creation narrative cannot entirely forego this imagery: the waters mentioned in Genesis 1: 2; the motif of the separation of the light from the darkness, of the waters below the firmament from the waters above the firmament, etc. But such imagery in the Bible, and especially in Genesis, represents "anomalous fragments surviving from an age long past."[19] The writer has no other imagery at his disposal to describe a state of affairs prior to the coming into existence of our world.[20] The imagery has been "demythologized" and purged of any dualist bias. There is not the faintest suggestion of any struggle between God and the adversary: God speaks and created objects simply come into existence. There is not the faintest suggestion of any defective actualization of God's will either: God saw that it was good, that is, entirely in conformity with his will. "The execution follows immediately and is cast in the same descriptive mold as the words of command, to indicate that the execution was instantaneous and exactly conformed to God's command."[21] God is truly for the Israelite the sovereign Master, the Almighty, the Creator. This precludes in principle any dualism, exorcises all demonocracy from the world: nothing is evil as such, no matter how material it may be; everything is the work of God. More than ever do suffering and evil become a mystery and a stumbling block. Still Israel refrains from any search for a solution in a limitation of the power of God and finds the solution solely in the culpable infidelity of creatures.

The author of the creation narrative clearly indicates the absence of any attempt or intention on his part to instruct us in the concrete physical process of the origin of the world. He is proclaiming to us a creation theology: the whole world and all that is therein, no matter what its nature, are the work of God. The personal and sovereign will of God calls man into existence and all other things for the sake of man. Everything is comprehended in his will, from the highest to the lowliest, from the largest to the smallest. All things are sustained by this will and owe to it their very being. In the innermost nucleus of their essence resounds the voice of God fashioning them interiorly. The creative operation of God, even as his salvific operation upon Israel, comprehends everything and penetrates and permeates everything.

> Yahweh is . . . always that God who is simultaneously far off and near at hand, whose claims and whose mercy are so real and so absolute because he infinitely transcends every entity that is the object of his condescension. Such is the mystery of Genesis 1: the Creator there portrayed is unapproachable; he is anterior, exterior, and superior to everything created; but this is the very reason why his operation grapples onto the innermost essence of things and is the whole reason for the existence of all that is.[22]

This essential feature proper to the biblical doctrine and the Christian dogma of creation is not invalidated or even threatened by the doctrine of evolution.

We must also attend to another aspect of the biblical doctrine of creation that is of importance in relating it to evolution. This aspect can indeed be found in Genesis I, but there it is fairly veiled. It is what Lindeskog (and indeed the Scholastics as well) call the *creatio continua* or *actualis*.[23] The positioning of the hymn of creation at the very beginning of the Bible and the very structure of this hymn, which begins in a precosmic situation, leave the impression that creation is something that occurred just once before the dawn of the ages and has no further contemporary reality. The language of Catholic theology, with its distinction between creation and conservation, strengthens this impression still more. Yet such is not the intention, either of the sacred writer or of theology. The creative operation of God and the creation of the world are not limited to the initial origin of things; they are perpetually actual. For God's creative operation sustains and embraces the entire existence of the world and thus, likewise, the conservation and the development of this world.

The indication that this idea influenced the author of Genesis I stems, in the first instance, from the analogy between the salvific operation of God in Israel and his creative operation in the world. The word of creation is potent and effective athwart the ages, just as the word of the promise made to Abraham influences the whole subsequent history of his progeny, just as the word of the Sinai covenant channels and sustains the destiny of the Chosen People throughout the centuries. The creation hymn of the first chapter of Genesis may well have been of liturgical origin and read on the occasion of the new year or, later, on the feast of the Passover (as it still is in the Catholic Church). In the liturgical celebration the assembly of the faithful confesses that these events of distant times (deliverance from Egypt, call of Abraham, creation of the world) are always present and actual and exercise a powerful effect on the contemporary existents. From the unique and initial past event, God traces a line of force throughout the whole of history. Whoever commemorates the wonderful works accomplished by God in ancient times becomes a participator of these works. The believer who commemorates the deliverance out of Egypt is actually delivered here and now. The community celebrating the new year or the Passover, and commemorating on these occasions the original creation, is actually participating here and now in the blessing pronounced by the Creator once and for all time upon man, animals, plants, the entire world. When Israelite and Christian listen with the ear of faith to the reading of the creation narrative, they are confessing that their present-day world and their personal existence are being sustained and embraced here and now by the creative power and sovereign benevolence of God.[24] Does not the text itself indicate this in a certain sense? The writer probably intends to insinuate that the sun and the moon pursue their unfailing course because the ever actual word of God is efficacious for all time, that the fertility of field and flock and the blessing of human progeny is ensured by the perpetual efficacy of the initial blessing.

Theology usually distinguishes between creation as a bringing into existence and conservation as a maintaining in existence. But theology is aware of the superficial nature of this distinction.[25] The human artisan makes something new; that thing does indeed owe its existence to him, but it continues in existence independently of him. The single creative act of God imparts the continuation as well as the inception of existence. For God imparts to things their most intimate being and thus he imparts to them their being in time, their duration. This is why ordinary speech refers to all things perfectly justifiably as "creatures," whether they are the product of the powers of nature or of human industry. For their ontological status is not exhaustively described merely by stating that they are presently comprised of a fundamental matter that was created at the beginning; they are actually entirely dependent here and now on the creative will of God, in the most intimate and ontologically primordial nucleus of their "being."[26] The divine creative operation touches things not only in their origin but also in their continuing duration and their final consummation.[27] "Creation never stops."[28]

It is quite clear and generally admitted nowadays that the doctrine of evolution in no way undermines faith in the fact of creation. But it does entail a thoroughgoing modification in our picture of the operation of creation. Dogma teaches that all things depend on the creative act of God in their deepest and most all-inclusive "being": God is the First and Universal Cause. The doctrine of evolution holds that in the world of our human experience all things have been produced by natural forces: it limits itself to secondary causes and intracosmic relationships. It makes no pronouncement on the primary and ultimate foundation of the existence of the cosmic entities and operations. Philosopher and believer will say that all natural causes and forces are sustained by the divine Creator, but this statement does not deny that the natural causes have their own specific effect. On the contrary, it involves the supposition that the divine creative operation has imparted to things their proper nature and thus, likewise, their proper operation and causal capacity. The creative proximity of God does not render things destitute of their proper being; it constitutes them in that proper being. His operation neither limits nor duplicates their own operation; it sustains that operation. His creative word does not abrogate their immanent law; it promulgates that law. The creative power of God is not magnified by a cramping of that of creatures; it is the display of that creaturely creative power in all its splendor that most perfectly magnifies the creative power of those creatures' God. More majestic and more divine than merely making things is making things make themselves.[29] The immensity of the divine power manifests itself precisely in the supremely intimate inherence of that power in every created entity, "more intimate to my self than myself." By demonstrating the dizzying potentialities and powers resident in the primitive fabric of the cosmos, evolution guides us to the mystery of the creative Omnipotence.

It follows that, as Sertillanges has said, "the act of creation . . . is on no hypothesis a *phenomenon*."[30] Precisely because it is an act of creation, it can never be ranged on the same level as the phenomena nor yet manifest itself in a rupture of the chain of phenomena. Its essence lies in fact in the positing of the chain of the phenomena:

The distinctive feature of the divine operation exercised within the very womb of the universe is precisely that it cannot be pinpointed here or there (save, to a certain point, in the mystic congress of spirit with Spirit) but is rather diffused everywhere in the sustained, finalized and in a certain fashion superveniently animated complex of secondary operations.[31]

The creative operation of God is necessarily hidden in the operation and the laws proper to his creatures. We shall never find the act of creation at the level of the phenomena, not even in the very beginning of the world, since this beginning is never a "phenomenon." No matter to what point science delves back into the past of the world, never will it find the moment when this world did not exist. For pure and sheer non-being is not a reality, and apart from the world there is no time, and so there is no "moment," and there never has been a "moment" at which no creature existed. The novelty of being is no more susceptible to observation than is the radical dependence of being. The creative operation of God can be seen only with the eyes of faith and at the level of philosophical reflection. One of the features peculiar to the new spirituality will thus be the tendency to encounter the Creator in the operation of nature as such.[32] "God creates and shapes us through the process of Evolution."[33]

The doctrine of evolution certainly in no way undermines the dogma of creation. But it does oblige us to take a critical look at our own picture of the act of creation and perhaps revise that picture. Even though this act of creation is not a phenomenon and therefore cannot really be pictured, it does require a certain measure of plastic portrayal in order to be proclaimed and admitted by faith. The ancient view found this in the imagery of the artisan or the artist (the potter of Genesis 2, 7) making something new. And the special feature of the creative operations was that God made the world, not out of a pre-existing matter, but rather out of nothing. Undoubtedly creation was realized to have been more than a mere origination, but it was portrayed as an origination, as the first beginning of all things. For the new vision of the world and of the entire cosmos, this first beginning can be said to have lost all evocative force. For the primary origin has to be referred further and further back into a distant and inchoate past which defies plastic portrayal. In the entire panorama of the origins of things and of the earth itself, there is nowhere any clear-cut picture of a radical novelty. The time-honored portrayal of the initial creation has lost much of its evocative power.

Teilhard had to proclaim the reality of God and of his act of creation in a circle of naturalism and evolutionists. So it is not astonishing that he should have been particularly keenly aware of this awkwardness and tried to find new figures to express that reality. He found two. The figure of destiny occupies the place of honor in his writings: the existence *in fieri* of the world has an orientation, a destiny, and, as Teilhard enucleates in his deduction of the Omega Point, this destiny is none other than God. The Creator God "appears" at the end of the road being travelled by the earth and by man; he is the "God of the Forward March." The creative operation of God may be portrayed as the primary impulsion initiating the evolutionary forward march of the world. This creative operation likewise manifests itself as the force of attraction drawing everything to him, to an ever more perfect participation of his fullness.[34] God's creative act is like a lover drawing things out of nothingness by drawing them to himself. This image is just as good a representation of the doctrine of creation as the image of the artisan. Any doubts on this score merely serve to show how heavily the image often lords it over the doctrine. The total ontological dependence involved in creation is equally well signified by positing God as the final end rather than the artisan, at least in the first instance: "I am Alpha and Omega, saith the Lord."[35] Creation may be envisaged and portrayed either way, starting from its beginning or starting from its consummation. For the reason indicated, Teilhard prefers to approach creation from the latter point of view, an unusual approach. Hence the importance in his thought of this orientation toward the Omega Point and his preference, in his spirituality, for the motif of the edification of the Body of Christ.[36] God himself has indeed given us the supreme image for this motif: the Son becoming incarnate and constituting himself a Body which is the concrete end of the whole of creation.

The second image or figure sometimes used by Teilhard is that of the "Evolver God" or of the "animating type Creator."[37] These terms can easily be misunderstood.[37a] The term *evolver* here assumes a transitive sense and becomes the grammatical parallel of *creator*. God does not himself evolve (except insofar as he has become God-Man[38]); he makes the world evolve. And the "animating" operation of God ought to suggest to us, not the Stoic type world-soul, identical with the immanent laws of nature, but rather the impelling and vivifying power of God.[39] The cosmos is represented as a giant organism, comprehending all things and ever growing toward more elevated forms of being and of life. The action of God in this cosmos is represented as the permanent and fathomless source of cosmic life, sustaining and animating the interior operation proper to the cosmos itself. As opposed to the "old creationism"[40] which represented creation as the first origin of things, this image signifies that creation is the abiding and fathomless source untiringly nourishing the development proper to the cosmos. This image likewise conveys the ancient dogma of creation. But it uses a new form of plastic portrayal, centering attention on the abiding and uninterrupted influence of the divine creative operation, a feature always present in the doctrine as such but not brought out at all clearly in the old representation.

This new way of picturing creation incontestably merits the attention of present-day theology. Anyone who has ever had to explain the dogma of the creation to a mind molded by the natural sciences, and explain that dogma not simply as a formal doctrine but as a reality of faith of the greatest existential importance, will have felt how defective is the old picture. The heritage of the natural sciences is rapidly becoming accessible to everyone. The picture of creation offered by Teilhard corresponds incontestably better to the new scientific view. Theology will therefore have to take pains to elaborate it with more precision and to harmonize it more fully with the whole deposit of faith. But we must here enter two caveats. First, the new portrayal of creation as an abiding gift of being and of life will never entirely supplant the figure of creation as initial origin, any more than the figure of creation as initial origin could ever do without that of conservation. Secondly, the value of the new figure must not be exaggerated either. It remains a single particular representation of a reality which will never be able to be represented adequately. This Teilhardian figure will also have to be submitted to critical reflection, to the same critical reflection to which theology has always submitted the notion of creation as beginning. Teilhard's great merit will probably prove to have been that of having understood the necessity of a renewal and a different orientation of the plastic portrayal of creation, and of having made a first attempt, in the line of this renewal, to maintain the integrity of the true doctrine of the creation.

In our opinion, the same cannot be said of certain animadversions on creation which Teilhard explicitly presents as metaphysical deductions. He certainly does make laudable efforts to respect the data of the Catholic faith. But it seems to me that these efforts have not been entirely successful. These texts require a more technical discussion which would disturb the course of our exposition; and they do not appear to be of essential importance for the grand design of Teilhard. We have therefore chosen to deal with these Teilhardian reflections in an Appendix.[41]

THE SPIRITUAL SOUL AND
ITS CREATION

What is finally the most revolutionary and fruitful aspect of our present age is the relationship between Matter and Spirit: spirit being no longer independent of matter, or in opposition to it (provided, of course, that we do not understand "matter" in a "reduplicative" and restricted sense to mean that portion of the Universe which "redescends," escaping the rising stream of the Noogenesis), but laboriously emerging from it under the attraction of God by way of synthesis and centration.[1]

CHAPTER 4

It is one of the fundamental truths of the Catholic faith that man is not merely a material body but a spirit as well. In 1870, Vatican I summed up the dogma of the creation as follows: "The one true God . . . created out of nothing creatures spiritual and corporeal alike, to wit, the angels and the world, and finally man, who is a composite of spirit and body."[2] The Council was repeating almost verbatim the words adopted by another conciliar profession of faith nearly seven centuries before and expressive of the Catholic conviction of all ages.[3] But between the two Councils there had been effected a total change of aim, though the definition remained the same. The long-ago Council had aimed at proscribing the dualist heresies which held the soul to be man in the proper sense of that word, while the body was held not to have been created by God but rather to have been the work of the devil. Vatican I, on the contrary, was aiming its definition against the materialism of the nineteenth century, a materialism which was not prepared to see in man anything more than a more highly evolved animal and which denied man's spiritual nature. Evolution was and still is one of the most powerful weapons of materialism. Now Teilhard appears to be ranging himself on the side of the materialists by presenting even man's spirit as the fruit of pre-human evolution![4] Is he then sacrificing the essentially spiritual nature of the soul and its creation by God?

We are here arrived, there can be no doubt of it, at one of the most ticklish points of the encounter between the evolutionist doctrine and Christianity in the thought of Teilhard. Theology will probably have to expend much labor and engage in much careful reflection before it will succeed in separating, in Teilhard's remarks on the relations between spirit and matter, the nuggets of truth from the dross of less felicitous formulations and even errors. But Catholic theology and philosophy have every reason to proceed in this matter with the greatest circumspection, for both of them have often been content to repeat the old formulas without asking what significance these have for new problems. It is our intention here to attempt a modest study of the place Teilhard's intuitions may perhaps merit in a new reflection on the data of the faith.

The indispensable preliminary for any real understanding of Teilhard is the quite explicit admission that his hypothesis is exactly the contrary of materialism. The bias of his entire work is dictated by the desire to prove and render evident the "primacy of the spirit." Spirit is more than matter: that is the fundamental hypothesis, the "primordial option,"[5] from which he proceeds in all his philosophical writings and which he is always trying to justify, to make his reader "see." His demand for a thoroughgoing review and re-examination of the natural sciences is based upon this conviction; the natural sciences, after this renewal, are expected to culminate in this intuition.[6] The law of interiorizing complexification, in particular, is at the service of this truth.

But in order to grasp certain shadings of Teilhard's thought and to understand the forceful tone of the expressions he uses on this subject, the reader ought to know what a struggle it had been for Teilhard himself to reconcile in his own mind this fundamental truth of the Christian faith and of Christian philosophy with his own scientific intuitions. His initial inclination, by nature, by interest and by his scientific training, was to search for the deepest reality of the world in the material element, where were to be found the solid, the immutable, the inviolable, where reigned the primordial forces and fundamental laws of the physical world. But this attitude, fruit of a very definite idea of the natural sciences, came into conflict with Teilhard's Christian faith in the spirit. This conflict continued until, about 1910, his own reflections, reinforced by his reading of Bergson, led him to the discovery that an objective science of nature must also look toward synthesis, toward construction, life, the future, the spirit. At the denouement of the process of development of the world, as governed by the law of interiorizing complexification, the spiritual life of man flowers forth as a veritable crown. This spirit is the point of reference of the whole material world. In the spirit are to be found the true coherence and consistency of the world, even of the material world.[7]

Teilhard has many descriptions of the expansive and liberating effect produced upon him by this intuition. It was even a sort of "conversion" permitting him to love God thenceforth "with all his spirit." This inversion of perspective rendered possible the reconciliation between the scientific and the Christian orientation of his thought and finally the consecration of the natural sciences to Christ. He described this conversion, for example, in a sermon at a Nuptial Mass in 1928:

Originally, I had been as much impressed as anyone by the sort of priority accruing, in events, to the Lesser and to the Past. But then I had either to abandon all life of understanding anything within me or around me or else invert the perspective and accord total pre-eminence to the Future and the Greater.

I believe firmly that the consistency of the universe about us derives not from the apparent solidity of the ephemeral materials of which bodies are compounded, but rather from the flame of structuring which has, since the beginning, been traversing the world and diffusing itself in that world. The earth's whole gravity inclines it to a center still before it. Far from being fragile and fortuitous, souls and their unions and their powers are alone assured of infallible progress and alone fated to endure.

What is imponderable in the world surpasses what we touch in that world.

. . . Believe in the spirit.[8]

The spirit spoken of by Christianity and proclaimed by it to be of predominant value is not the enemy of matter, but rather matter's crowning consummation. Corporeal nature is nowhere more perfectly actualized than in man, who is spirit. Indeed, in man, matter regains its highest dignity, essentially human and authentically Christian, by being the "matrix,"[9] the root from which springs and is nourished the spiritual life of man, even though this spiritual life essentially surpasses matter. Henceforth, the natural sciences and technology, entirely ordered as they are to the material world, can be placed at the service of a true enrichment of man and even of the edification of the Body of Christ.[10]

It is a total misunderstanding of Teilhard to reproach him with an "imperialism of matter."[11] It would be far more to the point to speak of an imperialism of the spirit. In the whole of the fabric of the universe, spirit is present *in fieri*, as the end and highest actualization, as the real foundation of being. The reproach is based on a failure to realize the change of perspective accomplished in Teilhard's thought. This failure leaves the critic still imprisoned in the ordinarily accepted perspective of the natural sciences, in the *"materialist illusion,"* which consists in regarding "the elements of analysis as 'more real' than the terms of synthesis."[12]

Despite the repeated and insistent assertions of the primacy of the spirit, more than one reader will feel less than completely reassured on hearing it declared that spirit and matter are the two states or the two faces of a single fabric of the universe; that spirit is not opposed to matter nor yet independent of it; that spirit rises laboriously out of matter by the force of attraction of God; that spirit must be considered *"not* as an exclusion but rather as a transformation, or a sublimation, or a climax of the matter."[13] Is there any point in underscoring the primacy of the spirit if the traditional description of spirit as intrinsically independent of matter must go by the board?

A correct assessment and appraisal of such statements on the dependence of spirit with regard to matter requires a preliminary reminder that the essence of spirit is defined but indirectly, and very imperfectly at that, by saying that spirit is intrinsically independent of matter. This is merely a negative description, whereas any being, and especially spiritual being, should be conceived positively. A germane, positive definition of what spirit is should not posit, in the first instance, its distinction from matter; rather such a definition should proceed from the degree of being proper to spirit. From this point of view, philosophy probably disposes of no better description than that borrowed by Thomas Aquinas from Greek philosophy: spirit is "what reflects upon itself in a perfect reflection."[14] Spirit is therefore something, or better someone, so intimately and so compactly unified in himself as to be really present to himself and have operative control of himself: "to coincide with itself, to be present to itself, and therefore to be capable of knowing itself by way of reflection . . ."[15]; and so, to know via himself and to know himself in his knowledge, in his act of knowing; to determine in his own free will the thrust and bias of his own will, so that for him to love something means to will to love it.[16] Spirit is raised above matter by this unity of being, manifesting itself in reflective, reflexive knowing and in freedom of willing. For matter is quantitative, extended, having parts outside of parts, various parts which are exterior one to another. In other words, matter is partially alien to itself, is but very defectively present to itself. Matter exists in a lesser measure than spirit because matter is less unified than spirit.

In the second place, it must be realized that the human spirit of which Teilhard is speaking cannot be said without any reservations to be independent of matter. According to Catholic dogma, the spiritual soul itself is, in its own essence and not by virtue of some extrinsic influence, the substantial form, that is, the principle of being, of unity, and of life of the human body.[17] It follows that the corporeity, the physical nature, informed by the soul and the vehicle of expression of the soul, pertains to the essence of the soul, and that the human soul is not in full possession of its natural perfection without the body. The soul is not fully itself, is not fully realizing its own essence, unless it is living that essence in a material body. Or, more precisely, the implication is that it is not the soul strictly speaking which has an essence but only the human being, at once spiritual and material, composite of a soul and a body.[18] Now, in view of this stricture, the term *spiritual* cannot signify unreservedly a negation of corporeity. Otherwise man is made into a living contradiction.

There is another implication as well. If, as St. Thomas held, the soul in itself is not a specific nature, but rather a component of human nature, then we cannot speak in the strict sense of the "spiritual nature" or "spiritual essence" of the soul. Any definition of the essence of the soul is, in the final analysis, a definition of the essence of the human being, of man. Thus, the doctrine of the spiritual essence of the *soul* signifies, properly speaking, that the human being, *man*, even though corporeally and interiorly constituted by matter with its alienation from itself, is nevertheless just as truly spiritual, that is, subsisting in an interior unity, a possession of himself, which essentially raises him above the alienation from himself. The expression "spiritual nature of the soul" is simply an elliptical and practically manageable expression of this complex truth. It is implied, as an evident fact, that man is just as really and essentially corporeal, rooted in the material world.

In contrast to the ordinary simplified Catholic anthropology, Teilhard feels obliged to posit explicitly the two elements of this complex truth. His interlocutor is, after all, the modern scientist. This modern man of science is not usually a materialist in the old sense, but he has the impression that man's union to the material earth is not taken entirely seriously in Christianity with its insistence on the spiritual soul. Furthermore, the modern scientist is immersed in the study of material phenomena and of their enthralling depths to such a point that the idea of a spiritual soul has for him an aura of extreme vagueness. Though he may not deny or combat this idea, it conveys nothing to him. Teilhard wants to make this modern scientist *see* that he cannot neglect with impunity the spiritual aspect of man, that he must take it seriously. A decent respect for the full scope of the material phenomenon of itself entails the mandatory recognition and admission of the spiritual. The human spirit is not an intruder on this earth nor in the sciences dealing with the earth and with matter. Teilhard is fighting on a different front from that on which the customary apologetic of the human spirit is exclusively concerned with proclaiming the distance that separates spirit and matter. For Teilhard, the solidarity between matter and spirit is of the greatest importance. He concludes logically, from the ancient traditional doctrine of the spiritual soul as the vital principle of the body, that man's corporeal perfection rests on the fact that he is a spiritual being, and that man's corporeal perfection is the expression and the form of manifestation of his spiritual essence. The highest form of corporeity, of physical nature, is attained in man, not in despite of the fact that man is spiritual, but because of this fact. In the face of the altered situation in science and human communication, Teilhard has to underscore the ancient traditional truth that man's spirituality neither denies nor belittles physical nature, corporeity and matter, but rather actualizes them in the highest degree. In man, "the body is drawn to the being of the soul."[19] As a result, the body becomes more perfect as body and as material organism. The fact of the supreme actualization of the material in man by the spiritual being involves the supposition that the self-possession typical of man as spiritual being signifies a perfecting of matter as such. Thus, all matter is oriented toward human consciousness and in all material reality there resides an implicit thought which prefigures the spiritual. Thus, in treating of all the evolutive processes today classed in the field of chemistry or biology, St. Thomas declares: "The desire of matter tends necessarily toward the highest and most perfect form of being of which matter can partake. . . . But the highest degree of all generative activity (*generatio*) is the human soul. Therefore it is toward the human soul that matter tends as toward its own highest substantial form."[20] In this sense, we feel that the spiritual (in the sense of the human spiritual, of course) can with perfect justice be said to be a culminating point of matter.

But one condition must be laid down: equal justice must be done to what is proper to man as spiritual being, thus essentially raised above matter. In the foregoing, we have insisted so strongly on the continuity between the material and the material-spiritual that the reader may be asking himself if there is still any room left for the essential distinction between animal and man demanded by Christian and philosophical reflection; if there is still any possibility of a definition of the specific nature of the human spirit as spirit.

In his *Descent of Man*, Charles Darwin wrote these words at the end of his chapter on comparative psychology: "There can be no doubt the difference between the mind of the lowest man and that of the highest animal is immense. . . . Nevertheless, the difference in mind between man and the higher animals, great as it is, certainly is one of degree and not of kind." Since then it has been the custom to use the doctrine of evolution to deny any essential difference between the higher animals and man: man is held to be simply the most highly evolved of the primates, the *primus inter pares!*

Throughout the whole of his scientific career, Teilhard was constantly combating this way of looking at the matter. The anatomical differences between the other primates and man may be relatively small, and man's psychic life itself may show traces of kinship with the animal kingdom; yet, for all that, there is a vast difference between the whole of animal life and man, a difference just as susceptible of objective verification as are the anatomical, physiological, or psychological points of likeness. This difference has led to a radically new form of life. It must therefore be accepted as a real "biological"[21] magnitude and cannot be neglected or belittled by a science whose object is the whole spectrum of life on earth.

Man is not simply *primus inter pares* among the primates.[22] It is indicative of a total lack of precision to be willing to recognize between monkeys and men only a difference of degree and not a difference of nature. Here a warning must be sounded against the abusive attribution of a genuine intelligence to the higher mammals. The bond between man and the lower forms of life is indeed intimate; the continuity between animal life and human life is indeed clear and important; nevertheless any objective inspection of the phenomenon of man is forced to admit a "major discontinuity," a "rupture," another form of life, an "absolutely new phase." With the origin of man, the current of life has passed a critical point, has attained a new level. The life of man is at once a continuation of animal life and something heterogeneous from it.[23] The phenomena of the lower stages of life do indeed appear again in man, but they have been elevated and transformed: "all the lower manifestations of life are renewed and superveniently animated in Man, so that they are at once recognizable and unrecognizable."[24]

Teilhard goes so far as to say that the appearance of reflection in man constitutes, in a sense, "a mutation from zero to everything" without any intermediate member.[25] The appearance of man liberated a new form of life upon the earth. It is a prodigious leap, worthy of ranking in the history of the earth as "an evolutive event of the first magnitude": a transiton so profoundly and radically novel as to defy comparison with anything short of the first beginning of life itself. What is opening up is "a new interior world, the world of the *mind-caught*[25a] Universal."

These last words furnish a preliminary indication of the line along which must be sought man's distinctive feature. Sometimes Teilhard tried to make his positivist associates *see* the revolutionary significance of the appearance of man by describing the extent to which man has renewed the face of the earth.[26] But he always comes back to the real nucleus, the source of this revolution: the opening up of a new dimension whereby, above the biosphere, there forms a new layer of being: "a human sphere, the sphere of reflection, of conscious invention, of the sentient union of souls (the Noosphere, if you like)."[27]

With man, the interiorization which characterizes the progressive elevation of matter and of life and manifests itself as a kind of consciousness, at least among the higher animals, enters into an entirely new phase. Man, and man alone, is conscious of his own consciousness, and this renders him capable of foresight and invention: "At a critical point of arrangement . . . life has become hypercentered upon himself, to the point of becoming capable of prevision and invention. It has become conscious 'to the second degree.' "[28]

These expressions, life to the second power, consciousness to the second power, keep recurring again and again.[29] Not only does man know; he knows that he knows. In Teilhard's eyes, this is a *phenomenon* admitted by all, even though natural science is not accustomed to seeing its *biological* importance.

It is generally accepted that what distinguishes man psychologically from other living creatures is the power acquired by his consciousness of turning in upon himself. The animal knows, it has been said; but only man, among the animals, knows that he knows. This faculty has given birth to a host of new attributes in men: freedom of choice, foresight, the ability to plan and construct, and many others.[30]

And so, although there may indeed be a certain degree of consciousness in the infra-human world, man is distinguished by "a consciousness sufficiently centered to be able to coincide with itself."[31] From this power of reflected consciousness and the resulting reflexive awareness in man, there derive freedom of will and an unlimited faculty of knowledge. Teilhard even concludes from this power to the imperishable and immortal nature of man, as will appear in his deduction of the Omega Point.[32]

Do not these two excerpts provide a sufficient answer to the question as to whether Teilhard succeeded in defining what characterizes and distinguishes the human spirit as spirit? This capacity for reflection, this centration of human consciousness which is so intimate that the consciousness becomes conscious of itself, this return upon itself, seem no different from what St. Thomas in his day was advancing as the distinctive feature of the spiritual person: "he who reflects upon himself in a perfect reversion." The extent of the coincidence of the Thomistic and the Teilhardian approach is well illustrated by the fact that such an eminent Thomist as J. Mouroux uses Teilhard's very expressions: "to coincide with itself," "centered upon itself."[33] It is simply that Teilhard's manner of tackling the problem is not the usual one. With an eye to his interlocutors, Teilhard has to recognize, admit, and even underscore the kinship of human life with animal life and with material reality, a kinship passed over almost in silence by scholastic thinking. Nevertheless, Teilhard does succeed in maintaining the essential superiority of the human spirit with its power of reflection, by means of which spirit dissociates itself from the alienation proper to matter.[34]

This unusual manner of tackling the problem has the advantage of preparing his evolutionist interlocutors to see gradually the special quality and grandeur of man as an immattered spirit. As instance of interiorization to the second power and on a higher level, spiritual man finds a place in the great ascent of matter and of life, the great upward thrust governed by the law of interiorizing complexification.

It thus becomes clear that the doctrine of the spiritual nature of man does not, at least in one sense, signify any belittling of matter, which is coming to impress modern science more and more with the vast dimensions of its magnitude, its age, and its potentialities. The potentialities that have been displayed for millions of years in a marvelous wealth and diversity of forms of being and of life find their final consummation, their supreme complexification and interiorization, in the fact that matter becomes the body of spiritual man. Man, as immattered spirit, appears as the ultimate crown of the evolutive process, as the supreme consummation and actualization of the tendency to complexification dominating matter. Man is the ripe fruit of the ancient tree of material development. Man is the instrument of a continuation of the development, henceforth upon a new level, the level of reflective consciousness and of freedom. This new phase of development will form the subject matter of our Part II.

The doctrine of the origin of the human soul is obviously most ultimately bound up with the doctrine of the spiritual nature of that soul. On the basis of the ordinary *magisterium* of the Church, it must incontestably be admitted as a doctrine of faith that every human soul, and therefore that of the first man as well, owes its origin to a special and immediate "creative" act of God. Pius XII has said: "The Catholic faith commands us to hold that souls are immediately created by God."[35] On this point the witness of ancient tradition is particularly strong, although this tradition does not usually employ the technical term "creation," using rather vaguer terms: the soul has been constituted, given, etc., by God. Only the Church in Africa seems to have had doubts, discernible in Tertullian and especially in Augustine—the latter caught in the cleft stick of the simultaneous desire to safeguard the spiritual essence of the soul and to render intelligible the doctrine of original sin. But despite the enormous prestige of Augustine, the Latin Church was soon unanimous on this subject.

Teilhard, for his part, does not cast doubt on this doctrine. In a note in *Le Phénomène humain,* he declares explicitly that he wishes to leave full room for a "creative operation" and a "special intervention" of God in the origin of the human soul.[36] This note is undoubtedly a later addition on his part, but it squares entirely with his thought. In principle he does not try to define philosophically the first cause, the prime mover of evolution, limiting his investigations to the nexus of intracosmic phenomena and causes; God, moving power of evolution, appears only at the term. In one of his earlier writings, addressed to his fellow Catholics rather than to questing outsiders, he had shown that evolution cannot deny the creation of the human soul because creation is not a phenomenon.[37] Finally, we would underscore the Teilhardian expression to the effect that the soul comes into being "under the power of attraction of God";[38] this expression should be taken in the context of Teilhard's practice elsewhere of expressing the creative action and operation of God likewise by such categories as "end" and "power of attraction."[39]

Yet a man like Hulsbosch, for example, writes: "It is difficult to reconcile the immediate creation of the human soul . . . with the Teilhardian design."[40] The difficulty probably arises not from the opinions peculiar to Teilhard but rather from the doctrine of evolution in general, a doctrine whose import is fully revealed only in Teilhard's own writings. Since experience shows that this point constitutes a serious cause of friction between the teachings of faith and the science of nature and since, furthermore, certain minds molded by natural science are most disconcerted by this notion of creation, we must treat this problem here.

Let us take as the basis of our examination the classical statements of the theologians investigating the question as to whether the human soul owes its origin to creation or to parental generation.[41] There seems to be a fundamental parity, despite the difference between the origin of the first man from animal life and that of the child from its parents. The problem has always been the subject of laborious disputation on the part of Catholic theology and philosophy. It has never been easy to reconcile the doctrine of the creation of the soul by God with the experimental datum of procreation. Sheer reflection on the creative operation of God has always demanded a more than ordinary effort on the part of the human mind.

The first caveat is that the doctrine must not be overlaid and smothered by vagrant elements borrowed from the human imagination. For instance, the quite common expression, *infusion* of the soul, evokes the picture of a God creating the soul in a kind of secret treasury and then pouring it from the outside into the vessel of the body formed in the mother's womb. Here there are three false images: the soul would exist before being united to the body; the body would exist before being animated by the soul; and the creative operation of God would penetrate to creatures from the outside. Now the creation of the soul *is* its infusion into the body. The formation of the body *is* its animation by the soul. And, above all, the creative operation of God is not "outside" but rather in the very heart, the innermost depths of the creature. In infusing the soul at the moment of conception of a child, God is not filling up a kind of vacuum left by the human procreative activity; rather he is activating and elevating *from the inside* the activity of the parents themselves. "So that the creative operation occurring in the case of man is immanent and not transcendent in nature, despite its totally transcendent cause. It is the work of God 'mingled with his works.' "[42] Or perhaps it is better to say that, because God is transcendent Creator, his operation is most deeply immanent. The creative operation of God is not positioned "outside of" the procreative activity; it is deep within this procreative activity, rendering it potent. St. Thomas here uses the figure of an instrument: the activity of the parents is creative in the hand of God, even as a pen in the hand of a man writing a letter is expressing human sentiments.[43]

This figure has still another advantage: it shows that the creative action and operation of God and the human procreative activity produce one and only one being, the child. The figure of the infusion of the soul seems patently dangerous. But even in the hallowed and indispensable expression *creation* there is hidden a subtle poison. For it may evoke the picture of the parents by themselves producing the body and God by himself producing the soul, with the result that God and parents each give being to a part of the resulting human child. And since generation and creation are both ordered to the imparting of "being," it would follow that man has a double "being." Now this is false: "there is not in man a double being."[44] Body and soul are not two "parts" of man which are mutually independent; the being of the soul is essentially a "being in the body,"[45] the being of the body is a being informed and animated by the soul. In the strict sense, there *is* not a body and there *is* not a soul; there *is* only man, composite of body and soul, of *a* body and *a* soul. The picture of the parents as producing (="making to be") the body alone and of God creating (=also "making to be") and infusing the soul, therefore, seems defective. Pushed to its logical extreme, it would lead to a dualism of being. The parents are not simply the parents of the body; they are the parents of the child.[46] And God does not create only the soul (although this could be said with more justification); he creates the body by giving the soul to the body as its substantial form. "Therefore," points out St. Thomas, "the fact is that nature which prepares the body and God who creates the soul are not acting as two independent causes but rather in concert and in the fashion of a single principle."[47]

The refinement of the notion of creation and its purgation of imaginative accretions can thus help to avert useless conflicts between the doctrine of the creation of the soul and the view of the natural sciences. But can anything be done along the line of a further determination and specification of the positive sense of this "creation" of the soul? Can we specify a positive sense which would have enough religious weight and meaning to be admitted to the Church's preaching? Let us try.

Creation implies that God is the cause of being and, therefore, that the creature, to the extent that it is being, depends on God as its principle. Now Catholic doctrine speaks of a particular and immediate creation of the soul. This means that the human soul (or more exactly the human being inasmuch as he is soul) differs from other creatures. But it is evident that no distinctions can be made in the creative operation inasmuch as it designates the operation of God. The creative operation of God is one and simple; it is a single act of his will, comprehending and sustaining the whole cosmos and the whole of time with all that they contain. Distinctions can only be introduced into creation to the extent that creation signifies dependence of being with regard to God. Thus the only thing that the particular creation of the soul by God can signify is a particular dependence of being. A particular dependence of being, in turn, can signify nothing other than a particular mode or manner of being, to the extent that this manner of being is seen with reference to God. For the dependence of being which is called creation includes the total being of things; outside of that there is nothing but non-being, nothingness (so there *is* no "outside"). Thus a particular creation of the human soul or of the human being inasmuch as he is soul signifies a special relation of his being to God.

In the light of all this, we can perhaps look for a definition of this particular and special character along the following lines. The human being is born of the generative activity of his parents, a biological activity. Inasmuch as he is produced by them, he is an individual of the human species; for generation is ordered to multiplication, and multiplication implies reproduction. Inasmuch, therefore, as man is the product of generation, he is an entity which repeats itself, which differs numerically from his fellow men. But the human being is more than an individual in a species. He is a person, and as such, he is one, unique, and cannot be reproduced. This comes out most clearly in the fact that man has his own end within himself. His existence has more than the merely relative value of an individual, existing only as a member of its species and having as its end nothing but the preservation and consummation of this species. Man is an end unto himself, for he can know and love God personally, and can therefore be called personally by God.[48] Man has an absolute value as such, as individual human being. In the singularity of his essence, he can neither be reproduced nor be replaced. The existence of the individual human being is not entirely exhausted in his relations with the human species and with the cosmos of which he is part. He has an absolutely personalized, unique, direct relationship with God.

This brings us to the essential paradox of the person considered in relation to humanity at large. Insofar as he is spirit informing a body, he is *drawn* toward the conditions of material substance: he is a member of a species and exists for the sake of that species. Insofar as he is a spirit transcending the body, he shares the condition of the spiritual creature: he is marked by direct relation to God and surpasses a species made for his sake.[49]

Inasmuch, therefore, as the human being is a person, he is raised above the series of generations, the chain of reproductions to which he belongs as an individual. As a person, the human being is a unique and immediate creation of God, willed by God for himself and in himself, personally called by God's creative word and drawn out of the abyss of nothingness, personally invited by the grace of God to the vivifying encounter with his Creator and Father.[50] In every human being there is an element whereby he is an individual and, as such, the fruit of generation and biological heredity; but there is also an element whereby he is a person, in direct relation to God, the origin and destiny of his existence. He is more than a child of his parents and a member of his race; he is a new and original creation of God. This element is precisely his spiritual soul, the deepest kernel and nucleus of his being, by which he surpasses the alienation of matter and is actively present to himself, by which he is open to the horizon of the infinite and to God.

75

We have already said that God and the parents do not impart existence to distinct parts of the human being. Yet the paradox of human generation, like the paradox of the essence of man, is that it produces an individual of the species who is a person and, as such, is raised above the biological faculties of reproduction and generation. Here there becomes apparent the great wisdom of St. Thomas' comparison of the instrument. Inasmuch as human parentage is not uniquely ordered to biological reproduction, but rather to the animation of a new person, the parents are the servants of God in his immediate solicitude for their child. This is doubtless the reason why biological heredity will play only a subordinate role in the molding of the personality, compared to the influence of the person of the parents on the person of the child, i.e., the influence of the parents in their unique, conscious, and voluntary relation to their fellows and to God.[51]

If the doctrine of the immediate creation of the soul can be understood in this sense, the importance of its religious significance, according it a place in the Church's preaching, leaps to the eye. It expresses the revelation that man in his personal individuality is the object of the creative love and solicitude of God, and that every man has a personal and unique assignment, which no one else can fulfill, set by the God who formed him in his mother's womb.

Applying this thinking on the origin of any human child to the first origin of man out of the living prehuman world, we must affirm with still greater emphasis that the biological generation culminating in man produces a living being raised essentially above the series of the generations. A new creation has occurred. This creative intervention of God need not manifest itself in a discoverable break in the chain of phenomena, even though it does signify a profound transformation of the body itself, which can now be enlisted as an instrument in the service of righteousness. The break becomes visible only when man reflects on his own essence, only when he knows himself spirit and called by God, and when he meditates, on the basis of this knowledge and awareness, upon the fathomless change his appearance has entailed upon the face of the earth. Man comes into being in a real and intimate continuity with the current of life that is bearing him along. But at the same time his relation to God and his dependence with reference to God cause him to surpass essentially the power of the waters out of which the creative voice and the force of attraction of God have called him into existence. Man enters the world on the one hand as a superior form of animal life, so intimately linked to that life that the boundary between the two eludes our observation; on the other hand, as an absolutely new, original and definitive creation, minted by God in his own Image and Likeness.

If the doctrine of the creation of the soul can be understood in this way, then Teilhard's thought, especially on evolution, far from trammeling this doctrine, actually includes it. For Teilhard's insistence that man is really the product of evolution is matched by his insistence that man's origin really does signify a new degree of being, raised essentially above the current of animal evolution. And, as will appear in the sequel, this new degree of being is distinguished by the uniqueness, the irreplaceable worth, the inescapably personal assignment, and the radical personal relation with God of every member of the human family.

APPENDIX I

A Metaphysic of Creation?

In some early writings from his years at the front, only excerpts of which have survived, Teilhard attempts a bold effort at defining creation and its essential properties by a kind of metaphysical deduction. The writings of the last years of his life contain allusions to these ideas,[1] and a synthetic exposition of them is to be found in *Comment je vois* (1948). This latter will serve us as a guide in our own exposition and critique. The first part, entitled *Physics*, recapitulates the ideas developed in *Le Phénomène humain;* in the second part, which amounts to four pages and is entitled *Metaphysics*, Teilhard proposes to "reconstruct deductively, i.e., *a priori*, the system thus observed."[2]

Teilhard reproaches classical metaphysics with proceeding from a statically conceived "being," treated as a primary and irreducible notion. The science of nature and analysis of cosmic development makes us aware that being is a definite sort of movement, to wit a movement of union:

> Being can in fact be defined (at least genetically, if not ontologically) by a special sort of motion, indissolubly associated with it, that of *union*. So that being could be equated as follows, depending on the type of the individual case:
> being = uniting oneself or uniting others (active form);
> being = being united and unified by another (passive form).[3]

Here there can be recognized the principle of classical metaphysics, according to which *unum et ens convertuntur:* "being" and "being one" are interchangeable. There can also be recognized the law of interiorizing complexification, according to which the existence of the fabric of the cosmos is a growth along the line of progressive interiorization and unification. And the disturbing question arises, for anyone at all familiar with the history of philosophy, as to whether this experimental law can be converted uncritically into a metaphysical principle.

Using this notion of "being" as a basis, Teilhard develops his ideas in four moments. His starting point is the datum of the existence of a "First Being," entirely and absolutely sufficient unto himself and existing in himself. But, in a second moment, we must picture this God, in conformity with the data of revelation, as constituted of more than one distinct person; even in God, therefore, the principle finds application, for the divine being is likewise a movement of internal union to his own life:

> In a first moment, we must begin by admitting as an outright given fact . . . the irreversible and self-sufficient presence of a "First Being" . . . But, for this initial and final Center to subsist in himself in his splendid isolation, we are compelled to picture him (in conformity with the "revealed" datum—second moment) as in trinitarian tension. Thus, the principle we have taken as the basis of our Metaphysic proves valid and enlightening, even in these primordial

depths: God himself, in a rigorously veridical sense, exists only in uniting himself.[4]

One must respect Teilhard's prudence in avoiding any statement to the effect that the mystery of the Trinity could be deduced from the principle of the identity between being and unity. Although there can be no doubt that the trend of his thought runs in this direction, he is too well aware that such a deduction would be unacceptable to Catholic thought. This reasoning would be specially illegitimate in view of the fact that the intra-trinitarian union of the Persons is a union of abundance and of plenitude, whereas the union to which Teilhard's principle refers when applied to the universe is but a comm-union of potency and indigence, that is, a "becoming one" and a "making one."[5] There is incontestably also in the created universe a union of riches, to wit, the union of love, of which Teilhard liked to say that "union differentiates"; but his metaphysical principle is not sufficiently refined to warrant its application to the divine reality.

The third moment of Teilhard's argumentation is still less acceptable. God, being posited himself as absolute unity, opposes to himself an absolute non-unity or absolute plurality, namely nothingness, pure potency and creatability, which is, so to speak, an appeal launched toward God, toward unity, and therefore toward existence:

In the very act by which his reality is posited, God, we have just realized, is trinitizing himself. But this is not all. By the very fact of his interior self-unification in order to exist, the First Being *ipso facto* makes another kind of opposition spring up, no longer within his own depths but rather at the antipodes of himself (*third moment*). There is the self-subsistent Unity at the pole of being; and, necessarily, in consequence, all around on the periphery, there is the Manifold: the *sheer* Manifold (nota bene), or the "creatable Nothingness," which is nothing and yet, by passive virtuality of arrangement (i.e., of union) is a potency, a craving and supplication of being, to which (and it is here that our intellect is absolutely incapable, at such depths, of distinguishing supreme necessity from supreme freedom), to which, I say, everything happens as if God had not been able to resist.[6]

Tresmontant rightly observes that this is a recourse to the ancient "metaphysical mythology" and that this absolute Manifold bears a great resemblance to Aristotle's πρώτη ὕλη .[7] Now the Judeo-Christian doctrine of creation excluded precisely this principle of prime matter. So Teilhard is right is saying that the absolute Manifold is Nothingness: where there is no trace of unity, there is nothing. But he cannot refrain from attributing certain properties to this nothingness: it is a "virtuality," "a craving and supplication of being"; in the succeeding paragraph he is already speaking of "structure." His belief in creation compels him to say that the Manifold is Nothing, but his metaphysic hankers to make it into something. In his earliest writings, when he came more drastically under the spell of the mythological image and was less mature in his faith, Teilhard had even spoken of a struggle of God against this Nothingness: "The overflowing Unity of Life grappled, in Creation, with the inexistent Manifold which was opposing itself to that unity as contrast and challenge."[8]

Teilhard seems to have fallen victim, in this portrayal of the absolute Manifold, to a spatial non-metaphysical imagination. In positing himself as the absolute One, God would posit around him his contrary. This statement has no metaphysical justification. Augustine's statement that "God has no contrary"[9] *is* metaphysically profound. God is absolute affirmation, the absolute Yes! Even the absolutely possible, which Teilhard identifies with his own absolutely Manifold, has no reality apart from God. It is solely in virtue of creation, based on the free creative will of God, that the possible, the potential, becomes distinct from God. This would be the place for a resumption of the old Scholastic discussion on the reality of "possible beings."

Teilhard pushes his reasoning still further. He reproaches classical theology with making God's creative initiative an entirely arbitrary act of will; this, he charges, makes classical theology incapable of rendering intelligible the interior nature of the created reality. His own metaphysic of union would, on the contrary, he claims, assign an intelligible place to creation, filling a sort of void by the image of the divine unity. And the fundamental law of creation would be to mount toward an ever-higher union:

Always in . . . classical philosophy, Creation or Participation (wherein consists the *fourth moment*) has tended to be presented as an almost arbitrary gesture on the part of the First Cause, operating (on an analogy with "efficient" causality) according to a completely indeterminate mechanism. . . . In a metaphysic of union, on the contrary, while the self-sufficiency and the self-determination of the absolute Being remain intact (for I insist that the Manifold, the sheer, antipodal Manifold, is but pure potency and passivity), the creative act, on the other hand, assumes a perfectly defined meaning and structure. The actualization of participated being by arrangement and totalization—Pleromization, as St. Paul would have said—becomes the fruit, in a sense, of God's Reflection, no longer now within Himself, but rather outside of Himself; this Pleromization appears as a kind of symmetrical antiphon to the Trinitization. It serves to fill a void, in a certain sense. It assumes its own proper place and it becomes, at the same time, capable of being expressed in the same terms which have served us to define Being. To create is to unify.[10]

Let us leave to one side the allusion to the Pauline *pleroma*. Let us do the same with the term *trinitization:* despite its grammatical form, it is not meant to signify a real *becoming* in God, but rather that, in the mystery of God, trinity and unity are not a crass and static datum, but rather life; Father, Son, and Holy Spirit are eternally positing themselves in a way that is divinely necessary and divinely free.

Nor is there any difficulty about creation being held to be an image of God and a reflection of the Trinity, nor about this being held to express a necessary metaphysical structure of created reality; this is a classical thesis of theology.[11] And the thesis that to create means to unify is self-evident for Thomistic metaphysics, even though this Thomistic metaphysics sees the unity of each creature in itself and of creation in its totality as somewhat less forthright and simple than Teilhard presents it. But the main difficulty again resides in this spatial imagining, which would make creation fill a "void" constituting for God what amounts to a challenge to which he is held to have to respond.[12]

Another difficulty is the attempt to find something other than the divine good pleasure as the basis for the act of creation. All such attempts are clearly repudiated by the Christian doctrine of creation: "God has created all things in perfect freedom."[13] Teilhard dreaded anything arbitrary and perhaps the philosophical and theological training through which he had passed gave him good reason. In this case, a deeper and more thorough meditation on what is meant by the will of God might have taught him that there can be no question of anything arbitrary here. God's will is the expression of his innermost essence, which is abiding goodness and perfect wisdom. God cannot create anything other than a reflection of himself, a creation which is good and in process of becoming good, wise and in process of tending toward wisdom, unified and in process of unifying itself. But the road taken by Teilhard is a blind alley blocked by the Christian dogma of creation.[14]

An integral part of the creation Gospel is the tenet that the whole of creation in its "entirety" and without remainder is sustained and embraced by the love of God; the joy of the believer lies in knowing himself to be enfolded in that love and by that love alone. As a pious Catholic, Teilhard knows this and professes it: "if he did not feel so completely swept away in the divine ocean that no initial point of support would be left him."[15] But in another context he is inclined to find an ultimate intelligibility which would not depend on God.[16]

Finally, his speculation leads him to see creation as a kind of consummation and fulfillment of God himself.[17] God is evidently the fullness of being and therefore suffices unto himself, as Teilhard repeats insistently. But the image of "empty space" leads Teilhard to a portrayal of a sort of complement to God, God realizing himself over against this void, filling it with the reflection of his glory in his act of creation. This may well be in part a protest against the idea that creation signifies nothing for God, leaves him "indifferent," an idea whose logical consequence would be that man's actions would have no absolute, "divine" value. Teilhard dreads the resultant belittling of man, which would take all the heart out of Christianity. In his specifically religious and phenomenological writings, Teilhard contents himself with seeking this meaningfulness of man in the edification of the Body of the God-Man.[18] But in his metaphysical essay he seeks for a deeper ground, capable of constituting the basis of the creative act itself.

There is real justification for opposition to an opinion which would slavishly introduce the "Unmoved Mover" of Aristotle into the Christian notion of God. Scripture is outspoken in its insistence on God's deep and lively interest for his people, for all men, for his whole creation. It would involve a distortion of the revelation of God to see in this insistence nothing but so many instances of naive anthropomorphism. God betokens an impenetrable mystery which is a transfiguring reality. And is not the Incarnation of his Son a tangible proof of this real and intimate relation of God with the world? But Scripture also seems to be showing us the path we must take in our explanation of the mystery. This relation rests exclusively upon the impenetrable power of the goodness of God. If God, even God-made-man, has need of us and of our collaboration, it is because he wills it, not by compulsion and need, therefore, but out of his overflowing abundance.[19] The fact that men can serve God, gladden him or wound and sadden him, rests upon God's initiative, on the covenant he has willed to make with his people and with creation and which he has crowned with the Incarnation of his Son. Love makes itself vulnerable by the very fact of loving. In a mysterious but real sense, men can expand or contract the divine being of God, in function of the extent to which they allow him to be God for them. But this faculty rests solely upon the covenant which God has established with man in creation and in grace. This "power" of man over God is not a motive of creation; on the contrary, it is the result of creation, or better it is creation itself. By addressing himself to man in creating him, God makes it possible for man to address himself to God. The figure of a "nothing" craving and imploring creation by God, and that of the possibility of any fulfillment of God are pure figments of the human imagination.

We shall return later to the rest of this attempt at metaphysical synthesis, in which Teilhard tries to "deduce" in similar fashion the mysteries of evil and of the Incarnation. The above exposition and critique will suffice to show the nature of this "metaphysic." As Tresmontant well puts it: "Metaphysics is a technical science, and anyone tackling it must make it his craft and profession. All the evidence militates against metaphysics having been the craft and profession of Teilhard."[20] Metaphysics is a branch of philosophy which looks at reality as reality *is*, and so finds itself being at once extremely abstract and very concrete. It demands of its initiates both a great respect for the whole of the real as given, and a prudent critical attitude in the explanation of the data. Teilhard's attempt to "reconstruct deductively, i.e., *a priori*, the system observed,"[21] built as it is upon the narrow basis of his definition of being, borrowed uncritically from the practical experience of the natural sciences, and making use of images just as uncritically employed, does not satisfy these conditions. To Teilhard can be applied his own remark: "I distrust metaphysics, because I scent geometry in it."[22] The best apology for these metaphysical elucubrations of Teilhard is perhaps to be found in his own estimate of them: "Its philosophical significance is obviously very roughly worked out,"[23] "dubious and tentative."[24]

The chief aim of this discussion has not been to point up the limitations of a very great mind, a very intuitive and original thinker in less ethereal spheres. It was primarily to persuade the reader that these Teilhardian observations ought not to be taken too seriously in the context of the whole of his thinking, despite the great importance attaching to the topics at issue.[25] Among the thousands of pages comprising his entire writings, only a minor multiple of ten treat of this area (the entire extent of *Comment je crois*, from the first notion of being down to and including the mysteries of sin and of the Incarnation, amounts to but four pages!). Our special hope is that we have shown that there is no mandatory nexus between his "phenomenological" insight and design and his metaphysical reflections. Even where Teilhard does use philosophical principles in his phenomenology, these principles have been borrowed not from exalted "metaphysics" but from more down-to-earth and generally accessible levels of philosophy. And, in the phenomenology, Teilhard remains faithful to the data of experience and of revelation, accepting the fact of the creative and salvific operation of God. What Teilhard calls metaphysics is a bold but fruitless effort to go beyond this complex of data, to dictate in some sense a law to God himself. Teilhard may well himself have contributed more than any other single person to compromising in the minds of his readers his own sweeping intuition of the world and of history, by pushing it to this abortive issue.

PART II

The Way of All Flesh

UPWARD TOWARD OMEGA

---

*Many biologists, and not the least eminent among them,
... undoubtedly still believe that the human species,
having attained the level of Homo sapiens, has reached an
upper organic limit beyond which it cannot develop, so
that anthropogenesis is only of retrospective interest. But
I am convinced that, in opposition to this wholly illogical
and arbitrary idea of arrested hominisation, a new concept is arising, out of the growing accumulation of
analogies and facts, which must eventually replace it. This
is that, under the combined influence of two irresistible
forces of planetary dimensions (the geographical curve of
the Earth, by which we are physically compressed, and
the psychic curve of Thought, which draws us closer
together), the power of reflection of the human mass,
which means its degree of humanisation, far from having
come to a stop, is entering a critical period of intensification and renewed growth.*

*What we see taking place in the world today is not
merely the multiplication of men but the continued shap-
ing of man. Man, that is to say, is not yet zoologically
mature.*[1]

CHAPTER 5

Since man emerged, toward the end of the Tertiary or the
beginning of the Quaternary Era, from the current of evolution,

89

he has undergone very little anatomical development. The single human phylum did indeed spread over the whole of the earth's surface and branched out into the present-day races; but modern man still bears an astonishing resemblance to the oldest specimens known to us of Homo sapiens or Praesapiens. Mankind, as a biological species, presents another characteristic connected with this fact. For mankind has not divided into several species, despite man's dispersion over the whole of the earth and the protracted isolation of distinctive groups and races. This is a striking exception in the world of living beings. Everywhere else, we see an ancestral species ramifying, under the thrust of evolution, into divergent races and these races veering off progressively further one from the other as a result of their distinctive evolution, to solidify eventually into new independent species. In the case of man, there are indeed racial divergences, but these do not split the human family into autonomous species. Biological cross-fertilization is possible across all racial boundaries and so is spiritual creative communication.[2]

Does this mean, as some scientists think, that evolution has stopped at man and that life has lost its original power to engender new species? Impossible, retorts Teilhard. Never has a species of living being shown as much vitality as mankind, never has a compact mass of living matter known such effervescence. Human life has always been inventive; the vital movement of interiorizing complexification continues its progress. With man, this movement attains a new level. There does indeed appear to be a stoppage of anatomical and physiological development. But if we consider the new "biological" dimension that has opened up with man, the conscious-reflective or reflex-conscious level, we shall there rediscover the age-old forward movement of life. A new form of complexification and interiorization, a new form of "arrangement," of involution of life upon itself, takes over where the older, former forms have left off. Life's dynamism is still operative, stronger indeed than ever, but at the level of the psychically reflective and of the socially conscious.[3]

Thanks to the marvellous and ingenious expedient of socialization in a reflective environment, a new type of "psychogenic" arrangement (educational and collective in nature) has come onto the scene of Nature's drama together with man, at the ideal moment to understudy or take over from the older and perhaps partially outdated forms of cerebralization.[4]

For a better understanding of these Teilhardian ideas, we must here recur to a phenomenon of infra-human life which we have not thus far treated. We have described above the growing complexification solely at the level of the individual. But the vegetable and animal world likewise presents to us a phenomenon of complexification at the level of the community, expressed in the progressive formation of social groupings: colonies, tribes and herds practicing division of labor and community of life as between individuals of the same species; and ecological associations in which different kinds and forms of life complement one another and ensure one another's existence. In proportion as the individual corpuscle attains a higher development and becomes more centered upon itself, and thus more radically specialized, it is also bound by multiple and more varied ties of mutual dependence to other living beings, within and outside of its own species. The higher forms of life cannot exist outside of a complex web of kinship and of reciprocal relations and dependence: in its fully unfolded state, the biosphere forms a "collective inter-complexity" of an extraordinary density.[5]

With the appearance of man and of his reflective consciousness and awareness, this grouping activity likewise enters a new stage. We need not, for our present purpose, enter into greater detail concerning this new form of dependence with regard to other living beings which is typical of man. The crucial role played in the cultural and social development of man by the domestication of animals and edible plants of all kinds is immediately evident. We can limit ourselves here to the new look imparted to the grouping activity among men themselves. Reflection can be said to furnish a new communal link.[6] The new look can be summed up succinctly as the transition from heredity to education. In the infra-human world, the formation of groupings is almost entirely determined by biological procreation which links every individual to his fellows in the series of the generations. Man can transmit his qualities to posterity not only by physical heredity but also by conscious education. In man, personal qualities and psychic experiences can, so to speak, become hereditary, capable of being transmitted and communicated to the next generation: "Now that the old chromosomic heredity is henceforth paralleled by an extra-individual 'educational' heredity, the conservation and accumulation of the *acquired* suddenly assumes an importance of the first order in biogenesis."[7]

And what is perhaps still more important, these acquisitions and these experiences become capable of communication and transmission even apart from the generative chain; they can be handed on to all human beings. This new capacity alters the aspect of the human formation of the group. The tribes, peoples and states of human history have not been constituted solely by physical consanguinity; this kinship has been reinforced, complemented, even supplanted at the higher levels of human development by the ties of education, exchange of ideas, juridico-social structures consciously erected and consciously accepted.

Thus, the development and flowering of the great cultural entities of mankind, the building of states, ancient and modern, follows and continues the old line of evolution. Spengler and Toynbee have brought to modern historiography a liking for the use of images borrowed from biological life (birth, growth, maturity, senescence, and death) to describe the origin, apogee, and decline of civilizations. For the historiographers, these are but metaphors which do not really effect any ontological bridge between biology and history. But Teilhard thinks that, in actual fact, human civilization is nothing but the prolongation of the old dynamism of evolution in the animate sphere, on a higher plane, that of the humanly conscious and psychic. The formation of tribes, peoples, and kingdoms of antiquity and of modern-day states (and, latterly, of international communities) is a prolongation of the age-old mechanism which gave birth to the animal species. There is this difference, however: the mechanism is henceforth operative on a higher plane, the plane of the conscious and the voluntary. And so the psychic element now assumes a more important role than that of the physiological and morphological element.[8]

Man now sees that the seeds of his ultimate dissolution are at the heart of his being. The *End of the Species* is in the marrow of our bones.

Is it not this presentiment of a blank wall ahead, underlying all other tensions and specific fears, which paradoxically (at the very moment when every barrier seems to be giving away before our power of understanding and mastering the world) is darkening and hardening the minds of our generation?

As psychiatry teaches us, we shall gain nothing by shutting our eyes to this shadow of collective death that has appeared on our horizon. On the contrary, we must open them wider.[9]

Teilhard distinguishes between two different phases in the development of mankind, and from this distinction derives his own forecast of the future. These phases can be graphically represented as meridians on the surface of a sphere; their origin is coincident at one of the poles, then they diverge, rapidly at first and then more slowly, until they reach the equator. When both have passed this equator, the divergent movement becomes a convergent movement proceeding more and more rapidly toward the opposite pole.

During the first phase, the divergent or expansive one, the development of mankind follows the process of a living species of the animal kingdom. Homo sapiens, probably born in Central Africa, has known a considerable development, numerically and geographically, in a relatively short time. From the new home he built in the Mediterranean area, he has spread in less than 20,000 years and with no important changes in anatomy or culture, over southern Asia, northern Europe, Siberia, and thence into North and South America.[10] Like every other living species, mankind has branched out into the present-day races and covered the earth with different cultural groupings, peoples and states. The expansion of the technical, social and juridical communities was accompanied by a similar growth in the interior wealth and unity of each individual. By membership in the social, cultural, and juridical grouping, every member is able to acquire the qualities of the group and so to enrich his own interior life, via education, language, literature and all the other forms of contact with his fellows. "When I read the great books, I become a thousand men and yet remain myself."[11] Indeed, I become more thoroughly myself. In the great cultures, the human individual has matured into a conscious and autonomous personality, with a value all his own and irreplaceable. The high point of this development was attained in the nineteenth and twentieth centuries, when on the one hand mankind had penetrated to the ends of the earth and, on the other hand, the political units were organized to perfection, while, finally, the ideal of the autonomous and inviolable personality attained its highest development within the social group.[12] This phase has thus been dominated and governed by the old law of evolution, by the association of complexification and consciousness in process of development.[13]

But the equator seems to have been passed already and the new phase, the convergent one, to be beginning to come into view. The divergent lines of mankind's development are beginning to converge. Various factors are contributing thereto. In the first place, there is no longer any possibility of geographical expansion. The earth's surface has its limits and the whole of it has substantially been occupied by mankind. An interplanetary migration, were it ever to become possible, is still not going to ease the pressure to any sensible degree. At the same time, there has been a drastic increase in the human population of the world. The members of each group are more compressed and the groups themselves more closely packed one against the other. The growing pressure of the population is thus leading to a more intensified interiorization of each group, a stronger reciprocal influence of all the groups and of all the individuals. And finally this density is raised to the second power by the fact that mankind is constantly creating more perfected technical communications media which are expanding illimitably the radius of influence of each individual and bringing to each one the benefit of the action of all the others. Thus in recent decades there has been woven a web of economic, political, cultural, and ideological relations whose density is increasing at an accelerated rate:

It takes the form of the all-encompassing ascent of the masses; the constant tightening of economic bonds; the spread of financial and intellectual associations; the totalisation of political regimes; the closer physical contacts of individuals as well as of nations; the increasing impossibility of being or acting or thinking *alone*—in short, the rise, in every form, of the *Other* around us. We are all constantly aware of these tentacles of a social condition that is rapidly evolving to the point of becoming. You feel them as I do, and probably you also resent them.[14]

For the superficial observer, the development of communications media—the network of land, sea and air ways, of postal, telegraphic and telephonic communications, of radio and television—may be a simple matter of economy or a sort of game. In reality, it is a potent phenomenon of nature.[15] It means, in fact, that mankind is uniting and welding itself into a single whole, under the influence of such developmental factors as the limitation of the earth's surface, the population explosion, the intensification of spheres of influence and the greater opportunity for mutual compenetration.[16]

The noosphere is arriving at a stage of abnormally high pressure which in turn calls for a more intensive organization, strengthening the reciprocal influence and consequently leading to a sort of hyperconsciousness which in its turn increases the pressure:

This growth of mental interiority . . . to the extent to which it simultaneously and inevitably augments the radius of effective action and the power of penetration of every human element with respect to all the others, has the direct effect of hypercompressing the Noosphere upon itself; this hypercompression automatically sets in motion a hyperorganization, which in turn primes a hyper-cognizantization followed in its turn by a hypercompression—and so on. [The] system is in process of indefinite reflexive self-intensification.[17]

Mankind seems caught in a powerful current, a whirlpool of collectivization, of "totalization upon itself,"[18] a movement increasing relentlessly by its own inertia which it is becoming impossible to escape.

Our age is oppressed and disturbed by this phenomenon.

Until now, man, at least Western man, had the feeling of an opportunity of limitless expansion, of progress consisting in the occupation of new physical areas. He now has the feeling that the world in which he must live is shrinking and becoming too small, like a dam containing him or a dome closing over his head.

Very early in his life, Teilhard recognized this anguish. There were his own experiences of the war where the individual person was torn out of himself and hurled into the violence of impersonal powers and anonymous dynamisms; there was the confrontation with the numberless, inarticulate, staggering masses of the Chinese Orient. *La messe sur le monde* describes this foreboding of the existential agony of this "being hurled" into "an existence pledged to death":

It is a terrifying thing to have been born: I mean, to find oneself, without having willed it, swept irrevocably along a torrent of frightful energy, which seems as though it wished to destroy everything it carries with it. . . . I am afraid, too, like all my fellow-men, of the future, too heavy with mystery and too wholly new, towards which time is driving me. Then, like these men I wonder anxiously where life is leading me.[19]

Mankind has plunged, with all the ardor of an adolescent, into the game of the natural sciences and technology. But at the very moment when his knowledge and his mastery of nature and of the world have become almost limitless, the future is presenting itself as a blank wall and imminent ruin threatens like an abyss. The optimism which prevailed in pre-World War I days has melted away and changed into a deep despair: "we no longer expect anything."[20] Is not this lonely "metaphysical anguish"[21] the root cause of the snuffing out of idealism, of the boredom of modern man, of the flight into pleasure and of the faltering of the creative flame?

Some may hide their head in the sand like the ostrich and refuse to see what is happening. Others may minimize the phenomenon of our times as a mere passing break in the equilibrium of things. But can anyone sincerely believe that there is any possibility of making head against the rising tide of the masses, the machine, the collectivization of thought and of action?[22] To live as a man, a man must be fully aware of his existential situation. So he must look the present threat full in the face, try to diagnose the anguish of his time.

This anguish is really that of a kind of death throes. Over the long centuries of a painful evolution, man has broken out of the primordial twilight zone and discovered the sunlit uplands of intelligence and freedom. But the current of life seems now to be driving him into a new and still darker tunnel. The bondage of industrialization and mechanization, the irresistible ascendancy of the totalitarian state, scarcely curbed at all in the wake of World War II, seem to evoke the picture of a hive or ant-hill future in which the individual will be jelled in a functional serfdom.[23] The blind torrent of the masses threatens to engulf our personality, our independent thinking and our conscious freedom. We are clutched by a mortal anguish because our most intimate life is being threatened and we are exposed to the risk of losing ourselves, of being crushed by the monster we have unleashed.

A sheer "mortal" anguish stalks and threatens to seize us: the fear of losing, in the process of the heralded transformation, that precious spark of thought, so painfully kindled after millions of years of effort—our little *I*. The radical fear of the reflective element in the face of an *All*, apparently blind, whose enormous coils are twining round the tiny *I* as if to reabsorb him alive.[24]

This problem is rendered still more knotty by man's feel for the responsibility devolving upon him and his kind. In man, evolution has become conscious of itself; but man has also become conscious of the fact that he makes the future.[25] Hitherto man regarded his world as the maternal womb in which he was safe, as the home in which he could play his game of science and technology without running any risks. But man has grown up, he has passed through a developmental crisis, a "change of age."[26] The cables that anchored him in the Stone Age have been cut.[27] We are discovering that the world is in a process of becoming and that we ourselves are the axis of that becoming. We can and we must make the world of tomorrow. Like grown-up children, we are critical of the world that has borne and raised us. In the game of development, we are at once the players and the stake. We can no longer withdraw. Like the games of a child, the inventive power of man used to seem a simple, harmless, even salutary thing. But we are suddenly discovering the mortal gravity of this game. The sorcerer's apprentice has discovered the vital control levers and is overpowered by the agonized fear that he may destroy nature herself.[28] Such is the tremendous and oppressive crisis of present-day development: man may refuse to go on playing the game that has changed into a bitter reality.[29]

And on the other hand, finding that by his discoveries he has acquired certain keys to the mastery of the world, he begins to realize that if he is to be equal to the situation he is bound, in his role of "quasi-demiurge," to establish principles and a faith regarding the future and the value of the task that is henceforth imposed upon him.[30]

Henceforth man is the axis of development. His conscious and free action determines the power and direction of the current of life itself. But man's action is paralyzed by the anguish and uncertainty that are clutching at him even as the new responsibility closes in upon him. To get rid of his anguish, man would have to know that he was on the right road. Can he ever be sure of this?

"What is most radically disturbing for the modern world . . . is not being sure and not seeing how it ever could be sure if there is an outcome, *a suitable outcome*, to that evolution."[31]

Teilhard feels himself obliged and called to give his answer to this uncertainty. He is convinced that science can provide the starting point for an answer to the question as to whether there is a way out of the impasse in which mankind presently finds itself deadlocked. Modern science, which is succeeding in lifting a little the veil of the future, which is daring to outline and elaborate certain plans for that future, must pay attention to the direction its path will take. Convinced of the task and the duty accruing to science, Teilhard, although geologist and paleontologist by original bent and training, feels a steadily rising interest in the future development.[32] What, indeed, can be the use of a knowledge of the past of evolution if not to light the road for mankind into the future?

Prehistory and the history of life's origins henceforth are of interest to Teilhard only in the measure in which they can provide directives and laws for the future. Hence his intense effort to construct a new and general science of the *fieri*, the developmental process of humanity. On the success of this new *hyperphysics* depends ". . . the preservation of courage and the joy of action."[33]

Man is developing himself and developing the world by his own acts. What must be done to maintain and even to fortify in man, not only the power, but also the desire and the joy of continuing to build the future? Such may well be, even more than the question of war and peace, the overriding concern of mankind today.[34]

At this moment, when for the first time he [Man] is gaining a scientific awareness of the general outline of his future on earth, his most urgent need may well be to assure himself, for solid *experiential reasons*, that the sort of spatio-temporal dome (or cone) whither his destiny is impelling him is not a blind alley where the floodtide of terrestrial life is going to be crushed and smothered against itself.[35]

Teilhard has a twofold expectation of the new science: the certainty, based on solid experiential reasons, that the road along which man is advancing does not lead to death but rather opens for man the door of life; and the opportunity for man to impart a direction to and establish a law for his work and his endeavor.

He believes he can find the needed certainty, in a quite generic sense, in the very fact of evolution itself. He cites in support of this view the words of Sir Oliver Lodge: "The transformist doctrine, properly understood, is a school of hope."[36] The whole sweep of history of the earth and of life on the earth ought to imbue us with confidence in the future. For this history shows us with what imperturbable assurance, with what potent and irresistible force the world has pursued its march toward life and toward ever more perfect forms of life, as it searched and groped its way across the narrow passes that impeded its progress. It is quite simply unthinkable that anything so powerful and so imposing could end by vanishing in a dismal suicide: "The World is too big a concern for that. . . . If it undertook the task, it is because it can finish it, following the same methods and with the same infallibility with which it began."[37]

This thought can be honed to an even greater keenness and given a still greater power of persuasion.

The new phase of human development, of mechanization, of scientific knowledge and technological mastery, of mass unity in thought and action, this phase which is unfolding before our eyes and wrenching us into a knot of anguish, is nothing else but a kind of collective complexification. It is thus nothing else than the genuine continuation of the old process of evolution. The whole of evolution has been governed by the formation of ever more complex unities. What we are now living through is the same phenomenon at the higher level of reflective consciousness. In the agonizing symptoms of our time, we can recognize the familiar phenomenon "of a Universe in process of involution."[38] Now we cannot doubt of the meaning and the force, the vital force, of evolution. We ourselves have been produced by evolution, for it is from evolution that we have received life. Doubting the meaning of evolution is doubting the very meaning of our own existence. No man can really take such a doubt seriously. The growth of interiority, of consciousness, the awakening of the spirit, are incontestably values of increasing magnitude.[39] If socialization as we are existentially experiencing it is a real prolongation of the old process of involution of the world upon itself, we cannot, in candor, doubt of the positive value of this socialization or of its forward march toward a higher realization and actualization of life.[40]

Let us consider things from a different angle. The history of life on earth, the history of millions of years and unnumbered efforts, certainly seems to have been a history that was traveling in a definite direction. It has succeeded in producing ever higher forms of life, crowned by man, by his ever more elevated individual manifestations, whose greater humanity derives from their higher degree of conscious awareness, and by man's social structures. Provided man remains faithful to the great over-all line of history and to the extent he remains faithful to that line, his present development likewise points to a destination beyond itself. It is leading to the egress from the momentary constriction of our present congested room to a door which will open to admit mankind to fulfillment and consummation:

> This planetization, which so affrights us, is nothing else than
> . . . the genuine continuation, the direct prolongation of the evolutive
> process from which the human zoological type has emerged in the
> course of history. . . . Well then, *no need of further proofs* . . . to
> be sure that the form of super-grouping toward which the continuing
> movement of Civilization is pushing us, far from being one of those
> material agglomerates ("pseudo-complexes") in which the basic free-
> doms are neutralized by the large numbers involved or else mechanized
> by geometric repetition, belongs on the contrary to the species of the
> "eu-complexes" (the "ideal-complexes") in which the arrangement is
> immediately identifiable as having a biological nature and value, be-
> cause of the very fact that it *generates consciousness*.[41]

All along the path of evolution, the growth of complexification has always entailed an intensification of consciousness. Does
not the constancy of occurrence of this phenomenon necessarily
involve the conclusion that the new phase of complexification, on
becoming conscious, will also lead to a new form of consciousness?

Teilhard is doubtless aware that this certitude on the subject of the future, though based on experiential grounds, differs in
nature from the usual certitude of the experimental sciences. It
rests on an option, a choice: that our existence and evolution itself
does have meaning. This must be accepted by an act of will, it involves a personal commitment.[42] It is a kind of faith, but a faith
rendered acceptable by scientific reasons: ". . . absolute optimism
or absolute pessimism . . . On neither side is there any tangible
evidence to produce. Only, in support of hope, there are rational
invitations to an act of faith."[43] "Our hope," "faith"—is this a
transposition of Christian values into the secular realm? We shall
have to return to this question later on, for we do have here what
may be one of the weak points of Teilhard's grand design. But we
must first see how the evolutionary doctrine offers us the opportunity of imparting a somewhat concrete mold to the future of
mankind, a mold whose necessity and existence have already been
demonstrated.

I have used this name of "Omega Point" to designate . . . an ultimate and self-subsistent pole of consciousness, sufficiently involved in the World to be able to collect within itself, by union, the cosmic elements arrived at the extreme of their own centration by technical arrangement, and nevertheless capable, because of its supra-evolutive nature (i.e., its transcendence), of escaping the fatal regression threatening every discrete fabric structure spatially and temporally tincted, simply because of the nature of such constructs.[44]*

Here the light of the Omega Point begins to appear on the horizon. This Point is in fact effected by the consummation and maturation of the Mystical Body of Christ, wherein the Holy Spirit will "full-fill" men and reconcile all of them in mutual love and in the love of God. Obviously the concrete content and cast of this Omega cannot be known save by the light of the Christian revelation.[45] But Teilhard believes he can essay an approach to it, too, in some sort, via his phenomenology. By reflection on human operations, phenomenology can actually formulate a set of conditions which must be satisfied by the mysterious Omega in order for it to fulfill its function in the human phase of the evolutionary process. Without the certitude of faith, Teilhard would quite possibly not be able to make out and pinpoint these conditions.[46]

* The original of this subtle passage, a major challenge to translation, is *toute construction à étoffe d'éspace et de temps.* Nowhere, perhaps, is the utter insufficiency and injustice of a facile or even too literal rendering of Teilhard in another language highlighted so strongly. One might be tempted to read here: "every material, spatio-temporal structure (or construct)" *but* this would reduce to insipidity precisely the novel in Teilhard's insight and be radically unfaithful to his constant use of "*étoffe.*" First, he is not obviously talking about merely "material" structures, even if we allow to "material" the less inert sense he attributes to it at every level, for man himself is here involved in the enumeration. Secondly, the structures or constructs are not in the least pictured as "spatio-temporal" in the inevitably evoked classical sense of a content in a spatio-temporal container; space-time is mingled in the very fabric of the structure, imparting to it a volatile peripheral consistency and the consequent danger of "fatal regression," i.e., dissolution, loss of the minimal consistency required for preservation of identity. Thus, here as throughout, we stand absolutely by our rendering which is not "free" at all but a genuine and meticulous "rendering" (i.e., giving again) of the sense of the original, which in the case of Teilhard must so often be "cast," as Mrs. Lowe-Porter so tellingly remarks of all poetic and creative writing in process of translation, "like a violet into the crucible."—[Translator's Note.]

Scientific reflection does not provide any adequate description of the Omega in itself; its description is but conjectural, based on tangential lines, whose direction is known from the past and makes it possible to calculate the future. It is in this sense that the description of the Omega is valid. In the following pages, we shall attempt to outline the paths by which Teilhard arrives at it and to show in this way the real meaning of the description.

The light of the preceding evolutionary process already reveals the nature of the present crisis of mankind. There have been such critical moments in the development of the earth: the first parturition of life and the awakening of human reflective consciousness. The condensation of the fabric of the universe, like a liquid approaching the boiling point, paved the way to these critical moments: that of the giant protein molecules led into the first critical moment; then, later, that of the animal consciousness of the primates led into the second. Does not this shed light on the phenomena of our own age? This age is distinguished by a rapidly increasing pressure, by an intensive complexification, by a feverish activity in the development of the human race. Everything seems to indicate that the "psychic temperature" of mankind is rising rapidly.[47] This rise in temperature may well be the symptoms of the approach of a "higher critical point."[48]

If the signs do not deceive us, this would be a "crisis point of socialization"[49] and of "collective reflection."[50] There is in fact still one striking lacuna in our human experience. Even though present-day man is beginning to take note and become aware of his ties with his fellows and to look beyond national and social barriers, the solidarity is far from having been globally realized and still remains on the surface of our essential humanity. Since the property of man is to live in the consciousness of himself and to cleave to his own nature, it cannot be said as yet that the human family is recognizing and accepting itself as such. The evolutive current of life has already given birth to man as an individual and autonomous person. Might the agonies and trials of our age, the wars and the atomic threats be the birth pangs of mankind? Of a human race that would consciously recognize itself and freely build itself up as the community of all men? "After Man, mankind."[51] Man as a "zoological species" could not yet be said to have attained his full maturity because the awareness of self typical of human existence has not yet matured into a consciousness of "species" or of community.[52] However, like all the magnitudes of nature, man is essentially multiple and can realize and actualize himself fully only by union with his fellows.[53] It can therefore be expected that, after the phase of full personal consciousness, a new phase will open for mankind: the phase of the awareness of humanity as an integral whole, the consciousness of mankind. At the height of World War II, Teilhard wrote: "The crisis through which we are passing has a 'positive sign,' a '+ sign' attached to it. Its features are not those of a break-up but rather those of a birth."[54]

Throughout the whole of the evolutionary process, the growth in complexity has, in fact, been accompanied by a corresponding growth in interiority and in consciousness. Now we have seen the present convergent phase of human history to be distinguished by an incredibly rapid complexification, which is enmeshing the autonomous human unitary entities in a more and more closely woven net of reciprocal relations. According to the general law of interiorizing complexification, this phase ought therefore likewise to entail an elevation of consciousness: "Evermore Complexity and thus ever more Consciousness."[55] A kind of super-individual consciousness, a consciousness of the human race as such.

This is no mere rational deduction. The symptoms can be seen already. The web of political, economic, social and cultural organization is steadily increasing in complexity and density, girdling the whole earth and penetrating every individual existence. Former generations were able to live within the limits of a family, a village, a nation, which satisfied all the vital needs of their members. Modern man, in order to live, has need not only of his ration of bread, but of his ration of metal, of electricity, of inventions, of news as well; and the whole of mankind has become his supplier. These economic, cultural, technical and scientific exchanges involve the accumulation within the human race of a common capital of knowledge, of convictions, of opinions, which are transcending the barriers of states and cultures to become the heritage of all men. "In the space of a few years, what is called modern civilization has spread impetuously over the entire face of the inhabited globe. In every country of the world, men today know essentially the same things and think essentially along the same lines."[56] The great organic body of mankind is in process of growth, with its own new senses, a kind of central nervous system and a diversity of functional organs.[57] Everything therefore seems to indicate that the higher degree of consciousness of the future called into existence by the new complexification will not lie in a further diversification of individual knowledge and effort, but on the contrary in a common perception and experience of the world which will be the common possession and a kind of common homecoming of all.[58] And mankind as such will be entirely actualized and realized only when the unity of the human family, in its whole existence, thought and action, has been consciously recognized and accepted by all its members: "Theoretically and ideally speaking, Mankind [Teilhard here has in mind the history of mankind on this earth] will be finished when it has at last *comprehended* and then, by a total and final Reflection, reduced this total comprehension within it to one common Idea and one common Affection."[59]*

After the actualization of the individual man, therefore, would come the transition to a higher plane of collective consciousness, a kind of new birth of mankind as community.[60]

In all the systems of human organization which confront each other before our eyes, the underlying assumption is that the final state towards which the Noosphere is tending is a body without an individualized soul, an organism without a face, a diffused Humanity, an Impersonal.

But this starting-point, once admitted, vitiates the whole subsequent course of the operation, to the extent of making it impracticable. How, if the Universe finally tends to become a Thing, can

* Again here we must insist that this rendering ("Affection") is incomparably more faithful to Teilhard's original "Passion" than would be the facile and literal "Passion." For "Affection" suggests (according to Webster): a) the feeling aspect of consciousness, etc., therefore pointing up the epistemological overtones; b) a settled good will, thus avoiding the volatility of Passion in English.—[Translator's note.]

it still find place for a Person? If the summit of human evolution is regarded as impersonal in character, the elements which reach it will inevitably, in spite of all efforts to the contrary, see their personality shrinking under its influence. And that is exactly what is happening. The servitors of material progress or racial entities strive in vain to emerge into freedom; they are fated to be drawn in and assimilated by the determinisms they are constructing. Their own machinery mechanizes them. And from that moment nothing is left to control the operations of human Energy but brute force—the force which, quite logically, some people today would again like to make us worship.

Not superior force, but Love, and therefore, *as a start*, the recognized existence of a Transcendent which makes universal Love possible.[61]

We have a natural inclination to try to picture this mankind of the future. But Teilhard warns us that this is impossible and even dangerous. Impossible, because we have here a new plane of life, involving a profound transformation of human existence; and because the transformation is so profound, its product cannot be pictured on the basis of our present experience. Dangerous, because false dreams might commit mankind to a wrong road. But one essential distinctive property of the future collective consciousness of mankind can be formulated; and it enables us to reject certain pictures and certain models of the future. This property is that the collective consciousness cannot be a smothering or an annihilation of the individual personal consciousness, but must rather be, on the contrary, the supreme fulfillment and consummation of this individual personal consciousness: "In this new (and therefore unimaginable) type of biosynthesis, the individual freedoms can only be conceived as being raised to their maximum by the very interplay of their mutual association."[62]

This damns National Socialism which tends to a unification not on the scale of mankind, the whole human family, but rather on the outmoded scale of the people, and which moreover stifles personal thinking and personal freedom by dictatorship over minds. It damns Marxist Communism. Though it dilates its ideal to a unity of men which would encompass the whole earth—and its very universalism is the explanation of the fascination it exercises on so many minds—yet its outlook is radically inadequate. In its reaction against liberal anarchy, it tends to annihilate the person and to convert the human community into an ant hill. It does not do sufficient justice to the spirit and thus reduces the human adventure "to the mechanical elaborations of a soulless collectivity."[63] At best, it dreams of a closed system of relationships in which man would find his fulfillment in surrendering himself outright to this collectivity.[64] It implicitly denies that man can open himself to the truly infinite and consequently that love can be the supreme fullness of his being. For "as such, the Collective is essentially unlovable."[65] The best elements of Marxism aim at a Humanism of the future which would be rudimentary at best and a caricature at worst.[66]

The Hindu ideal, likewise, reveals its inadequacy when measured against this essential demand of personalism. The unification of all men and all things has for long centuries been the object of Hindu religious preaching and endeavor. It is, therefore, no wonder that modern man, tormented by his own disintegration and that of the world, should be attracted by this ideal. But the unification offered by Indian mysticism is effected at the sacrifice of the personality and by immersion in the unconscious All. Man recovers unity at the loss of his autonomy and his particularity, his own selfhood, by plunging into the indeterminate fountainhead of being where there is no longer any distinction into separate entities: a kind of tensionless and formless divinity, which identifies man with it at the end of his path:

Make the effort and you will find, at the end of this descent *below all conceivable determination,* that there is a universal essence there, *subjacent* to everything, and only awaiting your return to it in order to absorb you and *identify* you with itself.

A kind of divine substratum, or again a "God of Heartsease," attained by relaxation of the effort of differentiation to which we are committed by the cosmic phenomenon.[67]

Not only does the whole of the external world here lose all value and significance (sheer alienation of proportionate being); even man's very personality is here just as drastically negatived.

These portrayals of the new consciousness of mankind and others like them are therefore unacceptable as terminal point and consummation of global evolution. It is already generically inconceivable, in the light of the known laws of evolution, that evolution would destroy its own best and finest product. The world is history and the essence of history involves irreversibility. But there is a further and special reason for saying that such a destruction is impossible. And we are here tackling one of the most original sections of Teilhard's thought. It is a section to which Teilhard himself attached the greatest possible importance and to which he wished to see devoted the lion's share of the attention of future science: "Human Power Engineering," which in fact constitutes the hinge of Teilhard's whole system.

The prospect that the human personality is doomed to dissolution in an impersonal collective would rob evolution of all dynamism and lead to a total paralysis of its impetus. In the final analysis, it is evolution which has produced the personality endowed with consciousness and freedom. This personality, as we have seen, is henceforth the sustaining power of evolution. Since man came into being, the center of gravity of terrestrial development has shifted from anatomy and physiology to culture, science, technology, and (as we shall soon see) to love, to the values with regard to which the free will and personal commitment of man play the crucial role. If, therefore, there were to occur a weakening of the personal will, then the upward thrust of evolution would slacken and its motion would come to a stop. The closer the Omega approaches, with the inevitable increase in critical tension and the inescapable aggravation of the laboriousness of the climb, the more too must the personal will to live be strengthened. With evolution in its present conscious and volitional phase, its further realization depends on the will to progress of the actors, their willingness to go on:

Again, if it be true that Evolution is rebounding on itself through the fact of human totalization, it must, becoming conscious, fasten passionately upon itself: which is to say that Man, to progress further, will need to be sustained by a powerful collective faith.[68]

It is becoming clear that one *supercondition* is required to sustain the tensile strength of . . . our freedoms and to keep them in operational order; and that is that reasons and a taste for life . . . shall be strengthened in the depths of the human soul at a rate that keeps pace with Evolution reflecting upon itself.[69]

This is one of the reasons for the great importance assigned in Teilhard's spirituality to the will to live and to develop oneself and the world.[70]

It is not enough by any means that Man have at his disposition the power required to synthesize himself beyond himself. He must also *will to do so*. And in order so to will, Man must have the *yen* to go on, that is he must be drawn by a kind of internal "gravitation" toward the heights via his own depths. A "yenless" Mankind, a Mankind with no yearning for more being would be certain to decline and die, even if spoonfed with astronomical mounds of calories.[71]

Now, the prospect of a dissolution or a crushing of personal consciousness in a blind collectivity would necessarily paralyze the will to persevere. It is impossible for a human being to commit himself with verve and enthusiasm to a task whose end will be not merely a threat but a fatal inevitability of self-destruction. If, then, Omega can only be actualized by the applied and earnest endeavor of all men, Omega cannot signify the total loss of man's individual personality. On the contrary, Omega must include the promise that our person will not be lost, that the deepest and most precious kernel and nucleus of our being will be preserved in Omega and will there reach its supreme development and consummation, its total fulfillment:

From the moment when Evolution begins to *think itself* it can no longer live with or further itself except by knowing itself to be *irreversible*—that is to say, immortal. . . . The second condition . . . is that the irreversibility, thus revealed and accepted, must apply not to any one part, but to all that is deepest, most precious and most incommunicable in our consciousness . . . a world presumed to be heading towards the Impersonal . . . becomes both unthinkable and unliveable.[72]

Did not the path of universal evolution, become conscious and voluntary and sustained by persons, show itself to be "an irreversible ascent into the Personal,"[73] then it would stifle all will to live and render its own further subsistence impossible, instead of generating enthusiasm and enlivening endeavor. Such a hypothesis would therefore cause the imposing structure of universal development to culminate in a radical contradiction.

This insight enables us to take a further step forward in our reasoning. Omega will be the supreme realization, actualization and unification of mankind as a universal community. But it, likewise, includes the promise of the highest realization and finest flowering of the individual personality of each and every member of this human race. This is why the future unification cannot be envisaged as an exterior organization which would entail the loss of all freedom for the individual person. This unity must be of the type consonant with a relation between free persons, a unity of concord, of sympathy, and finally of love;[74] a unity of minds and a unity of hearts; a voluntary union of all in the one truth and the one love. The mystery of love is that it can unite persons while at the same time respecting the autonomy and the uniqueness of each one of them, or better still, while making this autonomy and uniqueness more perfect in themselves: "Love alone is capable of uniting living beings in such a way as to complete and fulfill them, for it alone takes them and joins them by what is deepest in themselves."[75]

A union of love, as even our everyday experience attests, far from obliterating the distinction of persons, actually enriches that distinction in the deepest and most intimate being of those persons:

> There is no reason why we may not think that compressive Socialization, which at first glance seems so direly to threaten our individual genius and freedom, is in fact the most powerful means . . . of accentuating the incommunicable singularity of each and every reflective element and raising that singularity to its highest pitch. Is it not a fact of everyday experience that union not only differentiates but "centrifies" if it operates . . . radially, that is, from mind to mind or from heart to heart?[76]

A true union in sympathy and love neither diminishes nor congeals the respective components; rather it liberates them, enriches them, "superpersonalizes" them.[77] The Omega Point can therefore be conceived only as a union of love of all the members of mankind. Only to the extent that it is love can it promise the end of all discord, the realization and fulfillment of every man in his deepest personal existent nature. This twin promise enables Omega to fulfill its function as the crowning consummation of the evolution willed and actualized by the personal and voluntary dedication of men.

This means that love is coming to play more and more the decisive role in the human phase of evolution. In direct proportion to the closeness of mankind's approach to its final destiny must the zeal of Omega light the way and kindle the hearts of men. We can speak of an "amorization," an "affectionization" of evolution. Certainly there are other factors contributing to the unification of mankind. The common ideas being disseminated by science and the communications media, collaboration in tasks of common interest as instanced by the teamwork of science and industry, the feeling of the trenchant solidarity binding all peoples, a feeling capable of being aroused by the misfortune of a single one among them—all of these forces are contributing to the creation of the ultimate union of mankind. Teilhard stresses, especially in *Le Phénomène humain*, the influence for unity being exercised by scientific and technological "questing" (research), which is creating a universal culture and a social and economic unity that put an end to many oppositions. Nevertheless none of these factors are, in the final analysis, decisive. They leave the most intimate nuclei of the various individual persons still strangers one to another: "What we need is not a mind-to-mind or a hand-to-hand encounter; no, it is a heart-to-heart encounter!"[78]

And, finally, these various unifying factors must in the last analysis be enlisted in the service of love in order for them to make a genuine contribution to the realization of Omega. Mankind must so utilize them as to make them signify not an enslavement of individual persons but rather an aid to these persons in gaining a greater interior freedom and using this freedom for love of neighbor. This aim will play a major role in the outline of the new spirituality.[79]

Now at the end Teilhard thinks he can take one further

forward step in his approach to Omega, a step which for him is crucial. Hitherto Omega could be pictured as simply the internal unity of all men, limited to the human frame of reference. But in the last analysis the terminal point and consummation of evolution cannot consist simply of the human collective united at last in concord and in love. It must have a firmer, deeper footing in the union of love of all with a central pre-existing point. The force of attraction centering mankind at last upon itself must be a person: a person to whom all men can direct their love and in whom they can love their fellows. Teilhard gives due recognition to the measureless devotion to humanity which animates and fills the lives of innumerable workers and men of science; but the most perfect and perfectly emancipating devotion must be directed to a person, hidden perhaps behind these collectives. For devotion is love and love is always directed to a person: "For, after all, total giving requires the opportunity of loving. Now how can a collective, impersonal, even in certain respects monstrous, reality, like the World or Mankind, be loved?!⁸⁰ As such collectivity is essentially unlovable. . . . It is impossible to give oneself to an anonymous number."⁸¹

So long as mankind remains simply a thing, a collectivity, a centered system of personal elements, it is radically impossible and inhuman to direct to it a genuine love. For love is always directed to a face and a heart. Thus mankind in itself can be truly lovable as a community only if the central point of the community is a living person:

In order to achieve a "centric" grouping (i.e., to group themselves via their centers, their personal centers, by love), the human particles, no matter how compressed they may be, must in the final analysis love one another (love all at once and all together). Now there is no real love in an atmosphere of the Collective, that is, of the Impersonal, no matter how warm that atmosphere may be. Love cannot be born, cannot find purchase, save in the encounter with *one* heart, *one* face. . . . The only possible way for the cosmic involution to reach its true goal is for it to come to rest not upon a centered system of centers, but rather upon a Center of centers.⁸²

Teilhard does not in any sense want to imply, with these words, that the devotion to the great cause of humanity may not be sincere and genuinely loving on the part of those who do not admit a personal God. But this devotion is seeking, even at unawares, another reality, a person, behind the face of the collectivity; and this devotion cannot burgeon into true full freedom and joy until it recognizes the one who is attracting it.

The Omega Point must be of such a nature that it impels human beings, by its force of attraction, toward the unification which is love. It must be the point at which all love one another because all are loving the same personal central point:

> The generative principle of its unification is finally to be sought, not in the sole contemplation of a single Truth or in the sole desire for a single Thing, but in the common attraction exercised by a single Being. For on the one hand, if the synthesis of the Spirit is to be brought about in its entirety . . . it can only be done, in the last resort, through the meeting, *centre to centre,* of human units, such as can only be realized in a universal, mutual love. And, on the other hand, there is but one possible way in which human elements, innumerably diverse by nature, can love one another: it is by knowing all to be centred upon a single "super-centre" common to all, to which they can only attain each at the extreme of himself, through their unity.[83]

Failing such a center of universal coherence, not metaphorical or theoretical, but *real*, there can be no true union among totalised Mankind, and therefore no true substance. A veritable *Ego* at the summit of the world is needed for the consummation, without confounding them, of all the elemental *egos* of the Earth.[84]

Hence, the final conclusion:

> Omega can only be conceived as the *point of encounter* between the Universe arrived at the limit of centration and *another Center,* of still greater depth, a self-subsisting Center and absolutely ultimate Principle of irreversibility and of personalization; the only genuine Omega . . . .

> And here is the point where, if I am not mistaken, the problem of God, vanward Mover, Assembler and Consolidator of Evolution, is interpolated into the Science of Evolution (for Evolution to prove capable of functioning in a hominized environment).[85]

Teilhard sums up as "reasons of love" and "reasons of survival"[86] the ultimate reasons why Omega must be conceived, not as a magnitude to be realized by the synthesis of mankind, but rather as an eminently personal and eminently actual reality, ergo as a personal and transcendent God.[87] The function of Omega is to unify all mankind within himself as a loving and beloved hearth of home whose beckoning warmth touches the center of each and every person: "It must reach and act upon us . . . directly, from centre to centre (that is to say, from consciousness to consciousness), by touching the most sensitive point in ourselves."[88] But an Omega capable of this must be more than a future ideal, must in fact be an actual and real person, capable of personal compresence with all men: "A present and real Noosphere goes with a real and present centre. To be supremely attractive, Omega must be supremely present."[89]

To be able to offer the promise and the certitude that the personal consciousness and the collective superconsciousness of mankind shall not in the end fall prey to the ruinous disintegration threatening all things in time and space, Omega must transcend time and space; Omega, not being the subject of becoming, can be the fulcrum of the world in process of becoming:

It is not to say that it (the conscious Pole of the World) *emerges* from the rise of consciousnesses: we must add that from this genesis it has already emerged; without which otherwise, it could neither subjugate into love nor fix in incorruptibility. If by its very nature it did not escape from Time and Space which it gathers together, it would not be Omega.

Autonomy, actuality, irreversibility, and thus finally transcendence are the four attributes of Omega.[90]

In this way, Teilhard believes he can read the ultimate destiny of man to be a love union of all with the personal God, at once transcendent and intimate as this God is, within the range of evolution itself. Evolution would be absurd and impossible, were the conscious human personality, ultimate fruit and free sustainer of evolution, doomed finally to perish, were the upward thrust and march of mankind toward perfect unity doomed to abort into an inevitable alienation. Mankind is caught in an unavoidable current of complexification and involution around itself. And this complexification must involve likewise an interiorization, the final interiorization of every personal being, of all personal being into a great love, via the most intimate union with all the other personal beings.

By its discovery of that evolution which sired it, mankind is beginning to take cognizance of this ideal. Now, this ideal has already been revealed to us in Christ. In Christ we have come to know the personal God who is not only at the distant origin of the world but who is also present and operative in the most intimate nucleus of mankind by virtue of a personal heart-to-heart radiation;[91] a God who has, so to speak, created a purchase for himself in the very fabric of the created terrestrial world by way of his Incarnation and the sacrament of his Body and Blood, and who is using this foothold to unify all mankind in and into his Body.[92] Christianity is God's answer to man's anguish.

Seen in this perspective, the entire human phase of evolution assumes a new visage. At first glance, the human upward thrust and march toward Omega could be described as a "questing," i.e., an endeavor by mankind to arrive at a fully conscious and voluntary realization of the human community as such, by way of the advance of knowledge and the increasing mastery of the world and of self. But a closer examination shows that a purely objective "questing" is not enough; the moralization and "amorization" of human evolution become indispensable.[93] And then it becomes clear that even this is not the final word. For, in the last analysis, mankind cannot tend to a unity of mutual love unless it tends to the union of love with God, a union which has been given and promised to us in Christ. In proportion to mankind's advance on the road to Omega, the development must be consummated in adoring worship, in mystical union, in the edification of the Body of Christ.[94] Teilhard's science is animated and crowned by a spirituality.

CATASTROPHE OR CONSUMMATION?

We continue from force of habit to think of the Parousia, whereby the Kingdom of God is to be consummated on Earth, as an event of a purely catastrophic nature—that is to say, liable to come about at any moment in history, irrespective of any definite state of Mankind. But why should we not assume, in accordance with the latest scientific view of Mankind in a state of anthropogenesis, that the parousiac spark can, of physical and organic necessity, only be kindled between Heaven and a Mankind which has biologically reached a certain critical evolutionary point of collective maturity? (And it may be added, in perfect analogy with the mystery of the first Christmas which [as everyone agrees] could only have happened between Heaven and an Earth which was prepared socially, politically and psychologically, to receive Jesus.)

For my own part I can see no reason at all, theological or traditional, why this "revised" approach should give rise to any serious difficulty. And it seems to me certain, on the other hand, that by the very fact of making this simple readjustment in our "eschatological" vision we shall have performed an operation having incalculable consequences. For if truly, in order that the Kingdom of God may come (in order that the Pleroma may close in upon its fullness), it is necessary, as an essential physical condition, that the human Earth should already have attained the natural completion of its evolutionary growth, then it must mean that the ultra-human perfection which neo-humanism envisages for Evolution will coincide in con-

crete terms with the crowning of the Incarnation awaited
by all Christians.[1]

CHAPTER 6

Years of reflection may have caused all the objections against
the identification of the Omega Point, final terminus and crown
of the evolution of the world, with the return of the Lord in the
Second Coming, to disappear for Teilhard. But there will certainly
be some question marks in the reader's mind. And so in this and the
following chapter, we shall be examining the main problems raised
here that require perhaps broader reflection and some correction to
the Teilhardian design.

The reader will have to bear in mind that Teilhard was
operating apologetically and polemically in this area.[2] As we shall
be showing in greater detail in Chapter 9, Teilhard attacks the attitude of many Christians who talk as if our earthly and "natural"
activities and business had no importance for the Kingdom of God,
were devoid of value and even unworthy and beneath the dignity
of one who knows himself called to heaven. But this debate with
the faithful, however important it may be, is nevertheless subordinated to another more positive aim. Teilhard is, in fact, afraid lest
such an attitude create a still deeper gulf between Christianity and
modern mankind; that it give rise to the impression that the Church
is indifferent and hostile to the highest and best aspirations of
modern man; that it result in a Christianity that fails to be in the
vanguard of technological and intellectual advance.

Teilhard saw his chief assignment here to be that of making
Christianity, with its fundamental truths (reality of the spirit, primacy of love and personal God), meaningful again for the modern
scientific and technological world. Modern science is itself building
up a global picture of the universe. Having learned to explore and
master the world and himself, man is beginning the systematic

building of his own future. Marxism is enthralling millions of men by the audacity with which it is planning another and better world. Teilhard wants to demonstrate that Christianity is likewise in the vanguard of human thought; he wants to do this by word and example. It cannot be true that "the children of this world are daily surpassing the masters and teachers of Israel."[3] The Christian must be in solidarity with the tasks of modern man who is building for himself a world substantiated by science and dominated by technology. Nor can Christianity content itself with a mere recognition of the value of this endeavor; it must show that endeavor the proper road, the value of the human person and the union of all men in one love and one worship. The light of this ideal cannot remain hidden under a bushel; it must be set upon the candlestick to give light to mankind aspiring to unification.

Teilhard has been reproached, not without reason, for such expressions as "Neo-Christianity" (1948), "Ultra-Christianity" (1951)[4] and other such terms. Such expressions might insinuate that Christianity's role is finished. But the whole of Teilhard's works indicates and proves the contrary. Christianity is the most progressive and forward looking of religions by virtue of its doctrine of God as the home of the world and its personal nucleus, of the primacy of man in nature, of the future union of mankind into a spiritual organism.[5] Far from being outmoded, Christianity provides the only vision of the world and of man which is bold and sweeping enough to encompass the whole of reality, even in its newly discovered dimensions, and to direct and animate the zeal of future human evolution:

. . . by providing an exact and extraordinarily living expression of the higher pole of cosmogenesis that science postulates (i.e., by "amorizing" evolution [Christianity] is seen to be the form of "religion" most amazingly adapted to becoming the "religion of Evolution"—which alone can survive in the man of tomorrow).[6]

This "Neo-Christianity" has no desire to break with the traditional Christian faith; its contention is that the transformations of the face of the world and of man are imparting a fuller sense and meaning and a greater vital importance to a number of the basic truths of Christian revelation; we have seen what this means for the doctrine of creation and of divine providence (in Part I); and we shall be seeing what it means for the primacy of Christ over the whole of creation (in Part III). One of the aims of Teilhard's apologetic is to show his associates in the natural sciences that Christianity is in harmony with the deepest and best aspirations of modern man.

But the chief aim of this apologetic seems to be that of making the men of science "see" God: "my main interest in life has been for a long time now a kind of endeavor to better disclose God in the world."[7]

Various factors, to which we have already drawn attention several times, make it difficult for the man whose mind has been molded by the natural sciences of our time to see God as the origin of the miracle of life and of the universe. But might it not be possible to disclose God as the necessary crown and consummation of the path of evolution? Teilhard hopes to be able to show God to his agnostic associates in these stages: evolution, upward thrust to man, upward thrust of man toward union of love with his fellows, upward thrust toward common union with a personal, pre-existent and transcendent God. "Thus it is that there comes into view again, in our most modern Universe, above and beyond the rediscovered entity of Man, above and beyond the newly discovered entity of Mankind . . . the face of God."[8] If we hold that evolution has meaning, then we must hold to man as being the crown of evolution and to the fact that mankind can be fulfilled in union with a personal God, that a road is opened up to mankind by the force of attraction of God. God appears as the ultimate foundation of the meaning of universal history, not, as is usually said by Christian apologists, because he has originally set this history in motion, but rather because he is the fulfillment of every endeavor as final end and goal; he is not simply the God of the *Sursum* but the God of the *Perge!* as well.[9] "God is a very simple option, the option between a *Yes* and a *No*, between a *plus* sign and a *minus* sign."[10] Were not the end of the road for mankind the encounter with the personal God, then the road and consequently the whole of evolution would become absurd. Nothing would be left us save absolute and radical pessimism.

Such is, I think, the sense of the motto with which Teilhard prefaces *Comment je crois* (1934):

> I believe that the Universe is an Evolution!
> I believe that the Evolution proceeds toward Spirit!
> I believe that Spirit is consummated in the Personal!
> I believe that the supremely Personal is the Christ-Universal![11]

This text was most offensive to me at the point of my first contact with the thinking of Teilhard, for it seemed to invert the order and hierarchy of values, by placing "faith" in evolution before the holiest and most cherished central tenet of the Christian faith, faith in Christ. Actually these words are in no way offensive. They simply sum up the apologetic steps whereby Teilhard personally achieves the harmonious synthesis of his scientific tenets and his faith in Christ, and by which he hopes to convince his associates that religion and Christianity are not negligible factors but, on the contrary, the necessary condition and the indispensable power for saving human evolution from total pessimism. Many, if not all, of Teilhard's writings can be seen on close inspection to include this apologetic intention, veiled but undeniable: to make modern man see the importance of belief in God and of Christianity, to deepen and justify for himself the harmony between the Christian faith and scientific convictions. This bias explains in part certain peculiarities and certain gaps in Teilhard's presentation, such as the too-facile conjunction of the natural terminal point of evolution and the Second Coming of Christ, or the forced optimism concerning the eternal fertility of human activity.

Before proceeding to a more thorough treatment of these problems, it seems desirable to get rid of some of the suspicions sometimes still clinging to Teilhard's thinking on these matters as it is generally understood. First there is the fact that, for Teilhard, human nature as we know it is but a preparatory phase: he speaks in fact of a "super-humanity" and of a "second hominization."[12] Should this be taken to mean that the future is to produce an entirely different sort of human being? The best argument against this interpretation is Teilhard's own principle to the effect that personal consciousness, reflective awareness of the I, such as comes into being in man, cannot perish. Every man constitutes an irreplaceable and definitive value. And Omega, as we have seen, is viable and conceivable only if it preserves this value. The birth of a new humanity cannot then signify that the human being will undergo any essential transformation, such as would entail the former human being ceasing to be himself. It signifies that every individual human person and the human family as a whole will realize, in a new and perfect fashion, in a total awareness and an unreserved gift of love, what they are: "a kind of 'super-humanity,' much more conscious, much more aware, much more potent, much more unanimous than ours."[13] Teilhard's evolutionism does not, therefore, lead to an absolute relativism.[14] With man, evolution culminates in a form of life which has an inalienable value, an irreplaceable and imperishable worth. Man can only surpass himself by becoming more and better himself: "Once formed, a reflective centre can no longer change except by involution upon itself."[15] According to the time-honored axiom of theology: "Grace does not destroy nature but rather perfects it." The future crisis point of the birth of a new humanity cannot consist in any annihilation of human nature such as it now exists in us, only in its complete flowering forth. It is the obstacles to a full realization of humanity which will fall away; the human family will really become a solidly based personal communion of all human persons, in a common love and a common worship. In conformity with the nature proper to the human phase of evolution, the future regeneration will consist less in anatomical or physiological modifications than in a moral, religious, and even mystical renewal.

More serious is the suspicion of pantheism sometimes leveled against Teilhard. This suspicion seems to rest on a sounder basis. He himself speaks in some passages of his autobiographical writings about the pantheistic tendencies of his first years.[16] Even in the later works, he shows himself to be receptive to the elements of truth which endow the great pantheistic religions with their power of attraction, to the possibility of finding in every thing and in every action a contact with the ultimate fountainhead of being, to the ideal of a total and universal unification.[17] He even goes so far as to call his own Christian vision a kind of "monism" or "pantheism."[18]

In the light of such expressions, the reader may suspect a latent pantheism in the use of the term *Omega* to signify at once God or the fullness of the Body of Christ and the terminal result of human evolution. Actually Teilhard is not identifying God with the fruit of evolution; he is simply trying to take a new approach to the mystery of the last end of creation and of redemption. This last end is at once God himself and the God-given and grace-effected but nonetheless active union of men to God, a union therefore to which a human action and operation does contribute too. This mystery deepens still further and becomes still more ineffable in the incarnation of the Son of God, which positions the union of all men to God in the union of the elect to the Mystical Body of the Incarnate Son, so that men approach the Father incorporated into the Son. Our human operation does, therefore, truly contribute to the building of a reality in the divine order, the Body of the Incarnate Son. But our operation does not have this divine power of itself, as a human action; it has that divine power because, by the grace of God, the Son has become man and the Holy Spirit been poured out in our hearts.[19] In the light of divine revelation, Omega cannot therefore be conceived save as a multidimensional notion. Teilhard has several passages demonstrating this multidimensionality: "Omega can only be conceived as the *point of encounter* between the Universe arrived at the limit of centration and *another Center*, of still greater depth . . . the only genuine Omega."[20]

Moreover, Teilhard is continually insisting on the essential difference between what he sometimes calls a Christian "monism" or "pantheism," and the false pantheism. Our God is not identical with the world, is not a "World-God,"[21] a formless substratum of being. He is a transcendent person, a supreme *I*.[22] For this reason, our union with him, that ultimate ideal of all forms of pantheism, is a personal union that does not obliterate individuality and distinction, but rather brings them out with supreme clarity.[23] Teilhard is continually recurring to this point. Like the monist, the Christian desires to lose himself in God. But our God is so perfect that the union with him does not obliterate the particularity and individuality of man; on the contrary, it perfects them.[24] Pantheism shares with Christianity the ideal that "God may be all in all."[25] Yet in their understanding of this ideal, Christianity and the pantheistic error are poles apart.[26] Pantheism conceives union with God as an identification[27] in which the human individuals are dissolved in the divine being or themselves constitute the divine being. The principle of union for the Christian, on the contrary, is love, which presupposes the real and abiding distinction of persons and which unites and differentiates at once.[28] By the union of love, the one becomes in a sense the other, while nevertheless remaining himself. Even the act by which he loses himself in God serves man as a perfect realization of his own individuality.[29] Although Teilhard may indeed have had inclinations toward pantheism in his youth,[30] he surmounted them in his own thinking by his doctrine of love, the sole form of true union between persons. Let us conclude this discussion concerning his alleged pantheism by citing a text that is unequivocal:

> Since there is neither fusion nor dissolution of the persons who are the elements, the Center in which they aspire to meet *must necessarily be distinct from them, that is, have its own personality*, its autonomous reality. . . . A different Center, different from all the centers he "supercenters" by assimilating them; a distinct Person, distinct from all the persons he fulfills by uniting them to himself.[31]

To my mind, there *are* really serious objections to Teilhard's notion concerning Omega in other areas: notably the manner in which he believes he can find the knowledge of Omega, the way in which and the degree of certainty with which he sees Omega being realized, and consequently the amount of confidence we can have in the advent of Omega. We must now examine these objections most intently and ask ourselves to what extent they pertain to the essence of Teilhard's design, or whether they may not simply be defects which can and should be corrected within his own system.

The first question, which we have touched upon already, is the deduction of Omega.[32] Teilhard, in fact, concludes on the one hand from scientific phenomenology and the necessary conditions of human operation to the existence of the crowning consummation of evolution; and, on the other hand, describes it as the consummation of the Body of Christ upon His Coming Again. Does he mean to say that this mystery of the Christian faith is deducible from natural data? In this case we would be faced with the difficulty of reconciling this with the solemn teaching of Vatican I: "There are proposed to our faith [some] mysteries hidden in God, which we would not be able to know, had they not been divinely revealed."[33] Would not the deduction of Omega be in conflict with the essence of the mystery of faith?

The reply could be made that, in Teilhard's acceptation, "natural science" is less abstract than what is usually understood by this term. The history of mankind is also a part of this science. Now history is always concrete; its point of departure is mankind as mankind exists in actual fact, in a state wherein nature and grace are intimately linked.[34] Perhaps a case could after all be made for deducing Omega from the concrete development of mankind, with its chronic discord and internecine broils and its persistent desire for unity and union.

But Teilhard gives another, more classical reply to this difficulty. On every occasion on which he is developing the dialectic leading him to the notion of Omega, he makes a distinction between the light of science and the light of revelation. His concluding *The Phenomenon of Man* with an epilogue on the *Christian Phenomenon* is no mere accident nor yet a concession to the touchy ecclesiastical censors. The scientific analysis of the phenomenon constituted by the history of man impels Teilhard to the conviction that this history is proceeding in the direction of a focus in which mankind will attain its unity, and each individual man the utter fullness of his own personality; he concludes from this that the focus must be the union of all human persons with the one and only transcendent Person. This is what Teilhard calls elsewhere "the natural arc of my interior trajectory in quest of the ultimate consistency of the Universe."[35] But natural reflection cannot pronounce upon the internal nature and the divine aspect of this focalization. We find these in the Christian phenomenon, the only religion which offers an ideal and a promise divinely answering to the deep aspirations of mankind: in the revelation of the Father, who created all men to gather them again into his house and into his love; in that of his Son, who becomes a child of the human family, so that the ultimate unity of the members of this family comes to be their union to the Body of this Son, "sons of God in the Son"; in the light of the gift of the Spirit, that Holy and Divine Spirit who is the reflection of the unity of the Divine Persons. This very concrete and at the same time divine and mysterious unification of mankind is known to us only by God's revelation and promise. Inversely, the light of revelation reveals to us the ultimate meaning and the depth of the anguish of man and of his longing for unification. So this Teilhardian thinking on Omega seems to do just what is done by all apologetics: show, on the one hand, the deep-seated natural desire of man, and, on the other hand, the unhoped-for and transcendent response of Christian revelation and grace. The only difference between the Teilhardian apologetic and the ordinary apologetic is that Teilhard pays more attention to the social dimension of the natural desire, attending, therefore, not only to the individual's desire for union with God but also to the common desire for the union of all among themselves and with God; and that Teilhard delves more deeply into the roots of this desire, finding them not only in the existent nature of man but also in the totality of the world of which man is the fruit and the crown.[36]

We reserve to Appendix II[37] the examination of a number of passages in which Teilhard oversteps the bounds of the apologetic approach to the Omega Point. In these passages, he seems to be proceeding from the datum of evolution to a kind of "deduction" of the mysteries of the Incarnation, of the Redemption by the cross and of the ultimate union with the Father in the Body of His Incarnate and Risen Son. Here he is, in fact, no longer speaking as scientist or phenomenologist; rather he is reflecting as a theologian in the light of faith upon the mysteries of revelation and seeking the intimate and necessary nexus of these mysteries. He does unquestionably also use the term "evolution," i.e., the notion of a world in process of gradual development, as a key to the synthesis. But here this notion is no longer simply phenomenological, it is at least "metaphysical," specifying a law of created being in time. Indeed the notion probably even becomes theological, including a salvation history as presented to us in the Bible.[38] The scientific and phenomenological notion of evolution serves Teilhard as an occasion for recognizing the organic character of salvation history; in the passages in question, this notion is raised to a higher dignity and meaning. The following text well demonstrates that the supernatural aspect of salvation is basically safeguarded:

> I admit *radically* that the consummation and fulfillment of the World is not effected save athwart a death, a "night," a realignment, an excentration and a quasi-depersonalization of the monads. The aggregation of a monad to Christ presupposes a kind of internal disaggregation, disengagement and break up within that monad itself, that is a recasting of its whole being, as condition of its re-creation and integration into the Pleroma. Union with Christ by mandate presupposes that we reposition in Him the ultimate center of our existence, which means the radical sacrifice of egotism.[39]

Teilhard seems less prudent in speaking of the actualization and realization of Omega and of the certitude man has of reaching Omega. His picture of the Parousia being sparked at the moment when mankind has attained an extreme degree of tension is an image of great evocative power. The growing complexification of the Noosphere causes an increase in the interior pressure of mankind. In proportion as mankind reflects more and more upon itself and upon the world, attaining an ever-greater knowledge, comprehension, and mastery of reality, it becomes more and more charged with psychic energy. There comes a point of saturation, of total maturation, of extreme tension. At this moment, the fire will come down from heaven, consuming and recreating the world that was, in a single operation.[40] In the Teilhardian picture, the "crisis point of human Maturation" and the "Parousia point" would coincide as the crowning consummation of the evolutive process of creation, wherein "a descendent divine involution would come to combine with the ascendent cosmic evolution."[41] The Second Coming of Christ, which will effect the definitive consummation of his Body and the ultimate establishment of the Kingdom of God, will be not merely a catastrophe devoid of any positive nexus with terrestrial history; it will also be a crowning consummation and perfection.[42] The chief merit of such a portrayal does not lie in its appeal to the imagination. It is capable of giving comprehensible meaning to the doctrine of creation oriented to Christ even in its natural values.[43] The upward thrust and the development of mankind acquire a positive meaning for the realization and actualization of the Kingdom of God, a meaning which seems indispensable in order to impart a Christian value and cachet to all our actions.[44] What stands in the way of our supposing, asks Teilhard, that the Parousia can be sparked only upon encounter of heaven and "a Humanity arrived at a certain evolutive crisis point of collective maturation," and from seeing in the perfect unfolding of evolution on the earth and the actualization of all the potentialities of creation a necessary condition of the final advent of the Kingdom of God?[45]

This rhetorical question does not, however, prevent Teilhard from considering certain difficulties which it may engender. We shall not pause in detail upon the objection arising from Scripture that insistently describes the end of the world as a catastrophe. Perhaps our minds have been so fascinated by the turbulent and highly colored narrative of the stars falling, the sun turning to darkness, the universal conflagration, and the angels trumpeting doom that we forget, because of all this, the necessary continuity there must be between the earth that is and the earth that is to come. This continuity is indicated by the essence of the Church and of the Eucharist as real prefigurations of the abiding city; it is also indicated in the homey image, devoid of apocalyptic overtones, of the Lord who, returning to find his servants zealously about his business, girds himself and begins to minister to them himself;[46] or again in the Pauline doctrine concerning the deliverance of creation.[47] Perhaps we are too forgetful of the essential difference between the expectations of the Old Testament, from which are borrowed the catastrophic apocalyptic images of the end of the world, and those of the New Testament. The New Testament expectations, in fact, regard the Second Coming of the Lord as the fulfillment of what has already been realized in his Resurrection and of what he is continuing to realize and actualize in us throughout the centuries by his Spirit. For the Christian, the Parousia is something which has already begun.[48] Since Catholic theology and exegesis have not yet arrived at any clear-cut results on this point, we limit ourselves to these remarks.

There is all the more reason for refraining from a more detailed discussion of this point, since there is no real difficulty here. For Teilhard himself in no way denies or rejects the catastrophic nature of the advent of Omega. We have already heard him say it will be a "crisis point."[49] It signifies the radical displacement of the center of gravity of evolution. After their long past history of concentration, mankind and the world are going to have to take in that future moment the step of absolute ex-centration. They are going to have to position the central point of their endeavor outside of themselves, in God, instead of within their own interior. They are going to have to cease tending to an ever-higher possession of themselves and lose themselves in order to be possessed by another.[50] In his earlier texts, Teilhard's description here was mainly scaled to the human individual, but it holds equally on the scale of the human collectivity. For always there is operative the law of love, which dictates that "to be united . . . is to migrate and to die in part in him whom we love"; this demand becomes more radical in proportion as the beloved becomes more towering.[51] Now the Omega Point consists in the union of love of all mankind as such with God himself. Mankind as well must thus lose itself, and precisely at this point. At the very moment when it is marshalling its last forces and energies to possess itself and master the world, it is going to have to come out of its familiar world, out of time, out of space, and out of itself: "Thought, arrived at its own uttermost limits . . . must in this paroxysm . . . succeed in piercing (as a result of hyper-centration) the spatio-temporal membrane of the Phenomenon, to the point of reunion with a supremely Personal Being, supremely personalizing."[52]

The paradox of the Omega Point consists in fact in mankind's inability to attain its own supreme internal unity, the love-union of all men, except in the act whereby it loves God and loses itself in giving itself to him.[53] Only athwart a final and absolute "dissociation point" does mankind find itself again in a perfect community. Whence the following paradox: in tending to its own proper realization as a perfect community, mankind is tending to its own dissolution into and in a higher love. The dialectic of death and life is repeated on the scale of mankind: loss of self is the narrow gate through which mankind must pass in order to acquire its best and deepest being:

> Before passing into the Beyond, the World and its elements must attain what may be called "their point of annihilation." And it is precisely to this critical point that we must ultimately be brought by the effort consciously to further, within and around ourselves, of universal convergence![54]

Mankind as a whole, therefore, is going to have to involute itself upon itself, into and in a single point, in a process similar to that which occurred at the birth of personal consciousness; and then, in this state of perfect possession of itself, essay the leap into God, or better, let itself be torn away (rapt) from itself. The end of mankind upon earth should be described as a dual phenomenon, the extreme of concentration of the human mind and spirit, and its perfect ex-centration.[55]

The end is a true fulfillment, for mankind will find therein the thorough unity to which its whole endeavor is tending. It is at the same time a catastrophe, a ruinous collapse for all the provisional forms of this unity, a forcible extraction (rapture, rape) from the familiar world and the hard-won possession of self. The potent force of attraction of the divine love will snatch (enrapture) mankind to the heart of God, there to restore it and recreate it.

This vision of the future involves various consequences of vital moment. In the first place, it explains the ultimate and deepest motivation of the mysterious dialectic of disengagement and commitment, of detachment and attachment, which constitutes the kernel of Teilhardian spirituality. For primarily in this spirituality is reflected the law of the end. The final fulfillment of mankind will be an ultimate sacrifice: a sweeping and magnanimous sacrifice wherein mankind will offer up itself as oblation and will offer up the world, from the vantage point of the fullness of mankind's possession of itself and of the world; a sacrifice of Christ who will accept the death that awaits him in the fullness of his maturity as man; a sacrifice of mankind which will let itself be harvested by God like wheat now fully ripened. The present consequences of this vision are, therefore, attachment and commitment to the earth and to mankind, intense love of all things, and above all love of God. The central axis of evolution is love, but a love that cannot remain confined within finite and terrestrial realities. The flowering of mankind, the ever more pronounced centering upon itself involved for mankind in this flowering, must find its central and ultimate point of reference in a transcendent love.[56]

This vision of the future thus furnishes the key to the sense in which "questing" and worship will ultimately be conjoined and even now are of mutual benefit in the upward march toward Omega.[57] The "questing" is the whole complex of sciences, technology, organization, and reflection whereby mankind is tending to penetrate and master the world and itself and to explore and stake out the future and its own destiny. If it is really "the loyalty to Being" that it aspires to be, then it leads ultimately to the recognition and admission that mankind seeks union with the personal God to whom it must surrender itself in love.[58] The more man penetrates to the fountainhead of his own existent nature and takes possession of it, the more will the necessity of this last surrender stand out for him as the radiant outcome. The quest must therefore become increasingly open to the prospect of ultimate adoring worship. And faith in God will be expressed in a mounting impatience for the perfect possession of self, for the ripeness unto sacrifice. The proud will to be master of the world and the humble adoring worship of God will merge into a single gesture, "a composite gesture of worship wherein a passionate desire to conquer and master the World and a passionate desire to be united to God will combine and inflame each other; *the vital, specifically novel act, corresponding to a new age of the Earth.*"[59]

This stance and gesture came to be the basic attitude of Teilhard himself. Worship must not be lost sight of in the questing; the questing must flower into a talent for worship.

Finally, this vision provides us with the answer to the question as to whether there is still any room for grace left in Teilhard's system. In the context of the realization of Omega as such, Teilhard is constantly reminding his reader that the immanent development of mankind, though it may well be a necessary condition of the Second Coming of Christ, does not suffice to bring about that Second Coming.[60] This Return is the work of God, the fulfillment of the grace of God. Teilhard's use in this context of the comparison with the Incarnation speaks volumes.[61] A certain social, political, and cultural maturation was necessary before Christ could become man; yet, for all that, his coming was entirely dependent on the initiative of God. The same holds for the Second Coming of the same Christ. Union with God is not something realized by mankind; it is something bestowed upon mankind from the heights of heaven. The ultimate realization of Omega is the work of divine grace (while yet seeming to require a providential historical preparation).

Does the same hold true of the upward march toward Omega? More than one reader of Teilhard has come away with the impression that the path to be travelled by mankind is determined by nature. The powerful and imperturbable current of evolution is bearing mankind toward its ultimate fulfillment. Is there any room left for man's freedom, or for that matter for that freedom of God which is called grace? Is there any room left for the drama of sin and redemption? "Teilhard's system is alleged to be a denial of freedom and of grace, everything being imposed by natural determinisms."[62] Our examination of the certitude of Omega and our perfect confidence in its advent are going to show us that Teilhard leaves himself open to these objections. But this is because, for secondary reasons, he does not himself remain faithful to his own principles.

The ascent to Omega is the prolongation of the great evolution of matter and of life. It would be a misreading to conclude that this ascent is accomplished with the same imperturbable assurance as the preceding evolutionary process. It would be to forget that the concept of evolution is used in quite different senses as applied to the prehuman world and to the human world respectively. Since man has appeared on the scene, evolution is unfolding on an essentially higher plane. It is no longer a "biological" evolution, in the usual acceptation of that term; rather it is an evolution sustained by freedom, by personal choice and commitment, in the final analysis by love. And this factor attains more strongly pronounced predominance the closer Omega approaches. At the lower levels of human development, more mechanical forces, like population growth or technological intensification, could play a decisive role. In the real ascent toward Omega, in the strictest sense, in the concentration of mankind and its excentration onto God, freedom becomes the decisive factor. Evolution is, henceforth, no longer determined and controlled; it is voluntary, sustained by the free talent for loving as actualized by human persons. There is, indeed, room for grace. Man's personal commitment is sustained by the personal force of attraction of Omega, "loving and lovable."[63] The path of mankind is even now lighted up by the encounter between the personal God and human persons, an encounter which reveals its full glory in Omega. The upward march is dominated by the powerful pole looming on the horizon, by the "flux of attraction, personal and personalizing,"[64] by the magnetism of a God who is love and who has revealed himself in the Incarnation of his Son as the love intimately present and efficacious within the human family itself. The God who created mankind to guide it to himself guides and impels each man personally, "not only indirectly, through the universal network of physical syntheses, but also, and even more, directly, from centre to centre (that is to say, from consciousness to consciousness), by touching the most sensitive point in ourselves."[65]

Teilhard's expressions sometimes leave the impression that the human phase of evolution continues in a straight line with the evolution that has gone before. But Teilhard's own principles state that the propellant force of the human phase is the love in which God and men meet. This leaves all possible room for the Christian conception of salvation as a grace and as an interplay of divine love and human freedom.

No doubt the critic of Teilhard, still unconvinced, will counter: "Teilhard is a Christian; he believes in grace, to be sure; but in his thinking it seems to coincide with the upward thrust of evolution."[66] True, but this does not mean any derogation of grace; it is, on the contrary, an elevation of the evolutionary process of development. The assimilation of grace to the evolutive thrust that is "amorizing" can create a difficulty only for someone who has not grasped the real nature of human evolution. The Christian who understands that the real progress of the human phase consists in the love of neighbor and of God must, on the contrary, recognize and admit that the impelling force here is grace. It is only the personal force of attraction of God presenting himself as love object to man which sweeps man and mankind forward. Man cannot truly love his neighbor and his God unless he is animated by the grace and the love of the Holy Spirit.

APPENDIX II

Nexus Between Creation, Incarnation and Final Consummation

In his outline of a "metaphysic," which we have already criticized,[1] Teilhard also tries to "deduce" the Christian doctrine of the Mystical Body of Christ and of the Incarnation which is the foundation of this Body. The passage in question and other related ones aim at expunging the impression of arbitrariness often surrounding the notions of creation, Incarnation, Redemption and Parousia:

A series of notions, long regarded as being entirely independent, here reveal an organic nexus before our very eyes. No God (up to a certain point . . .) without creative union. No Creation without incarnational immersion. No Incarnation without redemptive compensation. In a Metaphysic of Union, the three central mysteries of Christianity (Note: until now presented . . . as entirely separable one from another. Popular catechetics still generally admits: 1) that God could, *absolutely speaking* [*simpliciter*], either create or not create; 2) that, granting he did create, he could have done it with or without Incarnation; and 3) that, granting that he were to become incarnate, he could do so in a manner involving suffering or in a manner not involving suffering. It is this pluralism in conceptual presentation that

133

I feel must be corrected, on any hypotheses) appear as nothing else than the three faces of one and the same mystery of mysteries, that of the Pleromization (or unifactory reduction of the Manifold).[2]

These excerpts already indicate the striking environment and atmosphere surrounding Teilhard's "metaphysical" reflections. They aim at nothing less than the establishment of an inner and ontological nexus between the mysteries of creation, Incarnation, Redemption and eschatological union with God. This is a nexus between mysteries taught us by Christian revelation. Such a metaphysic is evidently not metaphysics in the ordinarily accepted sense of that term, i.e., a reflection upon the necessary laws of being in the light of human reason. It might rather be termed a metaphysic of the truths of faith, an extreme form of speculative theology. As a general rule, Teilhard does not take cognizance of the equivocal nature of these theories. He is certainly not aiming at arriving at a deduction, by purely natural means, of the data of revelation; on one occasion, at least, he expressly sets the natural approach of the consummation and fulfillment of all things "apart from any deposit or support of revelation" in opposition over against the much richer and deeper vistas opened up for us by revelation and which he then proceeds to develop in the "metaphysical" deduction we have mentioned.[3] This "deduction" may well not be aiming at being anything more than what Scholastic theology calls an argument *ex convenientia* (from appropriateness).

A few remarks on this method of argumentation will suffice. It is actually of fairly secondary importance to Teilhard's over-all design. As we have said, it aims at establishing an interior and ontological nexus between the mysteries of the creation, the Incarnation, the Redemption and the ultimate consummation in the Body of Christ. This is a laudable assignment, as such, and constitutes one of the principal assignments of theology in all ages. Theology "is called upon to exert itself, with the grace of God, to acquire some comprehension of the mysteries" of revelation, by making use of "the analogy of the mysteries with the truths of nature and of their analogy with one another."[4] Comprehension is always a seeing of unity; knowledge, being, and being-one are convertible. Later

Scholasticism, vitiated by Nominalism and the excessive yen for total self-justification, often neglected this assignment. Later Suarezianism, especially, in which Teilhard was trained, regarded this prime function of speculative theology with disdain and even distrust. The whole complex of the polemical writings against Baius laid the whole stress upon the distinction between creation and grace, no longer making any mention of the unity of the two. There was a refusal, in reaction against Petau, to see any nexus between grace and the Incarnation of the Son of God. The "pure and sheer possibilities" of Nominalism were exaggerated to demonstrate that the Son could have become man and saved us without suffering. The social dimension of salvation was lost sight of, the Church seen as simply a hierarchical organization rather than a vital organism, the living organism of a humanity saved from its own inner rent. It is no wonder that a man so haunted by unity as Teilhard was should have come out against such a system, or rather such a systematic lack of system. This may, indeed, be a favorable witness to the sincerity of his religious conviction; but his reaction was too crass and insensitive to the elements of truth contained in the tenets of these schools of theology.

This is the way Teilhard develops his deduction: When God creates, he creates a world moving from multiplicity to unity. This key point of Teilhard's system we have already examined.[5] The world is thus in process of unification, and in the final instance, of unification with God. So stated, this thesis is acceptable over-all. For St. Thomas, too, all creatures tend necessarily to the highest realization and actualization of their being, and accordingly to their supreme oneness. In attaining it, they find union with him who is the absolute One.[6] But here Teilhard introduces, perhaps without himself realizing it, a second principle. He supposes, in fact, that the only possible form of union to God is the one we know from Christian revelation, the grace that makes us sons of the heavenly Father by uniting us to the Son. Theology raises some substantial difficulties militating against such a supposition. It recognizes and admits that union to God does in fact consist in this filiation. It likewise admits that this sonship is the supreme form of union conceivable. But it refuses to admit that this is the *only* form of union conceivable. For theology believes that to do this would be an infringement of the gratuitous nature proper to grace. If the end of the creature is necessarily union with the Creator and if the only conceivable form of union with the Creator is the divine sonship, this sonship, and so this grace, would be granted to man in virtue of the creation. The creature as such would have a "right to the grace of the divine sonship; without this grace, the creature would lose both goal and meaning. Thus the gift of sonship would be included in the gift of creation. Now this is contrary to the most ancient Christian thinking on grace, which locates the mystery precisely in the fact that man, servant by his created nature, is become son by grace.[7] In reaction against extrinsicism, Teilhard commits the error of making man's *de facto* destination to divine sonship the only destination possible for him. His metaphysic tends to impose upon God certain *a priori* conditions elaborated by human reason. This error is the more serious for its establishing of a necessary nexus between the grace of our filiation and the Incarnation of the Son.[8]

Such is, in fact, the next step in Teilhard's reasoning. The adoption of men to divine sonship rests on the fact that the only Son, the eternal Son of God, has become man. All Catholic theologians admit that all the grace of sonship is a participation in the fullness of grace of Christ. This is, moreover, explicitly taught by St. Paul who says that our sonship rests upon the gift of the Spirit of the Son and the participation in his relation to the Father,[9] and by St. John, who teaches "we have all received of the abundance of Christ, grace upon grace."[10] Many theologians are prepared to admit, with Teilhard, that our sonship as an adoptive filiation is neither possible nor conceivable except as a participation in the Son become man. How, in fact, could the heavenly Father be our Father, were we not incorporated into his only Son? Or, as St. Augustine says, how could the Father love us with a truly paternal love, were we not members of his Son: "He who loves his Son, how could he fail to love the members of this Son? His love for the members has no other reason than his love for the Son."[11] Thus, many theologians will agree with Teilhard in saying that the adoptive filiation necessarily presupposes the Incarnation of the Son.

But the indissoluble nexus between grace and the Incarnation renders still more urgent the need of a sharp distinction between grace and creation.

Now, here is the next step in Teilhard's reasoning: the Incarnation necessarily means that the incarnate God shall suffer. For in the Incarnation he assumes a human nature within the family of Adam and is thus united to a human race upon which evil and sin exercise their hold. As a holy man, he will have to suffer the hostility of these powers. Teilhard is perfectly right in reacting against the extrinsicism that separates the acceptance of suffering and death from the Incarnation. This notion was arrived at by theology through a process of abstractly conceiving the human nature assumed by the Son. But, in actual fact, the Son did not assume simply "an entirely individual nature, composed of a soul and a body"; he assumed a human nature within the family of Adam. "He was reputed to be the son of Joseph . . . the son of Adam."[12] He becomes the brother of the sons of Adam and so their fellow: "He is not ashamed then to own them as his brethren . . . and since these children have a common inheritance of flesh and blood, he, too, shared that inheritance with them. By his death he would depose the prince of death. . . . And so he must needs become altogether like his brethren."[13] In becoming man, the Son accepted the lot of mankind; he willed to find life by struggle, suffering, and death, to acquire laboriously out of human division unity with his fellows. Becoming man signified for him accepting an assignment including within itself strife and suffering.[14] To the extent that Teilhard is insisting upon the fact that by his Incarnation the Son of God necessarily accepted the burden of human division and the re-establishment of unity as a cross, the theologian can, therefore, agree with Teilhard.

But here there slips in a foreign element, that is, a strong quantitatively tinged notion of evil and of sin, to which we must return in the next Chapter.[15] Sin is held to be a necessary epiphenomenon of the "multiplicity" which, in turn, is a necessary characteristic of the beginning of creation. The Redemption is more or less assimilated to the unification, the final end of God in creation. The consequence of this seems to be a levelling of the mysteries of sin and of the Redemption. For anything that can be pictured quantitatively can be subsumed without difficulty under our human categories. Teilhard does not wish to deny that sin is culpable.[16] But by tying it in too closely to the picture of multiplicity and the manifold, Teilhard is concealing the tragic and evil nature of sin, its essential malignity. He makes of it something self-evident, so to speak. Number and division are among our ordinary human categories. The mysterious summit of the Redemption is leveled in a perverse and exaggerated rebound from extrinsicism; it is reduced to ordinary human proportions, to an almost quantitatively definable unification of multiplicity, of the manifold.

Here the valleys are filled and the high hills brought low, in the bad sense; sin and Redemption become barely perceptible molehills on the landscape. But sin is not simply an imperfection and lack of harmony; it is real perversity. Jesus bore not simply the "burden of progress"[17] and of our lack of love; he bore the burden of our hate, of our opposition and of our refusal of the goodness that appeared to us in him. We denied him because we preferred the darkness to the light,[18] because we did not want to see.[19] We killed him because of the irrefutable sign he was accomplishing.[20] He bears this sin; it is for this sin that he is pardon and salvation: "Enemies of God, we were reconciled to him through his Son's death."[21]

Teilhard does not deny on principle the grandeur of the drama of the fall and of redemption. On the contrary, his own principles require that the upward march and access to Omega be seen as a gigantic crisis, blanketing the whole of history with its tragic implications.[22] But various reasons, which we shall be analyzing in the sequel, incline Teilhard to scale things down into an image which weakens these tensions. It is precisely his effort to arrive at a "metaphysical" synthesis which impels him in the direction of this picture; this picture affords him the opportunity of a homogeneous and systematic view upon the world, including the history of creation from its elemental inception to its consummation.

The theologian will readily admit that this effort at synthesis contains valuable elements of truth. When God creates, he wills to guide the creature to union with himself, and to the highest and most intimate union in which the creature can approach him as son of the eternal Father; there is no doubt about this point. This destiny can only be realized because the Son, God's own Son, becomes man, bestowing upon his brothers the power to become likewise children of the Father. In coming into the world and into mankind, the Son must submit to the fate and to the development of mankind. In coming into a sinful humanity, he must drain to the dregs the hostility of sinners against the Holy One. By his love, he triumphs over the division of men; he so orders things that mankind, athwart centuries of a painful climb, shall reach even to the Father, as his body, the body of the Son.

The intimate nexus between the great mysteries of Christianity, sought after and glimpsed by Teilhard, does in fact exist. But it remains hidden in the unfathomable mystery of divine love. Love alone is the motive for creation; love alone is the motive for the calling of the creature to adoption; love alone is the motive of the boundless mercy and condescension that causes the Son of God to come into this world, that causes the faithfulness of God to triumph over the unfaithfulness of men. But Teilhard presents things as if there were an objective necessity at the basis of all these mysteries.[23] His instinctive repugnance against all that is contingent seems to make him forget that the root of our existence and of our salvation is precisely a radical "contingency," but a contingency more solid than any necessity: the freely overflowing love of the personal heart of God. As believer and religious, Teilhard knows this and lives by it. His "metaphysic" takes no account of it. And so there is here a defect in his theological reflection; and the reason is that here he has not applied radically enough to the mysteries of the creation and the Incarnation this freedom of the divine love which he has nonetheless elsewhere exalted.

CERTAINTY AND UNCERTAINTY OF OMEGA—SIN AND HOPE

May we not suppose that when this time comes Mankind will for the first time be confronted with the necessity for a truly and wholly human act, a final exercise of choice—the yes or no in face of God, individually affirmed by beings in each of whom will be fully developed the sense of human liberty and responsibility? . . .

But the Scriptures tell us that at the same time it will be rent by a profound schism between those who wish to break out of themselves that they may become still more masters of the world and those who, accepting Christ's word, passionately await the death of the world that they may be absorbed with it into God.[1]

CHAPTER 7

One of the main motive forces of Teilhard's reflection on the future and accordingly of his notion of Omega is the need of mankind today for security. Man must be sure that the last stage of the process of development in which he is at once actor and stake will come off well. Teilhard believes, as we have indicated, that he can base this certainty upon solid empirical arguments, namely, the imperturbable and irresistible power which has been guiding evolution for millions of years toward ever-higher forms of being and in the end toward man.[2] Evolution has, in the past, won out over all obstacles, found a way out of all impasses; it ought to vanquish, in the future, the difficulties which would threaten its final consummation in Omega. The impressive spectacle of the current of life which has led to man is a school of confidence and of hope.[3]

"The World is too big a concern for that. . . . If it undertook the task, it is because it can finish it, following the same methods and with the same infallibility, with which it began."[4]

The preceding exposition has certainly given rise to some questions in the mind of the reader who has followed it attentively. In the text just quoted, he will have caught an echo of the Pauline words: "I am confident that he who has begun the good work in you will bring it to perfection";[5] he will wonder if Teilhard's words are not a secularization of Christian hope, a worldly substitute for this Christian virtue. Then he will wonder if the certitude promised is really solidly based after all. Love does indeed become the great factor in the human phase of development and in the final upward push toward Omega, that final thrust that will ultimately decide the success or failure of universal evolution. It is the force of attraction of divine grace and the voluntary and loving consent of man that will determine whether the future of the development is to be a success or a failure. Now precisely this human freedom introduces an element of uncertainty, frailty, and danger into the powerful and sure current of evolution. Evolution is threatened from within with shipwreck, or rather with collapse: man can refuse to love, to continue to forge ahead; he can shut his ears to the call of God to love of neighbor and of God himself. In short, sin can paralyze and even ruin the upward movement.

Teilhard may well have failed to take due cognizance of the difficulty inherent in his system. He was certainly not unaware of the problem posed by the possibility of evil in the strict sense of the word, that is, sin. But his replies show a lack of internal logic surprising in a thinker of Teilhard's stature. He allows himself to be carried away into makeshift or specious solutions which impress one as downright decrepit. Here, in our opinion, lies the weakest point in Teilhard's design, a real danger of failure to do justice to the doctrine of the Catholic faith. Let us try to outline the train of Teilhard's thinking in this area and to subject it to a critical examination. For we must see if the gaps involve a total vitiation of Teilhard's grand design or if they can be corrected within the framework of this design as he outlines it.

A word first about a point of which Teilhard does not himself speak but which is to be encountered among certain of his admirers. Is it still accurate, they say, to insist so strongly on the power and the danger of sin? Sin has been overcome by the Redemption and by grace: "Be of good cheer, I have overcome the world."[6] Our world is a world set free, a world in which the victorious presence of grace is manifest. The power of sin has been broken, because it has been compensated and surpassed by the power of grace: "Where sin abounded, grace did more abound."[7] The ascent of mankind to Omega will not long be seriously threatened.

It may come as a surprise to some that Teilhard should not have had recourse to this gambit. But in refraining from such recourse, Teilhard is giving evidence of theological discernment. It is undoubtedly true that sin has been vanquished in our world. Immediately subsequent to the fall, God promised the Redemption, and the gift of his Redemption is offered to the whole of mankind. From the very outset, sin was caught in the divine mercy which pardons and redeems everything.[8] But, despite these certainties, faith in the divine mercy cannot make us minimize the threat of sin or the power of evil. Christianity is a tension between evil and Redemption.

The effort to class redemptive grace among the empirical certainties relative to Omega entails the risk of making redemptive grace into an intracosmic reality and, therefore, an object of human calculation. Grace must remain the personal love of God, a free gift surpassing all human estimation, a miracle ever new. "In a mysterious fashion . . . grace is at once ours and really not ours, an eschatological reality, hidden within the eternally salvific and merciful operation of the Trinity."[9] The certainty we have concerning grace and its final victory over sin remains always founded upon the faithfulness of God alone. This certainty is Christian hope, the mysterious confidence in the heart of the Other. Grace has already been given to us. But the signs and realities which manifest and give it to us, the sign of the death and Resurrection of Christ, the figure of the Church, the celebration of the sacraments, lie like frail and unstable sunbeams across the old face and figure of this world. Compared to the cosmic powers, these signs and realities seem fragile indeed.

Catholic thinking and religious practice here grope forward along a narrow path between a pessimism that would see in the world nothing but dangers and a sanctimonious optimism that would pervert grace into an insipid certain evidence. Catholic thinking has steadfastly refused to enhance the power of grace by diminishing the power of sin. The lives and words of the saints are very enlightening in this respect. The saints believe more firmly than others in the Redemption; they radiate more limpidly the joy of grace. But the saints are precisely the ones who are constantly asserting that they are sinners who must be continually "being saved" from the threat of their own perversity. St. Francis of Assisi adjured Brother Leo to address the severest reproaches to the saint, though in fact the result was the exact opposite. What Francis wanted Leo to say was this: "Brother Francis, you have committed so many sins in this world that you deserve Hell. You have committed so many injustices before God that you ought to be damned." The last words of Bernadette Soubirous were these: "Holy Mary, Mother of God, pray for me, sinner that I am." The innocent Thérèse of Lisieux sighed that, had God not preserved her, she would have fallen like Magdalene. These words are neither affectation, scrupulosity, nor false humility. In the familiar near presence of God, the saints understand better than we do that all good comes from him and from his Redemption. In and of themselves, they are human beings full of perversity, threatened with the possibility of all imaginable sinning the instant they are left to themselves and their own unaided powers. Genuine Christian living includes more than the joy of grace; it

means also accepting the dark side. . . the possibilities of evil, which I have not committed but which I could have committed like any other, and of which I am partaker in the mysterious depths of my human being, like the Everyman that I am, that all of us are. Since all of us are, as Jesus himself has said, "wicked," therefore wickedness, every human wickedness, is my own real possibility if not my reality. I must know that no wickedness committed by men is entirely foreign to me, it is a real (not merely a theoretical) possibility of my own self.[10]

Since Christian grace is always a redemptive grace, the living awareness of this grace becomes the living awareness of the power of sin from which man must continually be saved. Teilhard was well enough versed in the great spiritual tradition of the Church not for one moment to forget that faith in the Redemption does not give us the right to despise the mortal danger and the fatal power of sin. The Christian knows himself to be set before a dread enemy; against that enemy our protection lies "in the omnipotence of God."[11]

But in this phase of his reflections, where he is still standing at the portals of Christian Hope[12] and seeking after an intracosmic and empirical certitude, Teilhard does not yet appeal to the Redemption.

Teilhard's two descriptions of the future ascent to Omega show us that he is not underestimating the power of evil in Christian life nor yet the real possibility of a reverse. We dream of laboring at the building up of a humanity where will prevail the reign of love. Reflection and the mastery and domination of the world and of self lead to a great unanimity of views and endeavors, and accordingly to a humanity really united in spirit:

Theoretically and ideally speaking, Mankind will be finished when it has at last *comprehended*, and then, by a total and final Reflection, reduced this total comprehension within it to one common Idea and one common Affection.[13]

Peace through conquest, work in joy—these are waiting for us beyond the life where empires are set up against other empires, in an interior totalization of the World upon itself, in the unanimous construction of a *spirit of the Earth*.[14]

In this first eventuality envisaged by Teilhard, the approach of Omega would be signaled by a lessening of the evil in the world:

Evil, on the ending Earth, at its final stage will be reduced to a minimum conquered by the sense of the earth and human sense, hatred and internecine struggles will have disappeared in the ever warmer radiance of Omega. Some sort of unanimity will reign over the entire mass of the Noosphere. The final convergence will take place *in peace.* Such an outcome would of course conform most harmoniously with our theory.[15]

It is to this ideal that we must tend. We must never cease to labor at the building of a world which is "a kingdom of truth and life, a kingdom of justice, love and peace," a prefiguration of the new earth and the new mankind.

But Teilhard does not conceal the fact that there is a less favorable possibility, a somber prospect more in accord with the apocalyptic images of the Bible and the repeated experience of human history: it is possible that there will be an increase in the magnitude of evil corresponding to that in the amount of good, that the approach of Omega will be accompanied by a floodtide of perversity.[16] Mankind will have found a titanic destiny, dominating the world as never before. Mankind will be capable of self-disposition in a reflective self-possession. This domination of the world and of itself, in which mankind will realize its terrestrial perfection and supreme human fulfillment, need not blossom forth into a gift of love to God. It may write finis with an ultimate refusal, a final *No,* a last separation of minds and spirits.[17]

The call of Omega will ring out clearer and nearer; mankind will better understand that its further unification demands union with the transcendent "other." But the last temptation to self-sufficiency and narcissism will assail mankind from the other flank. Never will the old lie, "you shall be as gods" resound with fuller-voiced insinuation, that temptation of the Prometheuses and the Adams of all ages, becoming more critical in proportion as mankind becomes more perfectly conscious of itself and of its hold upon the world: "Given the power he possesses, why should Man look for a God outside himself? Man, wholly autonomous and self-sufficient [Teilhard here uses the English word], sole master and disposer of his destiny and the world's, is not this an even nobler concept?"[18]

Omega in fact demands an overleaping of, a forcible extraction from, time and space, a sacrifice of the world that was. And this at the very moment when mankind is definitively subjecting this world to its dominion and service. Above all, Omega demands that mankind, arrived at the mature awareness of its own greatness and the perfect flowering of its freedom, shall *let* itself be divinized and led into God. Mankind must recognize and admit and accept its total dependence and its radical insufficiency over against God. Never in the whole of its long history will mankind be so ready to love God with all its powers and all its faculties developed to their extreme limit and possessed in perfect freedom. But never will the temptation be stronger to will to be sufficient unto itself. The image of God that mankind is will shine forth in all its splendor before the eyes of mankind itself. Mankind will have the power to be grateful for this and to worship God, laying down its royal crown at his feet. But it will also have the power of bending the knee before the image and making its own self its proper idol. In this sense the ascent will be a final crisis, an ultimate and total choice, a definitive decision, charged with all the weight of past history, of man's world domination and of his power over himself. Man will have the power of causing himself to flower forth and of opening up the world to give himself as a richer and more costly offering to God: "to become larger and stronger in order to give himself and compress himself the more"[19] in an outgoing movement to the last sacrifice. But mankind will likewise have the power of clutching the world and retreating into its proper self, seeking its final unification not in love, opening upon the infinite, but rather in "the material organization of the Earth,"[20] in a "mechanizing synergy under brute force."[21] The tremendous density and power of unity accumulated by mankind within itself may lead to the formation of two gigantic camps to clash with their whole mass in an ultimate and definitive decision.

Enormous powers will be liberated in mankind by the inner play of its own cohesion: though it may be that this energy will still be employed discordantly tomorrow, as today and in the past. Are we to foresee a mechanising force or a synergy of sympathy? Are we to foresee man seeking to fulfill himself collectively upon himself, or personally on a greater than himself? Refusal or acceptance of Omega?

A conflict may supervene. In that case, the noosphere in the course of and by virtue of the process which draws it together, will when it has reached its point of unification, split into two zones, each attracted to an opposite pole of adoration.[22]

The possibility, therefore, does exist that a portion of mankind will not in the end find life, because it will have refused the last invitation of love.[23] It will not relapse into nothingness but will rather live in alienation from God: "There is not only a *nether* darkness, there is also an *outer* darkness."[24]

For Teilhard, the awareness of this possibility derives not only from the teaching of the Gospel and the Church but from the basic principles of his own insight, of the design he himself finds in the world. In making love the summit of evolution and its propellant force, he is obliged to take into consideration the possibility of a reverse. For all love is a free decision and a voluntary gift. The human will upon earth has in it always the power to refuse.[25]

Evolution is thus threatened so far as its final success is concerned, and this threat comes from within. It has produced man and with man the possibility of a failure and reverse in the final choice. It remains burdened with inner weakness; the fallibility of human love renders its tip fragile. Within its own limits, evolution does not furnish any certainty in respect of its own ultimate state. The final success of the upward thrust of the world cannot be guaranteed by the world. It can be guaranteed only by a force capable of preserving human freedom against its own power for evil, of saving it from a lack of love, by the power of divine grace. In its aspiration for ultimate security and certainty, mankind must have recourse to the power of divine love; in this respect, likewise, it must manage to displace its center of gravity, achieving excentration. Mankind must be assured and preserved against itself, against the possible malice of its own heart.

Teilhard does not, however, draw the final conclusions from this insight, at least not explicitly.[26] On the contrary, he seeks with all his might for a security and a certitude within the world and within the limits of mankind. He seeks them, like the scientist he is, in the laws of prehuman evolution, namely in number. And so he has recourse to statistics:

As I have said elsewhere, the more we study the past, noting the steady rise of life over millions of years, and observing the ever growing multitude of reflective elements engaged in the construction of the Noosphere, the more must we be convinced that by a sort of "infallibility of large numbers," mankind, the present crest of the evolutionary wave, cannot fail in the course of its guided probings to find the right road and an outlet for its higher ascent. Far from being stultified by overcrowding, the cells of individual freedom, in a concerted action growing more powerful as they increase in numbers, will rectify and redress themselves when they begin to move in the direction towards which they are inwardly polarized. It is the reasoned calculation, not speculation, which makes me ready to lay odds on the ultimate triumph of hominisation over all the vicissitudes threatening its progress.[27]

The past stages of evolution were guaranteed at their crisis points by the insurance of the numberless multitude of individuals seeking a way out of the impasse; though there might be numerous failures and reverses and many might be held in check, some would always succeed in crossing the frontier and continuing the upward march. It would be almost the same with mankind. The compact mass being pushed forward toward a higher form of unity, this unity would be bound to be realized at all events. Each individual man, disjunctively considered, may fail; but mankind as a whole cannot fail. The success does indeed depend on the voluntary commitment of each individual, but success is unfailingly assured: "Man . . . must reach the goal, not necessarily, doubtless, but infallibly."[28]

Such a conviction is, in our opinion, unsatisfactory and untenable for various reasons. It can furnish no support to the personal desire for salvation. It would ensure the success of mankind as such, but not that of individual persons. And by its introduction of the law of the statistical certitude of numbers, it seems to be reducing the person to a mere number. It, therefore, cannot satisfy the basic demand levied by Teilhard upon the certitude concerning Omega: the promise that the individual personality will there find its full realization and its definitive flowering, its salvation.

A closer examination shows that this quantitatively based conviction does not even provide real certitude of the salvation of humanity as a whole. It is a curious fact that *Le Milieu divin* had already formulated this basic criticism: Teilhard sometimes sees more clearly as a spiritual writer than as a man of science. In *Le Milieu divin*, we read: "Not the rigid determinism of Matter and *of large numbers*, but the supple combination of the Spirit that give the Universe its consistency."[29] We must repeat with Teilhard, against Teilhard himself, that the definitive factor of the human phase of evolution, especially during its last ascent toward Omega, is love. Love is the most personal drama of each individual person, the encounter between the freedom of man and the freely given grace of God. The personal Yes or No cannot be the object of a statistics. Two levels can be distinguished in the unity of human action: "The total act of our freedom, in its fully developed state, is always accomplished on a dual plane: the deep-lying plane of the personal gift of ourselves, and the more superficial plane, empirically accessible, of the definite individual act of choice."[30] The external aspect of human conduct may in part be the object of a calculation; it is codetermined by the world in which man lives and by all the factors favoring or disfavoring him. It is possible that in the future the law of numbers and of evolution will lead man to avoid certain missteps; thus, the evil of drunkenness has diminished in the last fifty years. But the deepest root of our act, the acceptance or refusal of the invitation to love, necessarily eludes the law of numbers. The decision is taken in the most hidden and intimate heart of each individual person and is absolutely unique. In this final and deep-lying decision, the drama of good and evil is played out in all its scope, intensity, and power within the inner sanctum of each individual life. At the level of this personal choice, all calculation becomes impossible, all statistics lose meaning. It seems to us inconceivable that at this level the force of great numbers could ever ensure the rightness of the choice. Yet it is the deep nucleus of each personal attitude, each personal commitment, which will be decisive for the ascent to Omega.[31]

How did Teilhard come to allow himself to be carried away to this illusory solution, so contrary to the most fundamental principle of the whole of his grand design?[32] Can it be a case of the natural bent of the thought of the scientist asserting itself against all Teilhard's esteem and attention to the sciences of the spirit and avenging itself by this confidence in the statistical security of large numbers?[33] Teilhard is always coming back to this practice of looking at things "from very high up" from a vantage point at which the "disorders of detail" blur into insignificance.[34] But what is a good method for geology may prove a bad method for the study of mankind in its more spiritual aspects. History is literally made of these disorders of detail; personal unrighteousness and personal sanctity can change the face of the world. By placing conscious reflection and, in the last analysis, personal responsibility and freedom at the center of evolution, Teilhard is tracing a clear boundary line between the material phase and the human phase. Yet he proceeds to describe the freedom phase using material categories. This is a want of logic in the application of his own principles.

Another reason for these gaps may be found in the narrowness and limitations of his polemical and apologetic position, and Teilhard himself is only imperfectly cognizant of these. When we come to speak of Teilhard's spirituality, we shall have to return to a more explicit consideration of this polemic of his against a wrong scorn of the world. He suspects that many Christians are of the opinion that this worldly human progress is worthless or, indeed, even a danger and a disloyalty to the one thing needful! He proclaims as his own message the collaboration of the development of this earth with the building of the Kingdom of God. In order to make this message resound with more power and warmth of appeal he inclines, like every polemical writer, to propose a monolithic picture of this worldly human progress as cornerstone of the City of God and stone without crack or fissure! He covers up the faults and the ambiguities threatening the value of the stone. Hence, this tendency to present the power of evil as a secondary affair, merely adventitious in importance or in the danger it poses, for the ascent to the good.

His apologetic intent seems to push him still more drastically in this direction. He wants to make modern man "see" God, and modern man is enthralled by science, technology, and the prospect of a unified humanity. Teilhard wants to make God appear as the end and consummation of humanity's path. This original thesis of Teilhard, a stroke of genius whose fertility seems proved by facts and witnesses, leads him to propose to the unbeliever a kind of hope that does not explicitly appeal to faith in God and still less to the mysterious and personal encounter with God which is Christian hope properly so-called. Teilhard believes that modern mankind will rediscover God in proportion as it goes generously forward along the road of human evolution. For it will then become apparent that this evolution calls for a divine cornerstone. But in order to advance generously and with the breadth of vision necessary to discover God, mankind must advance with confidence and a sure hope. Discouragement and despair do not provide an atmosphere favorable to the blossoming forth of faith in God. Thus Teilhard is led to present a prospect full of hope before even broaching the mystery of Christian hope. Only the reserve and the prudence of the good apologist restrain him from invading the holy ground of the mystery of salvation, properly speaking, and thus also of the mystery of sin.

Finally, we are led to suspect here the power of attraction of Teilhard's own theory on evil and sin; it may well be sweeping him away with it! This is not the place to enter in detail into this theory which constitutes a part of his "metaphysical" synthesis and which recurs more often in his other works than do the other parts of this "metaphysical" synthesis.[35] In all ages, the presence of evil in the world has been a scandal, a stumbling block to faith, to belief in God, and to creation as a divine operation. It is a little astonishing that Teilhard, prophet of creative optimism and herald of the operative presence of God, should not speak more often of this problem. His own excuse for this silence is his intention of clarifying the positive value of human progress. It would invidiously affect this aim to insist on the somber aspects. These aspects are, incidentally, quite evident in Teilhard's writings. Anyone seeing in Teilhard's design nothing but a delightful idyll rather than the cosmic drama that in fact it presents would simply not be understanding Teilhard's system.[36] We should like here to point out that some of Teilhard's ardent admirers show little real understanding of him in this matter; and the kind of retouched picture they present offers little real assurance or security.

In the forties,[37] Teilhard believed he had really found a satisfying solution to the problem of evil from the standpoint of the evolutionist approach.[38] Let us leave this overestimation of the evolutionist approach to one side and come to the core of Teilhard's way of looking at the problem. He asserts that evil in its various modalities is an adventitious epiphenomenon inevitable in the evolutive ascent; in a sense it might be called the ransom demanded by this ascent. Our world is in process of becoming and of realizing, actualizing itself; necessarily, therefore, that world suffers from its own incompleteness and its own imperfection. The higher form of existence and of life is attained each time because some of the individuals involved succeed in crossing the threshold under the evolutive pressure of numberless individuals. The decisive step is accomplished only after numerous missteps. The law holds at all levels of being, in a world created by God to realize and actualize itself. Groping and struggling ahead, the world must search for the way out of multiplicity and discord and arrive at a final harmonious unity. As long as unity has not been actualized, the divergent forces will clash; there will be missteps, disorder, malice, evil. Evil is revealed at the level of inanimate matter as disharmony, at the level of life as pain and suffering, at the level of human freedom as a sin. The rational explanation of all the forms of evil thus lies ultimately in the fact that the world must proceed from multiplicity (and, therefore, according to the laws of multiplicity) to unity:

> Not because of any lack of power on his part . . . but rather in virtue of the very structure of the Nothingness over which he leans to create, God can proceed but in one fashion: arranging, unifying little by little under his power of attraction, utilizing the groping play of large numbers, an immense multitude of elements. . . . Now, what is the inevitable counterpart of any success scored according to a procedure of this kind? Surely it is that the success must be paid for by

a certain proportion of inevitable wastage! Disharmonies or decompositions in the Pre-Animate, pain and suffering in the Animate, sin in the realm of Freedom; there can be no *forming order* which does not imply, at all levels of formation, some *disorder*. . . . The Manifold, pure and utterly unorganized, is not evil in itself; but because it *is* manifold and, therefore, essentially subject to the interplay of chance in its arrangements, it is absolutely incapable of progressing toward unity without engendering (however free it may be) some Evil here or there, *by statistical necessity. Necessarium est ut adveniant scandala.* If . . . our reason sees that there is but one way in which God can create, i.e., evolutively, by way of unification, then Evil is an inevitable by-product and shows itself to be a penalty inseparable from Creation.[39]

There is nothing further to be added on the "structure" of the void, the primal nothingness, nor yet on the insoluble problem of the possibility of the creation of a world without evil.[40] But we must examine more closely the theory holding that evil in all its modalities, even the evil which is called sin, and, consequently, the redemptive suffering of Christ, are inevitable consequences of the "multiplicity" necessarily inherent in creation.

Let us note first that this notion of physical evil (disharmony in the inanimate world, pain and suffering in the conscious world) as a by-product of good, is not so new as Teilhard thinks. Even a man as early as Origen was but following in the steps of still earlier authors in speaking of wastes and wastage.[41] The thinking of the ancient world may not have extended the concept of physical evil very widely, may have limited it to rare malfunctioning in the animal and human world. For us, the phenomenon of physical evil is much vaster in scope and can penetrate deeply into human life properly so-called. To the extent that human life is governed by biological laws, a certain percentage of deformations is inevitable. A single genius presupposes a plethora of persons of average talent and some idiots as well. In nature, as in science and technology, no discovery is brought off without paying the price of numerous efforts accompanied by their train of reverses, disillusionments, suffering, and anxieties. A great part of our suffering, even our properly human suffering, has its roots in the material nature of our world. To the extent to which Teilhard reminds us of this time-honored truth, he can be said to "serve the purpose of showing us the natural aspect of evil."[42]

But Teilhard goes further; he also makes moral evil, which is sin, an inevitable epiphenomenon of "multiplicity." As long as creation is in process of becoming and has therefore not attained to its final destiny of union and unification, sin will be, says Teilhard, inevitable and statistically necessary.[43] Here again, the points of contact with the best classical theology might be noted. According to St. Thomas himself, man's freedom of choice *in via*—in a state where man has not yet attained his last end but is tending toward it in a "multiplicity" of actions and operations—necessarily includes the possibility of sin.[44] Man can be admitted, as several Fathers of the Church have pointed out, to plunge still deeper into dispersion and multiplicity by sin.[45] But it must be clearly understood that the multiplicity here being spoken of is not quantitative but rather existential. It is the division of the man who is not yet inwardly one, because he is still on the road to his own ontological perfection and has not yet attained the fulfillment and unity of his being; he is pursuing this fulfillment in a multitude of finite objects, divergent and often contradictory desires and acts. Nor is the union of men among themselves as yet harmoniously realized either; at this stage their desires and their plans necessarily keep colliding repeatedly. Such is the existential multiplicity as understood by Teilhard. For he speaks of a multiplicity which arrives at unity by way of a great love. But this understanding of the situation seems continually being overlaid in Teilhard's thinking and in his language by the image of a quantitative multiplicity. The root of evil then appears to lie in number, and quantitative considerations play a decisive role in the victory over sin. Teilhard's metaphysic becomes a mathematics.

These quantitative considerations are entirely insufficient to explain evil in the strict sense of sin. This evil is located in the spiritual inner being of the personal existent who is not governed by the laws of matter and quantity at this level. This evil strikes at the highest and most absolute value of our world, the relation of the human person with God. By saying in this connection and at this level that every success must be paid by a series of failures and reverses, the thinker is degrading the person to the status of a means, depriving him of his greatest honor, that of being his own end and that of the world.[46] In his effort to explain evil and even sin, Teilhard does not take sufficient account of the fundamental difference between physical evil and moral evil. Physical evil does play a great role in human suffering; Teilhard is quite right in bringing this out; but Teilhard's explanation does not hold for a certain hidden root of moral evil, its most intimate and deepest root.[47] He persists in thinking as a scientist at the very point where, in his own favorite expression, there is a need to have recourse to a mystical understanding of things. In the concrete, could anyone seriously believe that, in accord with the laws of statistics, a series of moral failures and reverses would augment the chances of a moral success, that in other words, a certain number of sinners would be required in order to produce a single righteous man?[48]

If, in fact, personal commitment in love to neighbor and to God is, as Teilhard has said it is, decisive for the felicitous outcome of evolution in its human phase, then there can in principle be no intracosmic certainty of this happy outcome. No power in this world is capable of preserving man from the danger he bears within himself. Man can refuse to love God and neighbor. Such a refusal is more serious and inauspicious, even disastrous, than any mere series of failures favoring a subsequent success. Man is not merely imperfect; he can be wicked, malign, and make himself the slave of his own malignity. The faith teaches us that the sinner cannot be converted and delivered by his own power. And human experience even now within the framework of this world is aware of deep-cutting options and attitudes which render man the prisoner of a decision once taken. This same human experience witnesses that these decisions can weigh very heavily on the conduct of other men. The success of evolution in its human phase would therefore seem to be being continually and fundamentally put in doubt. True progress, progress toward and in love, can at any moment, at every turn, become definitively shipwrecked: this can happen in the individual, whose initial refusal to love can wound and paralyze the power to love to the point of imprisoning the luckless one within the walls of this refusal; it can happen in the human family as a whole, where the wickedness and misdeeds of a few individuals can influence the whole community to the point where all accept as their own the sin of the leader. The refusal to love can kill man and mankind spiritually. And this refusal with the slavery and spiritual suicide that follow in its train is not a purely theoretical and remote possibility; it is a proximate and abiding peril. Even the saints are aware that the abyss of radical and mortal sin yawns just beside the path they are treading. It would seem that there is in the individual human being and in the human family an almost fatal inclination to prefer the false love of self to the true love of God and of neighbor. Original sin, in its deep and tragic essence, is a truth known to us only from revelation. But it is likewise a fact of experience, this strange force of attraction of a false love of self over a humanity that can live only in love.[49]

Against this threat we have no security; from this bondage we have no ransom, save the miracle of love and Redemption issuing from God. No power within the world can preserve or save mankind from the mortal peril residing in its own will. No power in this world is superior to freedom. Personal choice does not guarantee against the possibility of failure linked with the freedom of choice. The final certitude man is seeking can be found only in God. Man can feel truly secure only when he seeks refuge from his own inclination to evil in the grace of God. Only grace, which bestows upon man the Holy Spirit and love in the inner man, can so dominate man's freedom of choice as to confirm it entirely and freely in love. Grace can likewise recreate the freedom for a new love even when that freedom has been fettered to a bad choice. From the human point of view, the sin can be mortal and the refusal of love irreparable. For the all-powerful grace of God, nothing is irreparable but the final and total refusal of grace itself. All sins can be forgiven except the sin against the Holy Spirit, i.e., against the very gift of the liberating grace of God.[50]

The grace of God that makes men free has appeared in the person of Jesus.[51] In becoming man among us men, within the family of Adam, in delivering himself up to the death inflicted upon him by our revolt against God, he reveals to us the divine earnestness toward us and the unconditional gift of love: "As if God meant to prove how well he loves us, it was while we were still sinners that Christ, in his own appointed time, died for us."[52] To save us, Christ went down into the deepest abyss of our alienation and of our loss. Jesus bore more than "the weight and burden of . . . the universal forward and upward march";[53] he bore all the weight and burden of human malice; even where we condemn him to death, his love comes to seek us out. Teilhard speaks of "sorrows, pains and faults . . . often good for future use,"[54] as if reinstatement from sin were a self-evident affair. This reinstatement is possible only because Jesus humbled himself for us right down to our own level. Thenceforward the very abyss of our fault and our perdition can be the site of our encounter with our Savior. And sin can, therefore, as in the case of Paul or Magdalene, contribute to make us enter still more deeply into the unfathomable mystery of the divine mercy and compassion. But the love that springs from this encounter remains always a miracle.

In the Resurrection of Jesus, God has given us the sign of his power and his will to love "which justifies the sinner"[55] and "gives life to the dead."[56] God has "raised up Jesus from the dead for our justification,"[57] to the end that this Jesus, by triumphing over death in the name of life eternal, might be the prototype and source of the recreation of mankind and of the world. By sin, man can cause his own death and that of his fellows and bring the world to ruin. God is not only able but also resolved to make "new heavens and a new earth where will dwell justice and righteousness."[58] In the First-Born from the dead, the victory over the powers of sin and death is already realized; it is promised to us by this earnest and pledge.[59] Mankind is ever aware of how dangerously its own path skirts the abyss of ruin; but in our distress that robs us of all confidence in ourselves, we learn to rely upon the saving love of God: "Indeed, for ourselves we could find no outcome but death; so God would have us learn to trust, not in ourselves, but in him who raises the dead to life. It is he who has preserved us, and is preserving us, from such deadly peril; and we have learned to have confidence that he will preserve us still."[60] In the final analysis, it is only the sign of the Resurrection of Jesus that gives us certitude concerning the salvation of mankind and of the world, despite the fateful possibility of sin by man. . . . The use of the word *interesting* in the following Teilhardian text strikes one, in the light of all this, as far from strong enough to mirror the reality: "For a Christian believer it is interesting to note that the final success of hominization . . . is positively guaranteed by the 'redeeming virtue' of the God incarnate in his creation."[61]

No other certitude is accorded us, save that of the Resurrection. Whoever thinks to find this certitude elsewhere is deceiving himself.

The drama of sin is essentially graver than Teilhard makes it out to be in these texts. And the mystery of the Redemption is correspondingly more lofty, more divine, more enrapturing. There are darker abysses and more radiant summits on the path of each man and on the road of mankind than are shown on the Teilhardian map: "He has not been able (or at least not been willing) to encompass the human drama in all its poignant beauty. He gazes upon the cosmos with too much complacency."[62]

So we come back to the question posed at the outset of this chapter concerning Teilhard's endeavor to set the "hope" of mankind upon solid empirical foundations. We must conclude that he has failed in this endeavor. Our true hope rests upon the love of God, his promise and the sign of the Resurrection. It could be countered that true Christian Hope does not preclude the search for terrestrial assurances and this-worldy kinds of security as well. And this is indeed true; it is just that the final ultimate security will never be found in this realm. The Christian must never cease to realize that these assurances are fragile and insufficient; indeed, human experience helps him to this awareness. Man and mankind can find their ultimate security only in the shadow of the Father's hand. He has shown himself mighty and he alone is mighty to overcome the threat of sin and of destruction. Were Teilhard really intending to find the deliverance from our existential anguish within the limits of the world itself, then he would be presenting a false hope to mankind and the only outcome would be a still more drastic disillusionment.

It might perhaps be said in justification of Teilhard that he is aiming at presenting a kind of apologetic of hope. Just as Catholic apologetics does not prove faith as such but only the rational and obligatory nature of faith, so Teilhard would be demonstrating, in an argumentation proceeding from nature, that it is in conformity with right reason and mandatory to have confidence in the faithfulness of God in true Christian hope. He would be pointing up the indications from the history of the world that prove that it is justified and necessary to hope in God. He would be trail blazing a new apologetic, specially adapted to the present distress of mankind in search of a firm foothold of hope. Unbelief, as it manifests itself in our day, seems to stem less from intellectual motives than from a deep-seated pessimism, causing man, despite his apparent assurance, to lack confidence either in the future or in the meaningfulness of his own existence. As against this pessimism, Teilhard eloquently proclaims that man and mankind cannot live without faith in the meaningfulness of the world and without hope in a destiny for that world. He claims that Christianity alone gives an answer to this vital need. Only in Christianity is that death which threatens all our earthly accomplishments not an end but rather the door leading to new life and resurrection. The awareness of the impotence of the world to preserve itself against the ultimate threat may become the stimulus and impulsion to seek another and transcendent foothold of hope. "The foundation which has been laid is the only one which anybody can lay; I mean Jesus Christ."[63] Teilhard may well have things to say to us that are of importance for an apologetic of hope.

But is Teilhard himself taking sufficient cognizance of the fact that an apologetic of hope is not yet hope itself? In the deduction of Omega, he distinguishes between the natural approach and the science of revelation properly so-called. In the matter of hope, he does not make any explicit distinction.[64] In *Le Milieu divin*, he hit upon the felicitous formulation: "feel so completely swept away in the divine ocean *that no initial point of support would be left him.*"[65] The ultimate certitude and the ultimate foothold are thus not to be found within the cosmos but solely in God. And so the "strong empirical reasons" for hope in the ultimate success of the process of universal becoming can have value only to the extent to which they are for us signs of the transcendent solicitude of God. The potent drama of evolution carving a sure path for itself through countless reefs and straits to consummation in the life of man can become a school of apprenticeship in Christian hope, if it aids man to discover behind the figure of this world the loving countenance of God. *Le Milieu divin* has an appealing description of this drama, seeing in the tremendous cosmic powers of construction and demolition the creative hand of the Father, fashioning the Body of his incarnate Son;[66] and *Le Milieu divin* expresses the conviction that "the whole Universe, between the hands of the Creator, still continues to be the clay in which He shapes innumerable possibilities according to this will."[67]

Across the somber and agonizing torrent of life, Teilhard has heard the familiar voice of Christ: "It is I; be not afraid!"[68] As man and spiritual writer, Teilhard sees the world, even in the power and inexorable determinism of evolution, as having become transparent and letting the God shine through who has revealed himself in Christ.

But it is a matter for astonishment that these echoes become very rare in his later writing. Among the basic central dogmas of Christianity, Teilhard lists that of "God as Providence, directing the Universe with loving, watchful care";[69] he speaks of God as "Mover" of evolution;[70] he knows that "God . . . acts upon us via Evolution."[71] But he scarcely mentions the world as sign of God and of his loving watchful paternal care. How is this omission to be explained? It is inconceivable that the encounter with God, spoken of with such fervor and eloquence in *Le Milieu divin*, should ever have become blurred in his mind. It remained the glowing heart of home for him all his life, inspiring his personal endeavor and living, and bringing to the face of the world he was studying the countenance of God, Creator and Redeemer. It may be that this had become so evident to Teilhard that he felt no more need of saying it in so many words; but the result is that there is in his system a kind of short-circuit between the intracosmic signs and hope itself. May it be that his apologist's reserve restrained him from speaking overtly of the personal providence of God and of his solicitude for the course of evolution?[72] For the reasons expounded above,[73] Teilhard's endeavor was to make the modern man of science "see" God at the terminus of evolution. Did he, perhaps, fear that he would weaken the force of this message by any premature mention of the nearness of God during the course of that evolution? He may have been persuaded that if the searcher found God at the end of the road, the light of that discovery would stream back reflected upon the present and the past: "from this focus of irreversibility, once discovered, the light would stream backward."[74] The preliminary prerequisite is that the searcher discover, in the prospect of the progress of the personalization of mankind, a God who is the personification of love. Then will that searcher be able to learn to find the nearness of the love of this personal God in the unfolding of universal history as well.

Interpreted in this way, Teilhard's words about evolution as foundation of confidence become acceptable. This confidence would not be hope, properly speaking, but rather a preparation, a portal, indicating on the one hand the indispensable character of hope for mankind, demonstrating on the other how the history of life and of mankind serves as a sign of the abiding solicitude of God. The gap would consist in Teilhard's not having shown with sufficient clarity to his reader (and perhaps not having realized sufficiently himself) the distance always separating the preparation from the hope itself. The reader, not properly forewarned, would think he could found his hope on this reflection on universal becoming; he would have nothing more, when all was said and done, than a meager and inadequate substitute for the personal encounter with the personal God. Herein lurks a real danger for anyone accepting too trustingly and uncritically Teilhard's expositions. But such a reader would not have discovered the innermost and inviolable core of Teilhard's great design either. As the Teilhardian teaching on the ascent to Omega has already demonstrated, and as the study of his spirituality will amply confirm, this core of the design is constituted by the personal relation of man with the personal God, whose creative and redemptive power is active and operative within our world; and the whole design is oriented toward the peak of his presence by grace, in the Incarnate Son; and the radiance of the entire design issues from this peak.

APPENDIX III

Evolution and Original Sin

A study limited strictly to Teilhard's ideas could afford to be very brief on original sin and the problems therewith connected. But what Teilhard writes on this whole complex subject compels our attention in this study because it so well reflects the thoughts and the tendencies current among the minds molded by evolutionist ways of thinking. Evolutionism itself seems less the cause of this mentality than the catalyst which transformed a latent uneasiness into a crisis. The wider scope of our study, therefore, compels us to penetrate further into the whole complex of these ideas.

The problem of original sin has usually been treated on the basis of a view of the world directly opposed to the evolutionary one. For the traditional presentation started from a perfect first state, a paradise where the first man, endowed with great privileges, was lord of the world; whereas evolutionism presents all origins as most modest, imperfect, defective. The crisis of this traditional conception of original sin is accentuated by the movement of renewal in exegesis, which has become more sensitive to the literary, cultural, and historical forms and patterns and less ready to accept the narratives as a monolithic historical recital. Finally, the present-day trend in philosophy is afraid that the doctrine of original sin may involve a devaluation and derogation of human history, making of it a gigantic cycle, a return to the primitive situation. When taken in addition to the mysterious aura that has always surrounded the question of original sin, these factors explain the uneasiness felt by many minds on this subject.

Teilhard's endeavor to give the ancient doctrine a new form

must be positioned in this wider context. Teilhard's aim was not merely to adapt the doctrine to new ways of thinking; he also wanted to restore to it an existential meaningfulness which it had almost entirely forfeited in the Nominalist schools and in some of the schools of the Counter-Reformation. This intention comes out in Teilhard's angle of approach to these questions. Why does science find no trace of paradise or of the fall? Usually theology seems to be replying that this is because these realities are too tiny for our observation. Teilhard would prefer to reply that it is because they are too large. Original sin could, for instance, be conceived as a pre-temporal fall, situated outside of the world of our experience and encompassing the whole of universal history. From its very origin, our world would have been a fallen world; the whole of evolution would be the spectacle of a salvation, of an extraction from the fall, "a fallen world in the process of rising again."[1] Teilhard discards this notion as mere imagination. He prefers another explanation: the doctrine of original sin would, on this explanation, be simply a version of the generic law of sin deriving from the imperfection of a human race in process of development. We are already familiar with Teilhard's theory of sin as statistically inevitable.[2] This explanation recurs in an essay from 1933;[3] it is alluded to in a note to *Comment je vois*.[4] In his exposition of his theory of the inevitability of sin, Teilhard remarks:

> Let us mention here the principle of a simple and fruitful interpretation of original sin—the necessity of Baptism (theological necessity) being explained by the solidarity of all men in the womb of one single Mankind (impregnated with sin by statistical necessity), where the collective bonds are revealed as being still more real and still deeper-cutting than any other liaison of a strictly and "linearly" hereditary sort between individuals.[5]

Teilhard always seems to be searching for an explanation along these lines; but these ideas do not appear to have satisfied him entirely. For in all his passages on original sin, he always reaffirms that the universal necessity of Redemption and of baptism are demonstrative of the universality of sin, whereas the statistical law of sin could never lead to more than a certain percentage of evil. Teilhard says this outright in the 1948 postscript to *Le Phénomène humain*. After outlining the statistical law, he proceeds to write:

> But is this really the whole story? Is there nothing further? I mean, is it quite sure that an alert and sensitive enquirer, illuminated by another light than that of pure science, would not find that the amount and malice of Evil *hic et nunc* presenting itself spread out throughout the world betrays a certain *excess,* inexplicable to our human reason unless to *the normal effect of Evolution* there be added *the extraordinary effect* of some primordial catastrophe or deviation? . . .[6]

The interrogative form of this remark becomes intelligible upon reflection that Teilhard is here writing on the apologetic plane, this side of dogma.

So it seems superfluous to subject this notion of original sin to a detailed discussion. Besides it would be pointless, for the real difficulties would be constantly re-emerging from the discord between the usual presentation of original sin and the modern views. For precisely the dogmatic presentation is one of the main causes of these difficulties. More can be expected from a positive exegesis of the doctrine of original sin, an exegesis which takes due cognizance of the justified hesitations of the modern mind and integrates into the ancient doctrine the new attainments of thought. Despite the important exegetical and systematic studies devoted in recent years to original sin, the positive contribution must here be a very modest one and the continuity with the traditional doctrine can only be indicated in passing. The judgment on this subject matter is the office of those who have received, together with the charism of truth, the authority to provide an authentic interpretation of the faith.

1. Original Sin in Its Wider Context

"If the doctrine of original sin seems today simply not to be getting through to the average Catholic, one of the main reasons is, we think, the fact that we have been preaching it too much as a truth in a class by itself, split off from the whole body of revelation on sin and Redemption."[7] Theology is often obliged and always inclined to treat each and every individual "dogma" of the faith as a self-contained unity. But this always involves the threat of a real deformation. In Scripture, sin, in particular the message of original sin, is always subordinated to the preaching of salvation.[8] Even as late as the Council of Trent, the decree on original sin served as an introduction to the decree on justification, and there was already explicit reference to salvation within this decree.[9] But for the understanding of the faith today, this dogma seems to hang like a leaden cope upon mankind. What theological writing or writer would still dare to exclaim today in the words of our Liturgy: "Happy fault, which has merited us such and so great a Redeemer"? Ought not our present chronological presentation, in which original sin is first presented in itself and then the Redemption, give way to a more dialectical preaching in which the two elements would compenetrate, with the primacy being given to Christ the Redeemer?[10] Human original sin is surely inconceivable save within a humanity destined to become the Body of the Son of God Incarnate and, therefore, as a sin assumed and enveloped by the mercy of God. "God's plan of salvation in Jesus Christ dominates the entire history of mankind. The power of sin is not unlimited in this world."[11] The framework of the salvation Gospel is indispensable to the Christian preaching of original sin.

On the other hand, the dogma of original sin cannot be split off from the sum total constituting the doctrine of sin as such. Circumstances have biased attention upon two extreme cases in the matter of original sin: the single fault of Adam and the guilt of newborn infants. The main stem of the doctrine has been wellnigh forgotten. This main stem consists of the empirical fact, confirmed by the word of God and by faith, that all men are sinners and that they are solidary in their sinning.

In any proper understanding of the doctrine of original sin, we must not lose sight of the solid fact we learn from experience and which the faith presents to us in more precise and specific image. . . . The empirical experience of sin was for Israel the occasion to compose the narrative of the Fall. We must not believe that Israel was sinful as a result of the fault of Adam and that this was all there was to it; we must also grasp the fact that the belief in the Fall of Adam is rooted in the awareness the Chosen People had of its own sinfulness.[12]

If the awareness of personal sin and of the solidarity of all men in the sin of mankind should be attenuated, or if original sin be split off from the adult's own experience of sin, then the dogma of the original transgression is bound to become blurred and to lose its existential meaningfulness. By reducing it to the "guilt" inherited by the children, we are uprooting it from its proper context in the sources. Of Scripture can be said what was written about Paul's great and famous text on original sin: "Paul has before his eyes chiefly the case of adults and is not thinking specifically of that of infants of tender age."[13] The Council of Trent still was envisaging original sin as an empirical fact of adult life, as comes out in the speech by the Papal Legate, Cardinal Pole, opening the discussion: "What original sin is, we feel more strongly in ourselves by the reality than we can express in words."[14]

But since Trent there has been a serious shift in the presentation of original sin which has given rise to various anomalies and forced the preaching of this doctrine into a cleft stick. There has been a shift of emphasis from the vital adult experience of the empirical fact to the state of infants; from the fact of solidarity in sin to an individualistic conception which asks only what original sin means for each individual human being;[15] from an integral approach to a spiritualist conception which does not any longer consider "concupiscence" in practice to be an element of original sin;[16] from a notion of sin as a dynamic power, "less a state than an orientation toward ever new sins,"[17] to a notion of sin as a kind of static magnitude identical in infant and in adult. Whereas the dogma of original sin aims at awakening an awareness of the seriousness of the fault springing from the depths of our nature and of human history, this dogma serves for many present-day theologians merely in the office of an excuse.[18]

If we reinstate the doctrine of original sin once more in the broader framework of the awareness of personal and collective sin, we shall rediscover its whole real meaning. The fall of Adam no longer appears as an isolated fact; his single transgression is no longer a hideously oppressive problem. We see the possibility of understanding original sin as a reality, a capacity for sinning, which grows and develops with mankind itself, because every sinner imparts a new force and impulsion to it. The opposition between the dogma and the modern, historical and evolutionist view is attenuated. Let us attempt here an outline of the main points to be consided in a renovation and renewal to be operated upon the ancient doctrine. Unfortunately we cannot attempt here to position the belief in original sin within its organic context of a growing awareness of sin as such; we must limit ourselves to unilateral speculative considerations. But in so doing, we are taking our stand forthwith at the heart of Christian revelation and are doing so from the point of view of the modern problematic, notably, the point of view of an anthropology which takes due cognizance of the social and historical nature of man.

2. *Outline of a Dynamic Doctrine of Original Sin*

According to Scripture, the world and mankind were created by the Father in view of Christ, that is, in view of the Son of God who was to become incarnate:

He is the true likeness of the God we cannot see, his is that first birth which precedes every act of creation. Yes, in him all created things took their being, heavenly and earthly, visible and invisible . . . They were all created through him and in him (literally: toward him); he takes precedency of all and all exist (literally: have their foundation) in him.[19]

The Incarnate Son of God is the end and the cornerstone[20] of the whole world and of man in particular. In the plan of God everything is ordered to the Incarnation, to the glorification and consummation of Christ; the whole of the history of the earth and of mankind is embraced by this design. "Our unity with Jesus Christ is therefore, and has been since before the foundation of the world, the single design and plan of divine salvation. This design is executed by God against our sin for our justification and our glorification."[21] From its first origins, mankind has been destined and called to arrive at the fullness of the Body of Christ. All the operations whereby man actualizes and realizes himself as individual being and as collectivity are ordained to this destiny. In developing himself as person and as community, according to God's plan, man is collaborating directly or indirectly to the realization of the community in which all will be one among themselves and with the Father in Christ.[22]

But this collaboration is of a special and paradoxical sort. The Incarnation of the Son of God and the edification of his Body are divine grace: personal, free, and compassionate communication of God, making of creatures his sons. Man is to hope for the fulfillment of his destiny as a free gift of the love of God. The final fulfillment of man is the work of God. Of course man must, as a spiritual intellectual being, realize himself and actualize himself. But this *self*-realization and *self*-actualization is of a very special kind: man must *let himself* be realized and actualized by the grace of God. The supreme act of human freedom is surrender to a higher love, a Yes to the invitation and promise of God. There is the imposing task laid upon man: to see to his own flowering in strength and beauty, as the image of God that he is on the earth, while at the same time accepting this gift in gratitude, humility, and dependent subordination; to tend to his goal and end by his own unstinting effort and endeavor, while at the same time hoping for this end and goal as a free gift from God.

It is this against which man has sinned from the outset, as the Bible teaches us in the paradise narrative:

The first man had to choose his stance and attitude, as did every other man after him. Would he take due cognizance of God as the reality which ought to guide all his actions or would he choose himself as the final and ultimate norm of his own actions, arrogating to himself in his conceit the place of God? Would he be ready to surrender himself in faith, to put his hope in God, or would he prefer to have recourse to his own human power, to the means which would lead him to salvation by his own calculations and in accord with his own desires? . . . Would he choose his own road or God's road, the road of obedient faith?[23]

Everywhere we find again the same nucleus and kernel of sin, in the transgression in Paradise, in the Tower of Babel, in the idolatry impelling Israel to make to itself a golden calf and worship it as God, in the impious and unrighteous policies and politics of the later Kings,[24] in the incredulity prompting the Jews to demand a Messiah tailored to their own cut and their own style, in their refusal to accept him whom God sent to them with his overflowing mercy and compassion, in the self-righteousness which refuses the gift of divine righteousness.[25] In his own grandeur and dizzying power, man wills to suffice unto himself. He wills to set himself up as the supreme norm and find therein his security. He wills to realize himself by himself without recognizing or admitting that he is *himself* one given and that his freedom is ordained and ordered to Another.

In its deepest essence, all sin is a refusal of God's communication by grace and so, at least implicitly, a refusal of the Son of God made man. It is thus also a refusal to accomplish that building of self into the Body of Christ. The result is that man and mankind, by realizing and actualizing themselves under the sign of sin, build themselves up into a "body of sin," into what the Bible calls the wicked world.

Let us now pause for a moment on the nexus between sin and concupiscence. Concupiscence is a consequence of sin and becomes in its turn an occasion of sin. "It comes from sin and inclines to sin," says the Council of Trent.[26] By concupiscence must be understood, in the first instance, not an inclination to evil things but rather the inclination to good things evilly directed and ordered. When he declines the gift of God, man inevitably comes to seek for an infinite outside of God. By his spiritual essence and by his vocation, man is geared to an infinite fulfillment; in every free act, he tends to an unlimited good and happiness. If he does not accept the infinite promised him in God, he will unfailingly seek for an infinite compass and dimension in finite things. His inclination becomes disordered, inordinate, and unbalanced. He demands of creatures what only the Creator can give him. He fastens desperately onto creatures, never satiated and never satisfied, always wanting to dilate their limits and so transcend their limitations.

Such is the heart of the concupiscence of which Scripture and the Church speak to us: the inclination, rooted in freedom itself and tending to the infinite apart from the Infinite, wanting all the good things of creation without any restriction or moderation. This concupiscence wills to make of these things—pleasure, possessions, fame, power over the world and over the self—absolute values. It, therefore, wills to transgress the limitation inscribed upon their essence. All the finite values can be desired and used in a good way,[27] that is, in their relation to God and accordingly in their relative modality of existence.[28] Concupiscence, properly speaking, does not consist in attachment to and desire for earthly goods as such. It consists rather in the tendency to make of them an absolute and to seek in them the ultimate beatitude, to desire in an infinite way that which is of itself finite. Concupiscence, properly so-called, therefore resides in the will itself. The closest approaches to this infinite object of desire are the values constituting the proper object of the will, namely, power, knowledge, perfect personal freedom and even that "love of self amounting to contempt of God"[29] wherein Scripture has located the core of all sin.

It is, therefore, an error to see concupiscence principally or exclusively in the discord between the desires of the senses and the will of the spirit. It may be in this discord that concupiscence is most clearly manifest. But the root of concupiscence lies in the will itself, directed by nature and vocation toward the infinite God but inclined to seek this infinite in objects which are finite.[30] True concupiscence shows itself, for example, in the stubbornness with which self-love infiltrates the best intentions, in vanity, ostentation, ambition, pride. Not only the more external passions but also the deep-seated tendencies, the yen of the innermost soul, show man's complicity, the complicity even of a man of good will, with what he recognizes and condemns himself as egotism. The saying of St.

Paul always applies in a sense to the man who is reborn to a new love: "The things that I would, I do not, and the things that I would not, I do."[31] The conflict between the higher and the lower inclinations is fed and fanned by the conflict within the will, not entirely submissive in its inclinations to the one undivided love. Every good can be directed toward God, source and crown of all good. Every inclination can submit to this pull toward the cornerstone of love. But wherever love of God falters, there every inclination begins to stretch itself indefinitely far in its own direction, so that man becomes torn and disjointed by the dynamism of his own inclinations, becomes the divided man spoken of by the Fathers of the Church.[32]

Man tends with his whole being to the realization of his proper self as an independent person, to the realization of mankind as a community, to the edification of a world which will be his sort of world. In proportion as he succeeds in this, the world becomes the reflection of his humanity and is subject to it. The result is that the man who is torn and divided builds a world that is torn and divided, and a community that is torn and divided, the "wicked" world of which Scripture speaks and which St. John characterizes thus: ". . . gratification of corrupt nature, gratification of the eye, the empty pomp of living."[33] He who loves this world cannot love God.[34]

This involves no condemnation of the goods of the earth as such, for they are created and given by God; nor does it involve any condemnation of man's effort to put these goods to his own service, for this is an assignment he has received from God. The world is condemned to the extent to which man molds it to the shape of his own sin, putting its goods and wealth at the service of his own "vain"[35] existence and of his own self-love and unbridled ambition. This is just what man has done from the beginning and is continuing to do. He builds up a worldly power and society in which pleasure, riches, fame, and power are raised to the status of absolute values. The result is that these values, these goods which continue to be goods as such, are sought in infinite measure, without being integrated into the harmony of a balanced humanity. In the world, every desire is ceaselessly creating for itself new means of satisfaction, and these means in turn stimulate desire. Man is living in a constant state of excitation, chasing an ever-vanishing will-o'-the-wisp sort of happiness. Finite goods are transformed into idols; their worshipers are aware that these idols have feet of clay, but do not, for all that, cease to worship them, begging of them salvation and sacrificing to them everything, even fellow human beings. The result is an unbalanced world in which earthly goods are no longer a springboard from which to leap upward to God but have rather become the solid wall that shuts off earth from heaven.

Society is equally unbalanced in such a world. As soon as man shuts his heart to the gift of God who has summoned him to love God himself and to love his human neighbor, man inevitably tends to build a divided society, not open to true communication and communion in love but teeming with all manner of desires, from pleasure to spiritual pride. The Bible gives us a picture of this recurrent drama of a society without God in the story of the Tower of Babel.

The Tower of Babel is the expression of national pride, trampling on the rights of other peoples and binding everyone and everything together into a totalitarian state by sheer force of arms. Babel and the national idolatry of which it is the image are the cause of all hate and all war between the peoples of the earth; Babel is a corruption of God's initial plan for the world, that it should be one single great human family even as he is one God.[36]

Mankind's secularized endeavor is in fact issuing in an ever more closely knit union of individuals and peoples. But this union is giving rise to and being forged out of wars of ever-vaster extent and tyrannies of ever-greater cruelty. For men are refusing the love that comes from God and put neighbor on the same footing as self, thus constituting the only solid foundation for a just peace and order.

This wicked world, hard-hearted and blind to the things of God,[37] is being built by the sin of men who have from the beginning been refusing the gift offered by God and his message summoning them to the Body of his own Incarnate Son.

Saving grace has also certainly been active and operative since the beginning; let this point be clearly noted, although we cannot develop it further here. Man's unfaithfulness cannot destroy God's faithfulness.[38] God continues to build up the true body of mankind, but he is doing this, so to speak, by a divine stratagem. The Son becomes man, but he does so against the current of the normal course of human fertility. The Holy One comes into the sinful world, expiates its sin in love, and thenceforth the love of God is close to the sinner.[39] The ordeal of the obstacle of sin around us and within us becomes a holy cross whereby the Father renders men of good will conformed to his Son.

In this context, original sin might be described as the burden of evil weighing upon every human being by the mere fact of his birth, because of the state of mankind, the intimate solidarity of the individual with the human race; this is original sin because it is antecedent to any of the individual's own sins, but it is freely and inevitably ratified and accepted by each and every personal sin.

Theology usually employs the analogy of the *habitus* to describe original sin: the *habitus* is the inclination of the will resulting from personal choice and hardening into a durable mold via this choice. This definition of original sin is based upon its most inward element. But there may also be advantages in approaching original sin from its external aspect. Thus Schoonenberg describes original sin as "the situation in which man finds himself from the moment and because of the fact of his entry into a world in which sin prevails."[40] By "situation," Schoonenberg means the surrounding world, the environment in which man posits his personal acts, a world which is on the one hand anterior to these acts and on the other determined and built up by the acts themselves. This environment is not constituted solely of things and material factors but also of interpersonal relationships, institutional forms of interhuman relations, value judgments and norms, *mores* typical of a specific culture, people or social class. Obviously the atmosphere or environment in which the individual finds himself can have a decisive influence on the way in which a personality is molded and asserted. Man develops himself by contact and encounter with things and people. If certain values are absent from his environment, the individual will scarcely be able to realize them in himself. He does, on the contrary, adopt unconsciously other attitudes that determine his own conscious conduct in large part. This objective element penetrates the personal element as an environmental atmosphere, a mesh of facts, ways of thinking, laws, traditions, authorities, and institutions. Before the manifestation of the personal, before the encounter of the *I* and the *Thou*, countless qualities . . . and social structures, language, fashions, manners, etc., are already present and it is within this framework and by means of this framework that the encounter occurs.[41]

As a concrete example, we can take the case of the way in which children are trained in our Western culture, even prior to any deliberate schooling, even by parents who have overcome the spirit of that culture in their own personal lives but are forced to bring their children up in an environment where luxuries are the criterion of happiness and where the main end, aim, and goal of education, study or work has come to be the acquisition of money. It may well be this atmosphere of which Paul is speaking when he talks of the "prince whose domain is in the lower air,"[42] "in which men live and breathe, by which they allow their thinking, their willing and their actions to be governed." This atmosphere "condenses into specific situations. It becomes an intense and potent spirit of the times, whose influence no one can escape."[43]

In any search for a concrete and social form of original sin, an important role could certainly be attributed to this environment of the "world" and of sinful mankind, into which every human child is catapulted by the mere fact of his issuing from the womb. From this point of view, at least, original sin can assume various forms and degrees of virulence and can be posited as not caused solely by the transgression of the first parents but by the personal transgression of each individual as well.[44] Every sin strengthens the dominion of evil in the world and increases the weight of transgression burdening other men and posterity. This gives us an opportunity of conceiving of original sin not as a purely static quantity but rather as something growing and developing with the body like a parasite that has entered the seedling and propagates throughout the entire tree, to the tips of its roots and branches. "It is a state in which the world has been set by its own fault and in which it sinks a little deeper each day by its own free act, so long as it cannot get out of that situation. This increases the original guilt so much the more."[45]

Original sin can be presented in a concrete and vital fashion if viewed from its external aspect, its objective form in the changing shape of this "world." But the nucleus of original sin lies hidden at a much deeper level; it lies in concupiscence and deviation from the destiny set and appointed by God. Were original sin nothing but an external situation, it could serve as an excuse for our own missteps, whereas, in fact, it demonstrates precisely what deeplying roots nourish the perversity of man. The sin-pocked world is in a continual process of building up from the heart of man. "It is not what goes into a man's mouth that makes him unclean . . . all that comes out of his mouth comes from the heart, and it is that which makes a man unclean."[46] The world is so potent an influence because and only because it finds in every human heart a spontaneous echo and a ready accomplice. "When a man is tempted, it is always because he is being drawn away by the lure of his own passions."[47] In every man is concealed the tendency to evil or rather, as we have put it, the tendency to will and desire good things and attach himself to them in an evil fashion. The Old Testament describes this inclination by saying that the heart of the chosen people is stone or corrupt[48] and that "man . . . has all the thoughts and imaginations of his heart, even in youth, so bent towards evil."[49] Post-biblical Jewish writings speak of the "perverse heart" or of the "evil inclination."[50] Paul's favorite expression for this is *sarx*, flesh in the sense of the disordered, transient and perishable.

It is of importance that the modern reader realize precisely that the whole man is designated by this term *flesh*, that it is not at all synonymous with "body" as distinct from "soul."[51] "Flesh" and "carnal" mean for Paul the whole man as deprived of the Spirit (i.e., of grace) and given over to the powers of sin, of the law, and of death.[52] "The flesh lusteth against the spirit,"[53] for "the desire of the flesh is the enemy of God; it is at enmity with God, not submitting itself to his law; it is impossible that it should."[54]

John locates the center of gravity of the power of sin in the "world," thus evoking the image of an objective external structure, outside of man though built by man; Paul, on the contrary, locates it in the "flesh," and thus within man himself, in the revolt of the carnal passions but, above all, in the deep-seated egotism lurking in the will itself.[55] This concupiscence making man an accomplice of the power of evil which reigns in this world is for Paul a consequence of sin and even a kind of sin.

The *sarx* . . . is an obscure but invincible complicity which the power of darkness finds within us, inherited in fact together with our earthly nature and bound up with the present state of that nature. . . . Through the intermediary of this *sarx*, the power of darkness acts not only upon us but in us, infiltrating his own enmity to God into the very wellsprings of our action.[56]

Sin is not just imposed upon us; it springs spontaneously out of us, voluntarily—for otherwise it would not be sin—and inevitably—for man is really the slave of sin unless redemptive grace deliver him.[57]

We are here touching on the deepest and most mysterious root of original sin. In the heart of man lies a kind of will not to love God; anterior to every personal choice, it encompasses and fetters that choice. Created and destined to love, man always aspires, at least unconsciously, to love as the final flowering and ultimate fulfillment of his being; but he has set up a deep-cutting egotism in the innermost chamber of himself. He suffers from a "*curvitas*,"[58] a deviation that turns him back upon finite goods and chiefly upon himself. He lacks the uprightness of *justitia* ("righteousness"),[59] which ought to project his existence beyond itself to communion with God in the Body of God's Son; he lacks the Holy Spirit, the gift of God, enabling him to love the Father.[60] Man is spiritually dead,[61] for communion with God is truly his very life. From the moment at which he comes into this life, man is under the sign of the breaking of the covenant made by God with mankind.

The whole of creation, the entire existence of each individual human being still continues to be directed by God to the edification of the Body of Christ and to the communion with the Father. But there is on the part of man a kind of obstinate refusal to go beyond himself into this infinite love, a morbid tendency to close up upon himself, something that, although anterior to personal acts, must yet really be called a sin, if "sin constitutes a rupture, a closing in upon self, a refusal of the demands levied by inter-personal relations between the subject and God or neighbor,"[62] a kind of aversion to God who has created and called man with a view to his Son.

It remains a mystery that such a sin could pre-exist in man, before the personal choice of his own life. This point may be no more of a mystery than the vocation of mankind to build up the Body of the Incarnate Son of God and to build itself up into that Body. The covenant in paradise would have allowed mankind to build this body by its own development throughout the course of history: the preceding generation would in each case have transmitted to its descendants a positive orientation to this destiny and the rudimentary beginnings of it. History is a process in which what follows has an internal nexus with what precedes. Thus, if humanity were to be able to realize this fulfillment via its own history, the parents would each time pass on to their descendents an inner existential orientation or bias, both internal and external, bringing them closer to the fulfillment. The parents' *Yes* to the call of God, a *Yes* concretized in the building up of society, would have inclined the children's existence in a positive direction.

Inversely, it is not unthinkable that the *No* of ancestors, repeated over and over again by the descendants, could have communicated to succeeding generations an inner deviation and aversion from this fulfillment. Not simply each and every human being is thrown by birth into a world and a society branded by sin; the very existence received from the parents is deprived of the interior bias to faithfulness to the divine covenant.

In this way, original sin might perhaps be described as a deep-seated bias within the very existence of each human being, a bias stemming from the very fact that the individual has been born into the human family: this human family has in fact broken the covenant that would have permitted it to build itself up into the

Body of Christ, and thereby seeks inevitably but nonetheless culpably to arrive at perfect self-development apart from the grace-mediated communion with God; it is the pursuit of the infinite in finite goods, the building of a world and a society in which these disjointed goods prevail. In each individual human being, then, original sin is the lack of supernatural love, of the Holy Spirit who would have made of that human individual a member *in fieri* of the Body of Christ, and a tendency and inclination, born of this lack, to ascribe an infinite value to finite things, an enslavement to the world which man is building with his fellow men.

But it would be a poor presentation of the doctrine of original sin that would involve an evaluation of the history of mankind as nothing but a history of sin. For this history is still more a history of grace and of redemption. The paradise narrative ends on a promise of salvation whereby God takes the side of his guilty children against their seducer.[63] The consequences of sin are not simply a deadly train of transgressions and of guilt; there is also a divine punishment and a way whereby the sinner can find a new communion with God.[64] This communion is more intimate than that of paradise, because the heart of God is more utterly open in this new communion and man accepts that heart with greater humility. God continues to build up the Body of his Son, and mankind continues to collaborate in this building. But, henceforth, the collaboration presents a dialectical character, an ambivalent aspect, because the effort and endeavor whereby man is realizing himself and the world serves to prepare the holocaust which he will offer to God, with Christ, of both himself and the world.[65]

3. *Cause and Transmission of Original Sin*

This outline of the essence of original sin enables us to envision the problems posed by the confrontation of the dogma with evolutionist thinking. One of these problems is the discord between the humble origin of mankind postulated by evolution and the universal import and bearing attributed by dogma to the act of Adam.[66]

The fact that original sin was caused by the sin of the ancestors of mankind pertains without any doubt to the doctrine as revealed. The Council of Trent defines that "the dishonesty of Adam injured his offspring" because he "lost for us also the sanctity and justice [*justitia*-righteousness] which he had received of God" and because he "transmitted to the entire human race the sin which is the death of the soul."[67] Paul summed up this doctrine in these words: "By the disobedience of one man, all are become sinners."[68] This is, likewise, what the paradise narrative intends to teach us. The inspired writer does not simply intend to delineate for us the tragic condition of every man[69] in the figure of the ancestor to whom he gives the name of Man.[70] He further intends to give us an understanding of the cause of the misery and unrighteousness from which mankind is suffering. "The sacred writer has a real desire to *explain* our present situation; this is of the very essence of his narrative. This Adam is not only a figure or a type; he is the *real cause* of our condition."[71] The believer asks for an explanation of the break between mankind and God, as manifest in the continual infidelity of the Chosen People and the perversity of the heathen. Since Israel tended to look at human history as a road rather than a cycle or spiral, a transgression committed at the outset, at the start of the road, is the only possible explanation for the fact that sin is now a general and all-encompassing human condition. Once the first step had been taken, there could be no going back.

> The sacred text . . . includes a narrative. It is not, at least directly, a doctrine but rather a story; it describes a beginning of the road on which there could be no going back. It must therefore be held that we here have a narrative of facts, very mysterious and obscure facts to be sure.[72]

This genuine causality of the single act of Adam does not preclude other sins as accessory causes of original sin. Such a way of looking at the matter is not in contradiction with the Tridentine doctrine on the unity of original sin[73] and is confirmed by the views of Scripture. For Scripture knows of other sins of ancestors which were handed down to the descendants, giving a more precise shape and a greater power to original sin in general: the Tower of Babel, the worship of the golden calf, Solomon's idolatry. When Paul speaks of original sin, we cannot forget that he refers to the description he has just given of the sinful society of pagan Hellenism and of Judaism.[74] The sin in the Garden of Eden is crucially significant as the *first* breaking of the covenant by the *universal* parents; but it is, on the other hand, merely "the beginning of sin,"[75] the breach through which sin entered into the world of man to continue thereafter relentlessly to strengthen its dominion.[76] It would, therefore, be inaccurate to isolate the first sin from the "picture painted by Genesis of a succession of falls, all of which affected more or less seriously the fate of a more or less numerous progeny."[77] The generic original sin is strengthened and intensified each time in the sin of later ancestors.

A similar state of affairs likewise applies to the life of each individual person. Personal sins committed inevitably but nonetheless culpably by the children of Adam, except to the extent to which they accept God's redeeming grace, are not committed apart from original sin; they are rather the actualization and fulfillment of it. By his own personal sins, every adult ratifies and makes his own the breaking of the covenant once perpetrated by Adam and allows it to dominate his own existence. The doctrine of original sin does not say only that "one man commits a fault, and it brings condemnation upon all"[78] but also that all bring condemnation upon themselves by "serving sin."[79] Original sin and personal sin cannot be separated into watertight compartments. Only in personal sins does original sin reach its complete actualization. Original sin is actually "described in the sources of revelation less as a state than as a bias toward ever new sins."[80]

Scripture and Tradition set up a very strict nexus between original sin and personal sins. With one doubtful exception, all the texts of the Bible in which tradition has read the doctrine of original sin speak of a deep-seated state of sin manifesting and giving evidence of itself in personal sins. Suffice it to mention, read in their proper context, the phrases of Psalm 51:7, Job 15:14, or the Epistle to the Ephesians 2:3.[81] Even the famous text from Romans (5:12–21) is closely tied in with the preceding description of the perversity of pagans and Jews. One single phrase in the

Bible could thus be held to speak of an original sin, adequately distinct from personal sins, namely Romans 5:12, and this only according to a very controversial exegesis.[82] Several contemporary exegetes see here as well a reference to personal sins. Lyonnet interprets this passage to be an even more precise Pauline definition of the relation between the sin of Adam and personal sins.[83] Personal sins would be the consequence of the sin of Adam, and at the same time the real and unfailingly realized condition whereby this first sin would be totally fulfilled and actualized in each and every personal existence. The fall of Adam lodges all his progeny in a state of alienation from God and accordingly under the dominion of sin and death. But this dominion is fully accomplished by the children of Adam in accepting the alienation from God personally and collectively and consequently in condemning themselves to "taste" the full terror of death.[84] "By their personal sins, the children of Adam, far from renouncing or denying in any sense the sin of their father, rather ratify it by making his revolt their own."[85] The condemnation and sentence which the fault of Adam involved and brought down upon his progeny "is somehow this same state in which the sinner finds himself, caught and pulled between the holy commandment of the Law and the infirmity of his own being; ceaselessly overcome as he is by his own perversity, he has no other prospect but final ruin, the full execution of the *katakrima*. Before achieving its perfect consummation and execution, the *katakrima*, the judgment, is rendered ever more manifest by the very multiplication of transgressions."[86] All personal sin is both a consequence of the sin of Adam and the somber set of links in the chain whereby the power of death is feeding itself to its "total expansion,"[87] or the sign making that power appear definitive and irrevocable.[88]

These considerations may clear away some of the underbrush in the subject under review here, for they get rid of various difficulties raised against the traditional presentation of the doctrine of original sin. The sin of Adam need not have been a kind of superhuman universal cosmic fault. It may well have consisted in fact in the primitive fault of a primitive man, though obviously one sufficiently evolved to be capable of a moral act, of a *Yes* or *No* to grace.[89] But "Adam's guilt may be said to have snowballed."[90] Not only do the children of Adam inherit the sin of their father; they ratify and intensify it at the level of their higher culture, with their more fully developed, mature, and adult conscience, their more potent possession of themselves and of the world. The weight and burden of the original guilt has grown. It is always growing and developing with the development of mankind.

In the light of all this, it seems pointless and even hypocritical to pose the question of how the fault of a distant ancestor could make us guilty in the sight of God! As if we had nothing with which to reproach our*selves!* We constantly make our own the revolt of Adam by our resistance to the grace of God. Our present-day sinning, personal and collective, proclaims, confirms, and perpetually strengthens the dominion of sin to which Adam opened the gate. We constantly set up the idols of money, pleasure, power, and pride, and build a society in which these gods are masters. Original sin is not an excuse for our sin. Only if we recognize and humbly admit how gravely we are rendering ourselves guilty before God, personally and collectively, will we be able to have a right understanding of the message of original sin.

Now a few more words on the transmission of sin. The Council of Trent says that the sin of Adam is transmitted to his "progeny," "by propagation, not by imitation,"[91] that children contract this sin by their "birth" and because "they are conceived and born of the seed of Adam."[92] But does the Council say that "the transmission of original sin must be attributed formally to bodily procreation"?[93] Is not the role of procreation simply supposed, as evident, without being part of the doctrine, strictly speaking?

There is no doubt whatever that the Council does wish to teach that every human being incurs original sin by his entry into the human race, so that every child is burdened with it from the moment of his conception. Education and example are not being addressed, as Pelagius taught, to a well-balanced freedom. Every human being is a sinner from the moment of his first origin *within* fallen humanity. Perhaps the Council wishes to teach further that he incurs this sin because he receives existence *from* fallen humanity. Procreation and birth assume here a central place; man can make no more active contribution to creation and history than by giving life to a new generation. Here is a nucleus from which mankind can direct its existence either to communion with God or upon a supreme self-sufficiency and self-satisfaction.

But procreation should not here be taken in its restricted biological signification. It can include the whole complex of factors whereby mankind makes a human being one of its members; among this complex belong the influence of environment and example, pre- and post-natal training. At the time of the Council, several of the Council Fathers would have preferred the formula: "by propagation and not *only* by imitation."[94] And although the Council did not adopt this formulation, it did not intend, for all that, to condemn the idea that it expresses.

Origin within and by the power of humanity signified at the time of Trent procreation and birth.[95] But in our day this point occasions hesitation. Technology may one day manage to produce a man without impregnation or, indeed, entirely synthetically. The inhabitants of other planets may one day be our fellows and become members of our family. Are these prospects already sufficiently proximate for a realistically inclined theology to take seriously the problems of such situations or answer them? For the moment, we cannot concretely imagine any origin within the human family except by conception and birth. The problem of other modes of origin can be safely shelved until it actually arises in the practical empirical order. Reflection upon the faith can also agree that "sufficient unto the day is the evil thereof" and that if tomorrow should bring, as it will, its peculiar cares, it will also have its own lights.

4. *Innocence in Eden*

The Garden of Eden narrative used to be considered an eyewitness account, handed down from Adam to Moses. Pascal wrote: "Shem who had seen Lamech who had seen Adam also saw Jacob who in his turn saw those who saw Moses; therefore the Flood story and the Creation story are true."[96] A decent respect for the dignity of the Bible compels us to abandon such illusions.[97] The writer himself gives us to understand in the sacred narrative that his description of the beginnings parallels that of the end. He speaks of the dawn of history in the same fashion as the ultimate consummation and fulfillment of God's plan for mankind, i.e., from the standpoint of Israel's experience of God and man and in motifs borrowed from Israel's life. The writer knows that in (and at) the end, God's grace will triumph over men's sin just as the plan of God was disturbed at the beginning by man's sin. The Eden narrative is history to the extent that the writer teaches the beginning of that history in which we are living. It is not history based on witnesses or documents concerning what transpired in those distant times.[98] The writer does not intend to provide detailed information; he aims to teach us that at the beginning of mankind there was a drama similar to that enacted at the beginning of the history of the Chosen People, a divine covenant of grace and salvation to which man was unfaithful from the very outset.

We ought not, therefore, to look for geographical, biological, or psychological information in the Eden narrative. The prophet of the beginning like the prophet of the end takes his data "from a picture contrasting with the actual world about him."[99] He is, therefore, not providing us with an exact description of the man of Eden. "The narrator is not furnishing a *direct* description, in a positive sense, of the state of man in Eden. He is concerned with *painting out* the great turmoils of our present-day life (shame, fear, the incongruities in relations between the sexes) and charging them to the fall of man."[100] These first pages of the Bible teach that the present state of man—his alienation from God, his concupiscence, his enmity and his death—are no more in accord with the original divine plan than were the discords, divisions, and humiliation of Israel. They are the consequence of an age-old sin, forever being renewed, whereby man has from the outset been breaking the life-giving communion with God. The inference is that there was a "time" when man was not bent, as yet, under the law of this miserable state. The Bible says nothing about how long this time lasted.[101] Neither does it encourage a curiosity that would seek for details on the state of man in Eden. On the contrary, "it is in harmony with the spirit of Genesis to abstain from excessive specifications concerning the state of primal innocence."[102]

This viewpoint may aid us in getting rid of some difficulties created by the opposition between the view of the primitive world and the traditional depiction of Eden. This traditional portrayal endowed the first human beings with great privileges, such as perfect knowledge, harmony between the life of the senses and morality, the gift of immortality. The evolutionist, on the contrary, can see in primitive man nothing more than a very undeveloped being, still tightly wedged into his animal prehistory. So the theologian must undertake a careful review of the traditional portrayal.

The Eden picture seems to have been strongly influenced by a principle that is more Hellenistic than biblical and one never sanctioned by the Church.[103] This principle calls for the ancestor to combine in himself all the perfections in which his descendants would participate. There is, therefore, no need to retain, in a revised portrayal, such a privilege as the perfect knowledge of Adam, which rests entirely upon this principle.

The privileges attributed to the First Parent simply because he was supposed to be the first, the active principle of all that would come to fruition throughout the whole course of human history, obviously belong to a portrayal of the world and of history which is not imposed by revelation and which anyone is free not to admit.[104]

The Bible and the Church have, on the other hand, spoken out on other privileges such as immunity to concupiscence and death. But even here the pronouncement has been an indirect one, consisting in the teaching that concupiscence and death are the consequences of sin. So we must not seek for details on the inner nature of the privileges, the preternatural gifts. More particularly, it can be asked whether the first man did not receive these more in the nature of a disposition and an assignment than as a full-fledged gift bestowed upon him. "Nothing would seem to compel us to hold that he had attained full-blown perfection forthwith, as a fully actualized state. Was it not rather a vast opportunity of progress that was opened up before him by the pristine vigor of his own nature, strengthened by such aids?"[105] The state of affairs might be presented thus: man could, by faithfulness to the covenant and to the union with God, have freed himself progressively from the laws of concupiscence and death linked to his earthly origin. The exact mode of these privileges and preternatural gifts is a question of human curiosity rather than of the faith. For the hard fact is that man was unfaithful from the beginning.

Above all, any excessively prodigious notion of these privileges must be avoided. Neither the Bible nor the Church teaches anything other than a preservation from concupiscence and death as these prevail in the world of our present experience. *This* concupiscence and *this* death are the consequences and the signs of sin. "The narrative limits itself to a global acceptation of death *as we know it:* the brusque and brutal termination of our life and our plans and dreams, with the accompanying gloom and anguish, and it asserts that this fact of experience has as its combined cause a punishment and our earthly origin."[106] It is speaking of that cruel death that snuffs out life in its first fine flower, the death that eats life away in a protracted decline, death in pain, loneliness and humiliation, a death like that suffered by Jesus. This kind of death *is* a punishment of sin, a judgment of God upon a "life of vanity."[107] But the peaceful death of a man full of years whose work is done and who survives in his posterity can scarcely be regarded as a sign of the enmity of God, except to the extent that it is indicative of a solidarity *in specie* with all those who suffer a cruel death. Such a death calls to mind rather the biblical image of a harvest ripe for the sickle and garnered home with joy.[108] The Bible and the Church teach that death as we know it, which alone really merits the name of death, is a punishment of sin and that this death did not reign over mankind before the fall. They do not appear to say anything one way or the other concerning a natural end of the man of Eden, a normal end of a terrestrial and bodily existence. Once again here it would be to no purpose to risk any speculations on such an end.[109] But it can be assumed that revelation does not oblige us to picture to ourselves the man of Eden as simply immunized outright against the law of decrepitude that holds for every living organism upon the earth.

The same train of thought can be applied to the preservation from concupiscence. This is usually presented as a perfect harmony between the lower instincts and moral endeavor. But the evolutionist, knowing the psychic life of man to be rooted in animality, can only imagine such a harmony as the fruit of a slow maturation, as the ultimate crowning consummation of the moral life, not as its beginning. Again theology may ask itself whether it is not laying itself open to a charge of oversimplification. According to the Pauline and Tridentine teaching,[110] the concupiscence experienced by fallen man is a consequence of sin. The man of Eden did not know this concupiscence. But we have already seen[111] that the core of concupiscence consists more in a division of the will itself than in a conflict between the inclinations of the senses and the moral tendencies, and that this inner division increases the virulence of the conflict. The preservation from concupiscence as it exists today does not therefore seem to imply that the man of Eden enjoyed a perfect harmony between the passions born of his animal nature and his will whereby he tended to communion with God and his fellow men. He might equally well have known the tension and conflict and struggle that gradually guided his inclinations to perfect moral integration and integrity.[112]

If then we have the right, as we seem to have, to take a much soberer view of the privileges of Eden, much of the shock and opposition aroused by the usual portrayal can be eliminated. The privileges of the first man must not be conceived as a complete and total break with his animal prehistory; they are rather a capability and a call to subject this animality to a specifically human destiny. They are rather an exemption from *our* concupiscence and *our* death, from the tyranny of both of these. They therefore contain the virtual capability of a harmonious integration of the instincts into morality, of an uninterrupted spiritualization of man's physical nature.

The privilege of the state of innocence which remains central is the supernatural vocation of building humanity up into the Body of Christ and the supernatural facility accorded by sanctifying grace and the infused virtues required for this undertaking. The first man had received the Holy Spirit, enabling him to love the Father above all and his neighbor as himself, and to accept his own development and flowering forth as a gift of God. The evolutionist cannot raise any serious objection against such a privilege.

If he admits the spiritual existent nature of man, he admits that man's appearance on the scene opens up an entirely new possible arena of action, that of freedom, morality, and infinite horizons, with the capacity for grace and personal encounter with God. This capacity may well have been covered with a carapace of very primitive psychological molds; but it was already the real capacity for a *Yes* or a *No* to the infinite. Without that there could be no real morality and therefore no human being as such.

In principle the awakening of the moral power and the first gift of grace imparted likewise a new and different function to the body and to instinct, both of which were now called to an integration of the moral life and love, to devotion to the service of righteousness and of the Spirit.[113] On the horizon loomed the opportunity of outgrowing the bondage of instinct and escape from the fragility of matter. The tyranny of death and concupiscence did not as yet exist. But this entire picture need not include or imply any sudden and total break with the physical nature and the psychic mechanisms inherited from animal ancestry.

APPENDIX IV

Monogenism

The most sensational perhaps, but certainly not the most serious, of all the points of friction between the doctrine of original sin and the evolutionist view of mankind lies in the problem of monogenism. The doctrine of original sin asserts that all men descend from a single ancestor, whereas the evolutionist tends to conceive of a multiplicity of ancestors, a whole portion of a population crossing the Rubicon of hominization. In what follows, we distinguish monogenism as over against monophyletism; in so doing, we are adhering to the terminology that has grown up in these intermediate regions between theology and the sciences. By monogenism and polygenism we understand respectively the origin of mankind from one or from several *ancestral couples;* by monophyletism and polyphyletism, the origin of man from one or several *phyla,* respectively. Thus monogenism presupposes monophyletism and polyphyletism would be an almost decisive argument against monogenism, although there would still subsist the possibility, in theory at least, that one pair of ancestors were born of the convergence of several phyla. But inversely monophyletism does not constitute a proof of monogenism. For a single species can have crossed the frontier of hominization in a great number of individuals, or prior to the crisis point the species may have split into several branches, each of which crossed the frontier separately. In these two events, we would have an instance of monophyletism without monogenism. For reasons we shall state later, the number of *pairs* of ancestors transcends the realm of natural science. From the strictly scientific point of view, writers do not make the distinction between "genism" and "phyletism" or they make the distinction in a sense different from that we have just outlined.[1]

In order to avoid any unnecessary exacerbation of the possibility of a conflict between theology and science, let us remind readers in both areas that the problem can be distinguished from the substance of the doctrine. Now, one more preliminary remark. The theological concept of the human family differs from that of natural sciences. In essence theology is speaking of *actual* humanity, the only humanity open to revelation and the only one spoken of by revelation; thus, theology is dealing with what biologists call Homo sapiens. Anthropology, on the other hand, speaks of a whole group of Hominidae, including, besides Homo sapiens, such specimens as Neanderthal man, Sinanthropus, Pithecanthropus, perhaps even Australopithecus. But it would have to be determined whether these fossil species could pass, theologically and philosophically speaking, for real man, or whether, on the contrary, they were still only "experiments in hominization, trials only."[2] They may not be direct ancestors of Homo sapiens at all, but rather "cousins," lateral branches which died out. Were they already rational and therefore immortal beings?[3] It can be asked whether hominization in the biological sense can be equated without reservation to hominization in the philosophical and theological sense.

But the most important point is to determine the nexus between monogenism and the doctrine of original sin, for the two cannot be put on an equal footing without reservations. This is the meaning of Pope Pius XII's declaration that Christians cannot admit various forms of polygenism, "in view of the fact that it is not clear how such a notion could accord with what the sources of revealed doctrine and the decisions of the magisterium of the Church propose on the subject of original sin."[4] The believer cannot hold a notion that would not accord with dogma; in the event of a conflict, he must even be certain, before giving his adherence to a certain definite notion, that it does not do any violence to the doctrine of the faith. But this is still not to say that monogenism is identical with the doctrine of original sin.

Nor do the sources of revelation give any indication of such an identity. The Bible does of course present things as if the whole of mankind derived from a single ancestral couple. The Garden of Eden narrative in particular "is built upon the strictest sort of monogenism."[5] There is no doubt whatsoever that the sacred writer intends to assert that all men are members of a single family; that all owe their origin to creation by God; that all are involved in the economy of salvation and of the ruin caused by an original sin of the man of the first days of humanity. This solidarity is expressed in the image of the single ancestor. But this still does not answer the question whether, over and above the structure of the narrative, monogenism pertains to the content of the doctrinal deposit of the narrative.[6] Considering the role of the Eden narrative in revelation and the transition of the name *Adam* from a generic meaning to a personal name, one can undoubtedly conclude with more probability that this involves less a question of doctrine than presentation. Among later texts, Wisdom 10:1 and Acts 17:26 refer specifically to this narrative; the text from Acts attempts to concretize the way in which all men, despite their national and racial differences, are included in a single economy of creation, fall, and redemption. The reference to the single first man seems in these texts to mean nothing more than it does in the creation and Eden narrative to which the text refers.

Can the same be said for Romans 5:12–21? This text also teaches the solidarity of all men in sin and in salvation, further stating that salvation is wrought by the single act of righteousness of the single Christ. It compares the one Christ and the one Adam by whose transgression all have become sinners. This text undoubtedly highlights the unitary character of Adam, image of the uniqueness of the Redeemer to come, in a way unparalleled elsewhere in the Bible. Thus the serious question can be put whether, in the light of the Christian economy of salvation and its decidedly unique character, Paul saw more deeply into what the Old Testament contained in an obscure fashion; whether Paul, therefore, teaches the unitary nature of the person of Adam as a revealed truth, or merely uses the literary figure of the single Adam as a parallel to the single Christ, without saying anything more about the one and only sin of the one and only first man than was said in the narrative of the fall. Personally I am inclined to the former conclusion. Paul seems to intend more than simply to use the figure of Adam familiar to the Bible and to Judaism, for before Paul there had never been this insistence on the unitary nature of Adam. Conceivably would not this primitive image of Christ, this prefiguration at the dawn of mankind's history, be historically accurate on the very point of the oneness that Paul sees in the prefiguration?[7] But better exegetes than we incline to the second conclusion.[8]

Should a more precise exegesis of Scripture be able to make the second conclusion admissible,[9] we should then have to posit that Scripture teaches that all men are sinners by the very fact of their membership in the human family, that is, by their birth, and that all men are one in the fall and in its guilt; that the cause of this guilt of the entire human family lies in the sin and defection perpetrated at the dawn of mankind and encompassing the whole of mankind's history; that Scripture is not saying anything one way or another on the nature of this sin as such. It is true that Scripture does ascribe this sin to the sole ancestor, but this concrete manner of presenting the oneness cannot with certainty be said to pertain to the doctrine itself; it may be nothing more than a literary form.[10]

Scripture is not, however, the only court of appeal for the Catholic. He must also ask himself what is said by Tradition and the magisterium. There is no doubt whatever that the ordinary preaching of all ages and the Council of Trent as well consider Adam as an individual person and the ancestor of all men. But the same question recurs: does this teaching simply assume the spontaneous *presentation* of the doctrine in Scripture or does it really *teach* the individuality of Adam? Hitherto little attention has been given to this theoretical question. Theologians usually appeal to the words of Trent: original sin is "one by its origin"[11] in all. But, as we have said above,[12] the Council probably intends to teach that original sin is not the same in all men by virtue of numerical unity but rather because it derives from one common source. The Council does not seem to take any definite stand on the question whether this origin is to be found in a single individual sin or in a multiplicity of sins that would have made primitive mankind into a sinful community, even though the Council itself sticks to the first of these portrayals.[13] Nor does *Humani generis* add any new light.[14] The encyclical does, indeed, sum up the doctrine of original sin according to the magisterium in the following words: "Original sin, which flows from a sin really committed by the one Adam, is transmitted to all by birth." But these words do not pertain to what the Pope here seeks to define; they simply repeat the current interpretation of Scripture and of Trent. They are normative as a summary of the thought of the ordinary magisterium; they are not intended to define more clearly what is contained in the statements of Paul and of Trent.

Theologically, then, it seems justified to conclude that monogenism merits a marked preference, at least in the portrayal of original sin as Scripture, the ordinary magisterium, and the Council of Trent propose it. But monogenism cannot be put, without reservation, on the same level as the dogma of original sin. The essence of the dogma, the guilt of all men, accrues to men by the very fact of their entry into mankind, and is the result of a primitive sin whereby mankind was unfaithful to the covenant at the outset; this opinion seems capable of defense apart from monogenism.[15] But, as we have said above, it seems probable to us that monogenism pertains to the *doctrine* of original sin. Nevertheless, it appeared useful to make the distinction between the main core of the dogma and its concrete form, so that any hesitation concerning monogenism will not immediately be interpreted as a doubt concerning original sin. This can render the discussion between faith and science more serene and consequently more fruitful.

The theologian, therefore, is fully justified in feeling some hesitation at putting monogenism and original sin on the same footing. Science, for its part, is far from admitting and accepting polygenism with no reservations.

Teilhard formulated a principle which has become the common heritage of evolutionism: "the automatic destruction of the peduncle of the zoological phyla."[16] Because of the enormous time spans of the past, paleontology discovers a new form of life only where the number of individuals is already quite large. The chances of fossilization and discovery are greatly, even drastically, limited. "*Paleontology* (like all manner of long-distance vision) *reveals to us only the maxima.* For an animal form to *begin* to appear, it must already be legion."[17] The critical evolutive phase, on the contrary, probably is passed through in a relatively short time and involves a relatively restricted number of individuals, even though this number may be absolutely very large.[18] Thus paleontology only discovers a new form of life at a point already far separated from the origin. Paleontologically speaking, therefore, the problem of a single first pair can never be posed directly.[19] The objections of paleontology against such a pair will always be indirect.

Natural science could furnish a proof against the monogenetic origin of mankind if it could establish either that mankind has come from different phyla or that, even though coming from a single phylum, it has taken the step toward hominization in different places or at different moments in time, or, finally, that the mechanism of the evolutive process requires that it be accomplished in more than one pair.[20] The first alternative, strictly a polyphyletic notion, was generally admitted prior to Darwin as an explanation of the divergences of the races and enjoyed a brief resurgence at the beginning of this century; it has now been abandoned by science. The UNESCO declaration on racial problems states: "Scientists have unanimously come to admit that mankind is a single whole; all men belong to the same species, Homo sapiens. Scientists have also reached a consensus of opinion to the effect that all men are probably offspring of the same common phylum."[21] On the second alternative, we do not find the same unanimity. Some scientists still hold it as probable that the original phylum from which mankind issued split into various branches before the hominization point, so that each of these branches reached this peak at a different point in time and space. Nevertheless, "it is generally admitted today that mankind appeared *but once*, in one single cradle."[22] Teilhard also held this opinion and thought he could point to Central Africa as in fact the cradle of mankind.[23] In some of his studies he envisions the hypothesis of two cradles of hominization, an African and an Asiatic-Melanesian one; but he maintains even in these writings that it was only in Africa that the step to Homo sapiens was accomplished.[24]

With this clear preference on the part of paleontology for the strictly monophyletic origin of man, the first two arguments against monogenism are hardly to be feared.

The third argument presents more difficulty. In 1930, Teilhard wrote that "for reasons of probability . . . Science, left to itself, would never dream (to put it very very mildly) of attributing so narrow a base to the enormous edifice of the human race as two individuals."[25] This describes well the attitude of the natural scientists. They think quantitatively and seek certitude in the laws of statistics, which by their very nature presuppose a large number. But later in the passage from which we have just quoted Teilhard observes that, precisely in the case of man, science ought to leave more room "for the powers of mind, freedom, and thus 'improbability.' "[26] Since 1930, the situation has changed: the difficulty has been further specified and accentuated. Most evolutionists consider that a macro-evolutive step is realized via an accumulation of micro-evolutive mutations that are aggregated and stabilized by natural selection. This theory requires that not only a few individuals but rather an entire population is developing progressively along a certain given line.[27] Should this Neo-Darwinian hypothesis of evolution prove to be accurate, then the monogenetic origin of mankind could only be explained as an exception in the kingdom of nature. But the scientists are expressing doubts on this Neo-Darwinism.[28] Some scientists are of the opinion that the origin of a new form should rather be explained by a macro-mutation, suddenly transforming the entire equilibrium of a living being. According to this theory, a new species would be able to come into being in a few individuals or even, indeed, in a single one. This would then offer the possibility of a strictly monogenetic origin of mankind.[29] These two conceptions are little more than theories as yet. Against the latter, one could object that such macro-mutations have not yet been observed; against the former, the objection could be raised that it has not been demonstrated that micro-evolutive modifications could really engender a new form of life. As we have said, the Neo-Darwinian notion is presently the predominant one; in this sense it can be said that "at the present state of our knowledge . . . science . . . thinks of the appearance of Mankind in terms of population, and anticipates a certain minimum thickness and density for its root."[30] This does not seem to favor the monogenist view. Yet in view of the uncertainty surrounding the explanation of the evolutionary process, "biology can as yet make no certain and definitive choice as between monogenism and polygenism."[31] All things considered, there is thus no reason to fear for the moment any real and serious conflict between the faith and the incontestable findings of science on the subject of monogenism.

PART III

*The New Spirituality—God
in the Cosmos*

THE NEED FOR RENEWAL
IN SPIRITUALITY

---

*Everywhere on earth, at this moment . . . are floating the
love of God and faith in the world, in a state of extreme
mutual sensitization. These are the two essential components of the Ultra-Human . . . generally not strong
enough*, at least not both at once, *to combine* in one and
the same subject. *In my own case, by pure chance (temperament, training, environment . . .) the proportions
of the two favored the fusion that was effected spontaneously, though it is as yet too weak for any spontaneous propagation. But it is sufficient to establish the fact
that the reaction is possible and that at some future date
the chain will form.*[1]

CHAPTER 8

Few writers and thinkers involved in the exchange of ideas provoked by Teilhard's work have accorded much attention to his
spirituality.[2] Scientific or philosophical and theological theories lend
themselves more readily to discussion than does a doctrine of spirituality; moreover, the interpreter and critic here finds himself in
the inner realm of personality with its unique and ineffable mystery
which compels the respect and restraint it engenders. Yet it would
be unthinkable to neglect this aspect of Teilhard's achievement,
for his spirituality is at once the crown of his thought and one of
the most powerful motivations of his scientific and philosophical

199

endeavor. In Teilhard's own eyes, the most important fruit of his own thinking and reflection was a new stress on certain aspects of the Christian life and the consequent renewal in the area of spirituality. Without doubt this was the principal message Teilhard believed he must mediate to his fellow men and fellow Catholics.

It is certainly no mere accident that Teilhard's first major work was entitled *Le Milieu divin* and called by Teilhard himself "a little treatise on the interior life." He compiled it during an interruption of several months in his scientific undertakings in China during the winter of 1926–1927. He kept recurring to this work to the last months of his life, specifying that, even in its somewhat immature form, it reflected exactly the basic intuition which inspired the whole of his life. We shall therefore use this little work as our chief source in this section, for it is the most extensive of his spiritual writings and the only one generally accessible.

Like all genuine spiritual writings, this work was lived before it was written down. Teilhard sometimes calls it a "narrative"; he describes his aim as "a simple *description* of a *psychological* evolution observed *over a specified interval*."[3] We thus have in this little work, in fairly systematized form, an autobiography, or rather a deposition, relating a personal experience and taking it as a point of departure. This book witnesses to a personal anguish and to vital enthusiasms that have lighted up a life. It bears witness to what God and Christ mean to man. It analyzes the components of this experience, the essential factors playing a part in its evolution. But it remains basically a witness, to such an extent, indeed, that some chapters gradually metamorphose into personal outpourings and prayer.

The reader must always bear this in mind. Such a book cannot be studied or judged with cold objectivity. Its truth consists in the authenticity of a Christian life. And Teilhard's Christian living towers far above the average in authenticity. His witness must be heard out with respect, meditated upon, even prayed over, and carefully, indeed painstakingly, assimilated. Any summary would involve an inevitable betrayal. While it might succeed in sketching the skeletal framework, it would mediate only the dead bones; only Teilhard's own words can communicate the warmth of conviction and inspiration permeating the whole. It is the message of a believer, proceeding from a faith living and lived, addressed to hearers and readers at once, in the hope that this witness may also aid others to see, to open their eyes to the discovery of forgotten or clouded aspects of the ancient faith, to live these newly discovered aspects and put them into practice with renewed joyous fervor.

Teilhard is aware that he is proclaiming a new spirituality. New, but not in that it denies the ancient and traditional heritage (for there is no difficulty in finding in the fundamental thoughts of this work several of the great themes of St. Ignatius' *Spiritual Exercises*, and attention has also been drawn to the kinship extant between Teilhard's spiritual teaching and major biblical and patristic motifs)[4] but rather in the sense that the perennial truth (or better still the truth that is eternal and therefore ever new) is seen in a new light; that the centers of gravity of that truth are shifted and consequently there is provided the possibility of a new equilibrium and a new harmony. This is what is at stake: finding God and Christ in all things in the new world being unveiled to man's eyes by modern science; and serving the Creator and the Redeemer in the new labor upon the world typical of our technocratic age.

Teilhard's spirituality was born of the anguish of his own interior life. As a Christian and Jesuit he pursued the voluntary and consciously deliberate ideal of cleaving to God with his whole mind, his whole complex of powers and faculties and an undivided love. At the same time, his temperament and his scientific bent are irresistibly drawing him to the earth. As a child, he had shown a deep and surprising veneration for all solid and imperishable things, such as a piece of metal or stones and rocks; later he was himself to see in this a kind of "religion," the search for an absolute reality. Here must be located the origins of his passion for geology. But he gradually became aware that the most solid element is to be found in the spirit, not in elemental matter; this was for Teilhard a total inversion of perspective, almost a "conversion."[5] Yet he always remained extremely sensitive to the kind of absolute enclosed within the material cosmos with its enormous vistas of space and time and its supratemporal laws. There also fell to Teilhard's lot a scientific assignment which demanded unreserved attention and dedication. He took part in one of the most thrilling explorations mankind has ever managed to undertake into the depths of pre-history. He came to feel in his own flesh and marrow the fascination of science as a result of his close cooperation with scientists of all persuasions, working together with him as friends at the most advanced outposts of science. The earth as a material entity, like-wise, demands of man a kind of dedication, almost a sort of love.

Teilhard felt himself torn and tossed about between these two simultaneous appeals to his loyalty and dedication, between these two ideals at opposite poles. As a young religious, he asks himself if he ought not to abandon the science of rocks in order to devote himself entirely to things supernatural. But his spiritual director reassures him by telling him that the Crucified Lord expects of him not only sanctity but also the natural development of his whole being.[6] A letter Teilhard wrote in 1916 still gives evidence of some disquiet. So the problem had been preoccupying him for about fifteen years at least; and for a man who had such a need of clarity and limpidity in his own life,[7] the clash must have been agonizing; only after such a prolonged battle did Teilhard succeed in reaching the conviction that there did exist the possibility of attaining the reconciliation of "the supreme and absolute love of God with the lower (but still legitimate and necessary) love of life embraced under its natural forms."[8]

Teilhard's great spiritual adventure lies in the effort he made to verify this conviction in his own life, to reconcile within himself the two great loves, the discovery that these two loves can mutually nourish and strengthen each other. His own personal vocation he considered to be the bearing of witness to this reconciliation.

Although Teilhard was aware that his own situation was exceptional, combining, as it did, a religious life of mature con-viction with an active participation in the most "earthy" of the sciences of the earth, he also realized that the same problem is faced substantially by every Christian dedicated to a worldly vocation. How can one who really believes in heaven and in the Gospel of the cross attach any importance to earthly business and occupa-tions? If true life lies in the beyond which man can enter only via the gate of death, then our earthly existence seems devoid of real importance or value. Christianity preaches detachment, renunciation, and sacrifice; by the very fact of his religious state, Teilhard continually gave conscious and deliberate assent to this Gospel. How could a genuine dedication to the things of this earth be reconciled therewith? Faced with this dilemma, the Christian can adopt several attitudes. Some repress their taste for the sensible and the earthly, do themselves violence in order to seek only after what is in heaven. Others revolt against the Gospel message and devote themselves to a life that appears more genuine and more human to them. The majority will abandon any effort at real understanding and seek in an uneasy compromise an unstable equilibrium between heaven and earth. A sorry state, this! Not wholly God's, not wholly devoted to the earth, such compromisers know themselves to be less than perfectly equilibrated, seem somewhat hypocritical to others, lead a double and divided life.[9] Teilhard assures us he has himself met many men suffering from this inner cleavage. Since this is the case, a solution must be found. No man can be truly mature, or *a fortiori* truly Christian, until he has managed to integrate into his own life the great values: God and the earth. Only an integral and mature Christianity can afford inner harmony, joy and freedom.

Only such a Christianity can save and conquer. "Holiness" and "wholeness" are synonymous;[10] the "Lord delivers us from division."

Christianity has always held the key to this dilemma, always found the way to make the synthesis into a living reality. This key is the first article of our faith: God the Father is creator of heaven and earth. So the earth is fundamentally good. "God saw that it was good." The earth is the gift and the assignment entrusted by God to man. The earth's attraction is a gift of the Father. Man's labor upon the earth is the assignment given by the Father. This principle of faith becomes a living reality in gratitude shown for the gift of God and in the "good intention" of our own labor.

"All that God has created is good and nothing ought to be rejected of what has been accepted with gratitude; everything is sanctified by the word of God and by prayer."[11] The earth itself will help us to encounter God if we accept gratefully the good things of the earth and the joys of life as gifts of God. God is found not only in detachment from the earth but also in the things of the earth. This awareness has remained vital and alive in Christianity, despite all the insistence upon renunciation of the world. Augustine, for instance, showed the way to a reconciliation, both in practice *and* in theory, of the two poles of earthly joy and renunciation: whoever is enjoying the gifts of God with gratitude is growing in the love of the giver and growing in the desire to abandon the gifts to find the giver himself.[12] The supernatural joy found by a Francis of Assisi, a Gertrude, or a Thérèse in the simplest things of the earth constitutes an imperishable treasury of Christianity. Finally, the *Spiritual Exercises* of St. Ignatius, in which Teilhard was trained, culminate in a powerful final harmony of grateful love for the gifts of the earth.

It remains a matter of considerable obscurity why Teilhard did not choose this classical way of gratitude. It may have been a question simply of natural disposition. It may also have been that Teilhard felt that many men in these days find this way difficult. Gratitude was relatively easy in the old picture of the world and the corresponding dispositions of man. This old view presented things as issuing directly from the hand of God. Their origin was conceived as being very close at hand. Every object and every event constituted a divine miracle. In our days, the origin of all that exists and all that happens has been pushed back to an immeasurable distance, to an initial point of evolution, difficult to picture at all. What has happened since is no longer a miracle for anyone. We penetrate the laws governing the processes and we bring them into subjection to us. Gratitude is no longer the food of a pusillanimous faith; it demands a robust and living faith.

Gratitude, furthermore, demands a certain contemplative peace of mind. Contemplation was a normal attitude so long as the world was regarded as a stable quantity. But modern man no longer adopts a contemplative attitude to the things that surround him nor to his own world. Science and technology have taught and are teaching him to master and dominate this world by his own power, to blueprint it and build it for himself: "The end which it [modern science] proposes to itself is not pure contemplation or simple intellectual representation; rather it is the mastery and domination of matter and of its forces for purposes of building the future."[13]

Preceding chapters have sufficiently demonstrated that Teilhard clearly discerned this revolution in the attitude of science and that he held it to be a gain, because it contained an element of human maturity. The man of today, and undoubtedly still more the man of tomorrow, sees his world not as an object of quiet contemplation but rather as a field of arduous labor. Christianity cannot discourage this imposing sense of responsibility, this proud ambition that man has to build himself up by his own powers. It must impart to this ideal a new meaning, a new attraction, a new zealous verve.[14] To the hardworking builder of today and tomorrow Christianity must show the way to encounter God in *his* world, man's world, being built and dominated by man himself. Teilhard is searching for a Christian experience applicable to this new type of Homo faber who is being born in our age. He is searching for the way to the "divinization of *human activity*."[15]

Christian spirituality has long been in possession of a source capable of Christianizing and sanctifying the most secular and insignificant of activities. It speaks of the "good intention": the *intentio*, the end or the desire to will to serve God alone and seek his will in all our actions, even the most ordinary and the most commonplace, to seek God and God's will rather than the fulfillment or satisfaction of our own desires and ambitions. Teilhard is, likewise, persuaded that this doctrine contains a large portion of truth. This intention is in fact the key to the encounter with God in daily life, because it directs everything to God's good pleasure.[16]

But Teilhard cannot be entirely satisfied with this approach. In fact, the doctrine of the "good intention" is usually presented, or at least understood by those to whom it is presented, as saying that *what* one does has no importance and that the only thing that counts is the *fashion* in which one does it. The only thing that counts is felt to be the inner disposition which animates the action; the action itself and its result are without importance and the Christian can be indifferent to them. Man's heart and mind rebel against such a divorce of motive and content in his actions. Teilhard explodes against such a presentation: I cannot believe that it is only my *operatio* (work*ing*) which is of value in the eyes of God and not at all my *opus* (work) which is dear to me as the offspring of my endeavor: "The divinization of our endeavor by the value of the intention . . . infuses a precious soul into all our actions; but *it does not confer the hope of resurrection* upon their bodies. Yet, that hope is what we need if our joy is to be complete."[17]

He is here touching on the weak point in this spirituality. Such a radical separation cannot be introduced between the spiritual end and the exterior realization of a human action. The fully human value of an act is not exclusively determined by the intention; it is also codetermined by the object and by the result.[18] Otherwise we fall into a false spiritualism, holding that only the "soul" and not the "body" of our acts is of value. Or to put it another way, if we posit as a general rule that we are accomplishing the good pleasure of God equally well by an insignificant action and by an important action, by a failure as by a success, we are making the divine good pleasure into a purely formalistic principle without any real content of its own. This is essentially a Nominalist notion of God, which in reality cannot be brought into accord with Catholic thinking.

The negative element in this doctrine of the "good intention," namely, that the result of our labor has no importance, may be a solution in extreme cases, a consolation for someone not able to grasp the meaning of his task, not attaining success in it but rather seeing an undertaking founder that was well intentioned and well done. Often the individual does not see the results of his own labor and endeavor: "One sows, another reaps."[19] Sometimes a man sees himself constrained to pursue a task that seems hopeless and senseless, to continue fighting for a lost cause. Such a man may then seek strength and comfort in the belief that God chooses perhaps what is weak and foolish and that he can be better served by a failure than by a success. But this naked faith is a last bulwark, not an initial position for the Christian in normal circumstances. So the negative element of the "good intention" may serve and be justified in extreme situations when the Christian finds himself trapped in such. And Teilhard then repeats the saying of Léon Bloy: "Everything that happens is a cause for worship."[20] But this cannot be raised to the rank of a prime and general principle of action. St. Ignatius teaches that "when the intellect becomes refractory, the will cannot long continue to obey with joy." One must grasp the meaning of an assignment, in the general course of affairs, in order to accomplish it with devotion and real dedication.

This becomes all the more true now that mankind has progressed to the point of commencing to build his own world in a conscious and organized fashion. As long as the world constituted a given quantity to be accepted as such, man could content himself with accomplishing the task that happened to fall to his lot in the world. But the new world *in fieri* must be built by man himself. It is man who must determine the direction history will henceforth take. It is man who must draft a plan of the future. He cannot do so unless he takes cognizance of the form given to the world by his own acts. His work and its result may well be of secondary importance for the realization of the Kingdom of God. But it does have some importance all the same!

In the next two Chapters, we shall try to sketch Teilhard's effort to make possible the divinization of our labor when we consider and accomplish this labor, even though it be an entirely worldly and secular undertaking, as a collaboration with God who is constructing the Body of his Son throughout the course of history. Collaboration with God, then, and edification of the Body of Christ. These are two forms, intimately interconnected, which allow the Christian to encounter God even in his worldly endeavor. The most ordinary and the most earthly of labors can be consecrated to God and become the sign of his nearness. "Whether you eat or drink, do all to the glory of God."[21]

COOPERATING WITH THE GOD
WHO IS OPERATING

At the heart of our Universe, each soul exists for God, in Our Lord. All reality, even material reality, around each one of us, exists our souls.

Hence, all sensible reality, around each one of us, exists, through our souls, for God in Our Lord.

So that "every endeavor cooperates to fulfill the World in Christo Jesu."[1]

CHAPTER 9

This passage enunciates the thought constituting the hinge of the whole of Teilhard's vision and spirituality, despite its insistence on the "soul," a reflection of the "rather egocentric and introverted period," as Teilhard himself later admitted in *Le Milieu divin*. All terrestrial realities exist for the sake of man who, in turn, exists for the sake of God. This commonplace truth again evinces the influence of the prologue of the "Principle and Foundation" in the *Spiritual Exercises* of St. Ignatius: "Man is created to praise, honor, and serve God our Lord and thus to save his soul. All other things on earth have been created for man and to aid him to pursue this end for which he was created."[2] Let us first consider the second part of this reasoning.

All things exist for man. This is proclaimed by the first page of the Bible.[3] The world, the sea and the earth, the plants and the animals, the lights in the firmament—all form the habitation con-structed and ordered for man who is to inhabit the world as God's steward.[4] Paul says: "All things are yours."[5] Never has the Church ceased to repeat this truth in her liturgy and through the mouths of her doctors and teachers. But this time-honored truth must be understood in a new and deeper way if it is to clarify the new notion of the world. The old saying must be given a new power and a new refulgence. In the old static picture of the world, the relations of all things to man were vague and obscure. God's plan in creation remained hidden, scarcely reflected at all in the visible shape of the world; but today the ancient doctrine is acquiring a visible and tangible form, and we can imagine the zest and zeal it carries with it.

The world has evolved, and the summit and crown of this development is man. The obscure and tremendous power that has pushed the primordial fabric of the universe toward life, the ir-resistible impulsion that has raised life to ever new and higher forms, an upward thrust over a period that must be estimated at billions of years, one that has triumphed by its slow and primitive power over all obstacles—such has been the orientation of all things toward man! A deep-seated immanent will, as powerful as our cosmos itself and representing nothing else than the very becoming of this cosmos, has engendered man. With all its existent nature, the cosmos "wills" man to exist and to become more and more man. Man is deeply rooted in the earth because the current that bears his existence springs from the very source of the earth. The cosmic power of the earth is prolonging its own course in man. Man's will to live, his inclination to fulfill, penetrate and dominate the world, his thirst for progress and his aspiration to achieve the full flowering of his human nature in this world—all of this is nothing else than the old impulsion pushing the world for millions of years toward ever-higher forms of being, life, and consciousness. By all the pores of our being, there is entering into us a thrust of existence and of life that is incomparably greater than ourselves.

The man who understands this, who takes cognizance of what is animating him beneath the superficial manifestations of his daily occupations and aspirations, will feel a boundless sense of forlorn confusion. Like abysses threatening to engulf him, immeasurable perspectives open up before him: immensities of space, innumerable multitudes, enormous time spans. Teilhard has a description of this experience in the first person; and if this is only a stylistic technique, nonetheless he, too, does hear from the depth of the somber abyss the voice of the Gospel: "It is I; be not afraid!"[6]

The believer can see God, hidden and enveloped in the world. His eyes can be opened and he can perceive in the primitive motion of being and life the creative power and will of God. Evolution itself, this great undertaking, actualized by a force as lumbering and blind as the world itself, can become the sign of the Creator. Man can hear the echo of the original *fiat* in the low note that resounds in the universe and vibrates in his own being. From this moment, the world ceases to be a cause of anguish; it unveils in its deepest center the face of the Father.

The world itself is consecrated as a result. The deep roots linking man to the world, the "sacred tang of being,"[7] become holy. The will to be himself, to develop himself, and to actualize himself as man to the extreme limits of his powers, the great vital thrust of man and humanity—all this is nothing but the echo of the creative word of God. Believing in the "active presence" of God thus signifies, if our faith is not to remain a mere matter of verbal assent, doing justice to the appeal resounding from the depths of our own being. Man *ought to* want to live and labor, to mount up to a more total actualization of his human being. This is a sacred duty, because it is the will of God, incarnate and embodied in the very nature of the world and of mankind.

First, to your deep inspiration which commands me to be, I shall respond by taking care never to stifle, nor distort, nor waste my power to love and to do. Next, to your all enveloping Providence which shows me at each moment, by the day's events, the next step to be taken and the next rung to climb, I shall respond by my care never to miss an opportunity of rising "toward the spirit."[8]

It is a grave fault on man's part to lack the will to live, to allow discouragement to get power over him, to buckle before the sweeping tasks imposed upon him by the world. For in so doing, he is actually refusing to obey the word of God resounding from the depths of the world and of his own being.

Here we must pause for a moment to effect a critical review of the foregoing. Teilhard's principle is none other than faith in creation taken in its fullest sense: creation that is not simply at the origin of things but continues to sustain their existence, even and indeed particularly, in its highest actualization which consists in the action and creative labor of man. God's omnipresence permeates the whole world, right down to and including the forces whereby the world moves itself. Although classical Catholic theology does indeed tend to consider only the faculty of beings for action to be the object of God's creative operation, Teilhard's position on this point, including within that object the action itself as well, can certainly be considered to be a classical Catholic doctrine. There can be no objection to this stand in principle.

But Teilhard's conclusion does create a certain uneasiness. A sanctity of "lust for life," the duty of being faithful thereto? This seems in flagrant contradiction to the Gospel message of mortification and renunciation. Teilhard seems to be forgetting the warning of the *Imitation of Christ* against the contradictory motions of nature and grace. Teilhard's position seems likely to end fearfully in a pagan vitalism canonizing all the passions springing from the dark crannies of our nature, the thirst for pleasure and enjoyment, self-love and ambition. Did Teilhard really intend man to let himself be so guided? To ask the question is to answer it.

When Teilhard speaks of the holy impulse of life, he means something more profound and genuinely human than the vital power of a Nietzsche or the motions of nature against which Thomas à Kempis declared war. He means the vital motion inherent to man's deepest and most unique essence, as it issues into existence from the hand of him who "has created man for immortality and as an image of his essence."[9] And we shall soon see that this can include an acceptance of the cross. Teilhard means the nature which, according to Catholic doctrine, cannot be entirely vitiated by sin and which is not destroyed but rather perfected by grace. There is in man, springing from the very source of his existence, a thirst for happiness, a desire for life, for an imperishable life, an aspiration to fulfillment, to the total flowering of his infinite capacities, a will to subjugate the earth and to enlarge himself. God has put these longings into man's nature; they are the first law of his being. Man's primary duty is to say *Yes* to this law with all the strength of his own will.

Catholic moral theology and spirituality as a general rule give little attention to this duty. It may be that they did not need to do so in an age when joy and the courage to live were still fresh and spontaneous, as in the age when these disciplines were in the process of elaboration. So in the disciplines in question men could content themselves with warning against the deformations and deviations of this primordial desire and longing. But the greatest among the moralists, an Augustine or a Thomas Aquinas, recognized the existence of this duty and saw in it the basis of all other obligations: "There is no doubt that we all want to be happy."[10] But in our age it seems really necessary to recall this sacred duty. Western mankind is tired and has lost to a dangerous extent the joy and the spontaneous zest for life. The spark still glows, to be sure, but it is hidden beneath the thick ash of disillusionment, failures and anxieties. The moment has come for man, for the Christian, to fan the smoldering flame. There must be a renewed diligent cultivation of the courage and joy of living, the will to make of life something great, something worthy of man and of God. Man will in all probability not recover the joyous optimism of his childhood. He must regain his optimism in mortal combat with the rising tide of anguish. He must rebuild his faith and trust in earthly tasks beginning with faith and trust in God. Outwardly the will of the Christian to live may well resemble that of the pagan; but inwardly it is differently motivated. The Christian attaches himself to the world because he has first attached himself to God, because he recognizes and embraces the gift and the assignment of God within that world.[11]

Thus the contradiction between Thomas à Kempis and Teilhard is but apparent, though both manifest a real difference in emphasis. When Thomas warns against the motions of nature, he means the human inclination to seek happiness in enjoyment, comfort, wealth, power, fame and reputation. Man always seems inclined to deflect and scatter the great current of longing for happiness into the manifold little channels of superficial lusts and thus to mire himself in a wilderness of unsatisfied desires and disappointments. Thomas à Kempis is warning against this tendency to become bewildered in trifles. He is not speaking of the great floodtide of life.[12] And Teilhard is! His ultimate goal is none other than that of Thomas and all the doctors of the spiritual life; he too wants to preclude man's dissipating himself, stranding his great capacity to love and to build up great things. But the point of attack differs as between Teilhard and Thomas. Thomas warns of the dangers; Teilhard shows the precious and impressive gift that has been confided to us as a mission. The best safeguard against the danger is the awareness of the deep-seated bias of our being, of the "end for which man has been created," the strength and perseverance in this bias. A great spiritual enthusiasm will certainly extinguish the trifling lures. Things will retain their attraction, for if they did not possess a real value they could not allure man so much in the first place. But for him who has become aware of his real and true destiny, they will remain a shadow and prefiguration of the great fulfillment.

One of the most typical traits of this doctrine of spirituality is the effort to awaken in modern man the awareness of this deep bias of his being and the will to be faithful to it. Hence the sketch and blueprint for a future domination of the world, true fulfillment of all the dreams of power; hence the sketch and blueprint of a future likemindedness of mankind, authentic satisfaction of every aspiration to community; hence the sketch and blueprint for the one great love, cleaving to God and loving in God all men and all creatures, ultimate cure of all human division. Teilhard wants to help modern man to understand his own unease. Man must be brought to see from what deep springs within the world and within his own being derives his desire for progress, for peace, for betterment, and toward what horizons this desire is impelling him. He will then be less in danger of dissipating the gift of God in petty satisfactions or of smothering it in disappointment and discouragement.

It would thus be a misunderstanding to think that this sort of spirituality has no room for asceticism, for victory over self and acceptance of the cross. On the contrary, all this is included in any real obedience to the great thrust of life within us. For it is the law of life to mount ever higher toward a greater interiorization and a higher unity, culminating finally in the losing of self in God. So man must accept the struggle against the dissipation of his desires and the motions of nature of which Thomas à Kempis was speaking; and this demands an ascesis. We must build up our personality by bringing "more and more order, more and more unity into our ideas, our feelings, our conduct."[13] Man must likewise struggle continuously against his conservative instinct. History demands of him that he be constantly breaking with the familiar and safe habitation of ancient forms of organization and culture, that he leave behind him what he has already attained and realized, dear and precious to him as these things may be. "To pause, so as to enjoy or possess results, would be a betrayal of action."[14] Man and mankind are being constantly obliged to seek new forms of truth and beauty, of organization and technology. Anyone who harkens to this demand for progress on the part of life will also come to know the sorrows and sufferings which accompany any creative labor.

In proportion as man penetrates to the heart of his being by a more perfect domination of the world and by a better building up of his own personality, he will also discover to what an extent his existence is tied to that of his fellows. We are never alone in our life; there is always the other, the millions of others. "We cannot break through to the very limit of ourselves without going out of ourselves by uniting ourselves to others."[15] So we must overcome ourselves, overcome the egotism whereby we isolate ourselves from others and lock ourselves into ourselves. There is need for a loyal cooperation with the others, a sensitivity to their needs, a dedicated service of causes higher than our petty personal private interest. The upward thrust of life demands that man open himself to the other and to the others in love.

And finally there is presented to man the ultimate demand of life: union with God. In God we shall find ourselves again, but only after having lost all that is ours and our very selves. The world we have built up for ourselves, those whom we have loved, our possession and ownership of our very selves—all this will be taken from us by death and by what precedes it. Fidelity to the law of life includes an acceptance by us of death, "the critical point of our ex-centration, of our reversion to God."[16] Teilhard summed this up briefly in a lecture given in Peking during the war years:

> Three successive movements, all mutually linked, can be distinguished . . . in the process of our interior unification, that is of our personalization. To be fully himself and alive, Man must: 1. center himself upon himself; 2. decenter himself upon "the others"; 3. supercenter himself upon a greater than himself. . . . No longer then is it a case of simply developing himself by himself, nor even of giving himself to another who is his equal; there is more, there is the need to submit and to refer his life to another greater than himself. In other words, first to be, then to love, and finally to worship.[17]

In this Teilhardian design there is thus really room for mortification and sacrifice. But its typical feature is the deliberate tendency to a harmonization of "development and renunciation, attachment and detachment."[18] The equilibrium point may be located to one side or the other depending on the vocation, the grace, and the development which fall to each individual. But both elements are mandatory.[19] Such is the second and very important feature of this spirituality: it proclaims the duty accruing to the Christian to be attached to the earth and to serve it. This obligation equally derives from obedience to the will of God. "It is in truth God who raises up the great benefactors and the great physicians in the course of time."[20]

The labor of physicians, educators, technologists, and economists can be a holy service, because it is serving progress; thus the creative will of God is guiding mankind forward. It is a sacred duty to fight against sickness and death, misery and ignorance, against everything unworthy of man. Certainly the Christian must also be ready, as we have said, to resign himself to the inevitable and to accept the cross, but resignation and acceptance should come only after a fight to the finish against the forces of destruction.

A positive attitude toward earthly values and a regard for them are thus proposed to us explicitly as a Christian duty; renunciation and the cross are preached against this background. This is not something radically new. The Church has never extolled the sacrifice of earthly goods by implying that they are valueless, worthless or evil. Virginity and celibacy are not recommended in a way that implies any condemnation of marriage, nor is monastic obedience a derivative of contempt for the free personality. What is being offered to God as sacrifice represents the finest of the flock, the purest of human values: "Honor Yahweh . . . with the first fruits of all thy income."[21] It is certainly inaccurate to present this section of Teilhard's writings, as some of his admirers do, as a protest against a latent Manicheanism considered to be a habitual infection in the body of the Church.[22] The great spiritual writers of past centuries considered this fundamentally positive attitude toward earthly values to be a self-evident truth. When Augustine had overcome Manicheanism in his day, the conviction appeared assured for all time that the goods of the earth were gifts of the Creator of all good, and that the Christian was offering to God his own gifts. But this basic attitude has undergone a profound reversal in recent centuries. The earth has become secularized and its goodness has been called in question. Existence upon an earth without hope deteriorated into a *Weltschmerz* or into a nausea. Repeating the words of the saints in such an atmosphere just as they were written makes them into an incomprehensible travesty. The noblest expressions of a proud and joyous Christianity take on overtones of a disenchanted pessimism. In our age, the Christian dogma of the intrinsic goodness of things must be recovered in faith and restored in practice. The message of suffering and the cross can no longer be proclaimed except in this harmonious equilibrium with the message of life. Teilhard understood the urgency of this shift of emphasis. One of his great merits seems to be the endeavor to maintain at once both poles of the integral Christian attitude, to provide a theoretical justification of the paradox of these two poles: the renunciation of the world and of self, combined with the joyous *Amen*, full of hope, spoken to the earth and to the whole of God's creation.

Whoever believes in creation must encounter God in earthly tasks and assignments. In the eternal dream of progress and the flowering and fulfillment which impels mankind in his science, technology, and economic activity, the faith perceives the echo of the creative *fiat:* "In action I cleave to the creative power of God, I coincide with it; I become not only its instrument but its living prolongation."[23]

EDIFICATION OF THE BODY
OF CHRIST

There's a prayer I'm fond of saying now, because it sums
up what I mean: "Jesu, sis mihi mundus verus." May all
that is elect in the world, Jesus, be to me a channel for
your influence, and be increasingly transformed through
my efforts into you."[1]

CHAPTER 10

The preceding Chapter was limited to one aspect of the Christian meditation upon action: the *Amen* and the collaboration with the great current of life passing through us, as with the creative will of God. Another aspect is more important and dearer to Teilhard. It is dearer because it is more immediately related to the heart of Christianity, the love of the person of Christ, at once divine and human. It is more important because it forces us to take cognizance not only of the principle that motivates our action but also of the direction in which it should be motivated, the end toward which it is directed and which it is contributing to actualize. Our action, all our action, is contributing to the edification of the Body of Christ. This perspective furnishes us with a norm against which to measure the goodness or malice of human action. It mediates to us the zest to accomplish our assignments with devotion and joy. Finally, it provides a Christian answer, i.e., the only valid

218

answer, to our ineradicable desire to labor at an imperishable, divine undertaking.

The Christian must understand the great importance of this last element. Teilhard believes he can point in the world to a new religion, a religion without God. In Communism, in National Socialism (he was writing in 1934), in the devotion to science and to progress as that devotion is showing itself, there is something closely allied to religion, including faith in an ideal, strong enough to give man's life a meaning and a bias, to demand total consecration even unto the sacrifice of life itself. The religion of progress and of human perfection has been exalted to the point where it requires unreserved devotion:

> The *humanitarian Pantheisms* around us represent a very young form of religion, a religion with little or no codification (aside from Marxism), a religion without any apparent God and without any revelation, but a Religion, for all that, in the true sense, if this word Religion designates the contagious faith in an Ideal for which a man may give his life. . . . A rapidly growing number of our contemporaries already agrees to admit that the supreme interest of existence consists in vowing oneself body and soul to universal Progress, as expressed in the tangible developments of Mankind. . . . What does this mean, if not that we are seeing a new faith, which has been positively coming into existence and being constituted around us for a century now, under various forms (communist or national socialist, scientific or political, individual or collective); this new faith is the Religion of Evoluton.[2]

Far from being a mere accident, this tendency to project and plan an absolute ideal (divine in its absoluteness) is a manifestation of an essential trait of human action. Man would not lift a finger, were he not sure, however unconsciously, that he is collaborating in an undertaking of permanent worth and meaning.[3] Or, to put it in the terminology of classical ethics, man tends, in every truly human (i.e., moral) action, to a *final* end, to that which represents for him the *absolute* good. The deep-seated nature of this human tendency manifests itself in the fact that the mass of men, alienated from all religion properly speaking, allow themselves to be fascinated by such ideals and although (or is it precisely because?) this devotion demands the greatest sacrifices. It is therefore of the greatest moment for the force of attraction of the Christian message that men be made to see how Christianity answers this profoundly human aspiration. It can have an expansive effect upon the Christian to understand how this aspiration, in which he is in solidarity with his contemporaries and, basically, with all human beings of any age, is capable of harmonious combination with his love for Christ and finds therein its loftiest fulfillment.

This understanding is provided by the identification of the Omega Point, the crown and consummation of all human activity, with the Body of Christ, the grace-mediated union of mankind with the Father in his Son. Teilhard thus considers it his mission to show the nexus between human endeavor and the coming of the Kingdom of God, between the final victory of Christ and the success of the undertaking mankind is trying to accomplish.[4] The greatest joy of Teilhard's life was to experience within himself that the synthesis was possible and viable; that the consecration to a human ideal and the consecration to Christ were not mutually exclusive; that the two poles of his existence were capable of reacting one upon the other, of fertilizing each other, of rising in a single flame of consuming love filling for him the whole world of Christ and found again in his earthly tasks as well: "The joy and strength of my life will have been to observe that, when brought together, the two ingredients—World and God—react inexhaustibly one upon the other, giving off a light so intense as to transfigure (or even "transubstantiate") for me the depths of the World."[5]

Our next and last chapter will have to recur to the allusion to transubstantiation. Teilhard's reader must understand to what an extent this view and, above all, this experience was for Teilhard a deep and universal, rich and transfiguring one. He will then realize why this experience cannot be evoked except in terms that do violence to the framework of stereotyped terminology.

That is why he opposes to the "God in the Heights" (the traditional representation), the *new* "God in the Van," if only to insist upon their identity;[6] to the traditional God enthroned above the world, the God of the future, building himself up in the history of mankind. Not of course in the sense that God in himself, Father, Son and Holy Spirit, were *in fieri*, or still more absurdly speaking, had to be actualized by our human action; but rather in the sense that within human history, by the secular, age-old and universal labor of mankind, a reality truly of the divine order is coming into being, the Mystical Body of the Incarnate Son, the perfect man, the *Christus totus* of Augustine, the *pleroma* spoken of by St. Paul. There is no compelling reason to be enthused over this use of the name of God. In current theology and spirituality, there is a felicitous tendency to reserve the word *God* to serve as the proper name of the Person of the Father, in conformity with biblical and liturgical language. But if the Son can and must indeed be called God, if this Son and God is the ultimate subject of even the human properties of the God-Man, and if finally the conviction is held that the God-Man and his Mystical Body constitute, in a mysterious but nonetheless real way, but one single person, then this terminology is perfectly justified. It expresses in pregnant fashion that Christianity presents in fact a fulfillment of the apparently hopeless and temerarious dream of mankind, of mankind's aspiration to actualize by its own efforts and endeavor an absolutely definitive good, worthy of our total devotion, of the unreserved gift of ourselves.

The progress of mankind serves the edification of the Body of Christ. Such is the sustaining thesis of Teilhard's spirituality. To preclude any misunderstanding, let us formulate the same thesis forthwith in contrary terms: only that which serves the edification of the Body of Christ can be of value in the sense of true human progress. This thesis, this main tenet, is already surprising as such. Human progress, connoting essentially technology, economics, and the sciences, surely belongs among the secular values that we are accustomed painstakingly to distinguish from the supernatural values productive of salvation. So this thesis must be cogently proven. Teilhard's own argumentation is deceptively simple. All things exist for man and for the perfection of his human life. Man himself exists for his final incorporation into Christ. Therefore all things exist for the incorporation of men into Christ, i.e., for the building up of Christ's Mystical Body.[7] In other words, the abiding creative act whereby God gives being and life to all things is none other than the act whereby he builds up the Body of his

Son. For the Father creates all things in him and for him and everything has its foundation in him.[8] Therefore nothing can exist, neither thing nor work nor action, which does not contribute in its own way to building up this Body, with the exception of sin, which is itself in another way put into the service of the same end and goal. This edification is the only end and goal giving a meaning and a destiny to all that is and all that lives. The active omnipresence of God, spoken of in the preceding section, is a presence which is building Christ, an *"omnipresence of Christification."*[9] The existence, life, and operation of all creatures, echoes of the creative Omnipresence, constitute the "network of organizing forces of the total Christ."[10] Obviously this is equally and pre-eminently true of the highest of earthly realities, the existence and life of mankind.

This thought is basically traditional, for it belongs to the ancient and time-honored heritage of Catholic theology. One of the first Latin theologians, Tertullian, was already writing: "All things are servants of man, they are subject to him and put at his service." And man in his turn is created in view of Christ, for "all that God fashioned in the clay of which he made the body of Adam was the idea of the Christ who was to become man. . . . This clay, formed as it was already to the image of Christ who was going to come into (and in) the flesh, was not only a work of God, it was also his pledge."[11] With the formation of the first man begins the formation of the Body of the Son of God, who will also become the son of David, of Abraham, and of Adam.[12]

This traditional Catholic doctrine is given a renovated meaning in the design of Teilhard. The classical static image of the world presented creation and therefore also the relation of this creation to Christ as a fixed order of things, which obviously did not exclude the operation of these things. If the world be presented, on the contrary, as developing itself, it is the operation, the labor of things and men which comes to occupy first place. In their works, echoes of the creative word of God, all things are oriented to man, to the first coming of Christ, and finally to the second coming of that Christ at the end of time. They are collaborating thereto in however remote and indirect a manner. This is a second difference between Teilhard's picture and the classical one. Teilhard's includes the obligation of taking seriously the whole history of mankind.

Christians are often tempted to see but the half of history. From Abraham to Christ, there is progress toward Christ; after Christ, there is neither progress nor ascent. In the history of the Chosen People, providence has indeed brought about the fullness of time. Not only in the formal sense that there was required a certain number of years, but in the full sense that the vicissitudes of God's people were to accumulate a certain definite number of experiences, of religious, cultural and social attainments, before the acceptable time should come. God's people was to mature with a view to Christ. That this maturation was not entirely positive, that it had its negative side as well, is of importance but in no way detracts from the reality of that maturation. A real sense of history pertains to the essence of biblical revelation: the living God is a God who makes history. He does not lead his people in disordered and goalless fashion through the cycles of the ages; he leads them toward an end, a goal. But it is a curious fact that Christians must be observed to take less seriously the history of mankind after the ascension of Christ. We cannot here pause over the reasons for this phenomenon: a belief that in Christ had arrived the fullness of time; awareness that in life and in death each and every Christian was placed immediately before the eternal Lord; the expectation of his speedy return in the community of the early Christians; repeated warnings that the hour of the end was unforeseeable and known only to the Father. . . . However this may be, there was scarcely any further questioning whether mankind, even after the ascension of Christ, was still continuing its march toward an immanent destiny. Its unique function seemed to be that of permitting the preaching of the Gospel to all peoples, or even, according to the greatest thinker of the Middle Ages, to multiply the number of human beings until the number of the elect fixed by God's decree had been accomplished.[13] Is this idea not even now latent in many minds: the earth, conceived of as a gigantic fruit tree, whose function is held to be that of bearing and nourishing the souls which are its fruit until they be ripe for eternity? There would be a real process of maturation for the individual man but not for mankind. Mankind would have no finality. Its end would be marked not by the accomplishment of a maturation but rather by an intervention of God, when the number of the elect should have been complete. Only this stark numerical fact would bring the fulfillment of the course of the ages.

Against this Teilhard is protesting, together with all those who, after Newman, see in the history of the Church a real and genuine growth. If the world in its entirety and up to the advent of mankind has been characterized by a true and genuine history, so that everything preceding was truly a preparation of that which followed, mankind too, as the highest life form in the world, ought to have a history. For mankind, too, it is true not only that there are future things but also that there are things that are coming, "not only a future scenario which is being run off, but a future state which is being built up."[14] The notion that holds the entire meaning of earthly existence to consist in the accomplishment of the number of the elect seems in essence a throwback to the old cyclic notion of universal history, from which man was delivered by the revelation of the personal God.[15] The cycle would be held to repeat itself indefinitely in the course of each and every individual existence; history would keep revolving ceaselessly round the same central point. Now any approach that takes cognizance of the fact that history is a becoming and that all men are in solidarity with their predecessors and their successors compels the admission that there does exist a real progress of mankind, with the endeavor of each preceding generation bearing its fruit for the following generation:

> The twofold sense of duration and collectivity has pervaded and reordered the entire field of our experience: with the twofold result that the future, hitherto a vague succession of monotonous years, awaiting an unimportant number of scattered individual lives is now being seen to be a period of positive becoming and maturing.[16]

If the foregoing reasoning is correct, this *genesis* in history must be nothing other than a maturation geared to the second coming of Christ and the perfect measure of the manhood of Christ.

To this maturation all our human endeavors contribute, even the most secular and those most directed toward the earth and things earthly.

How is this contribution of our secular activity to the fulfillment of the Body of Christ to be conceived? The thesis according to which not only the inner intention but also the exterior result of our action and operation have lasting value might lead to the conclusion that, for example, the material products of art or technology would be recreated to a new existence in the new world. With joy or terror, according to the individual temperaments of each one, some readers of Teilhard wonder if in the new world there would figure Michelangelo's "Moses," the pictures of a Picasso, the strains of Beethoven's Ninth Symphony or of the "Rhapsody in Blue," to say nothing of technological achievements. Their imagination drives them beyond the boundary line that Teilhard wishes strictly to respect. They do not fit with his extreme and conscientious sobriety. According to Teilhard, the new earth, "renaissance, rebirth . . . outside of Time and Space,"[17] is located beyond our power of imagination, which is geared to time and space. We have no other figure of the future reality save the Body of the Risen Lord. Below the horizon of the death of the world lies the promise of the new creation, but "this does not mean that we can see what lies beyond and behind that trans-phenomenal zone."[18] We must resolutely refrain from any concrete representation.

We cannot advance anything save one general principle: "All the good that I can do *opus et operatio,* is physically gathered, *by something of itself,* into the reality of the consummated Christ."[19] Something, some "particle and portion of chosen being"[20] finds its place in the final structure of the Body of Christ.[21] This "something" Teilhard does not further specify. He seems to mean that every thing, every good product of human action contributes in some fashion to the enrichment of our human being and is thereby incorporated into us. By a comprehension and domination of the material world through its use, admiration, enjoyment and even renunciation, the body of mankind assimilates the sap of strength, of beauty, of goodness running in all things. This something which is assimilated and incorporated by man and contributes to the total flowering of the human being contributes also in a more or less remote fashion to the edification of the ultimate Body of Christ. Humanity functions as a crucible, as a "zone of continuous spiritual transformation, where all inferior realities and forces without exception are sublimated into sensations, feelings, ideas, and the powers of knowledge and love."[22] Teilhard nowhere postulates a renovation of things in their crass reality but only insofar as they have been humanized or assumed into the very being of man.

We must, then, keep constantly in mind the warning that it would be erroneous to seek "divine love and the divine Kingdom *on the same level* as human affections and human progress."[23] Teilhard is always on the alert to underscore the difference between the edification of the Body of Christ, properly speaking, which consists in a growth of faith, hope and charity and actualizes itself in preaching, the sacraments, prayer and the practice of the virtues, and the progress of mankind, which includes science, art, technology and economics.

Teilhard gives an excellent summary of his thinking in the following passage from a letter to a businessman who had prospered well and was anxiously wondering if he could permit himself, as a Christian, to savor the joy of a successful undertaking:

You still experience a certain difficulty in justifying to yourself this euphoria of a soul plunged in "business." I would point out to you that the most important thing is for you to experience this well-being. Bread was good for our bodies before we knew the chemical laws governing its assimilation. . . . In what sense, you ask, does the success of a business undertaking involve a moral progress? My answer to you is this: In this sense, that, since everything within the world is in a process of unification, the spiritual success of the Universe is tied in with the good functioning of all the zones of this universe, pre-eminently with the freeing and release of all possible energies in this universe. . . . Because your enterprise (I am supposing it to have been a morally justifiable one) develops favorably, there is a little more health disseminated throughout the mass of humanity and, consequently, a little more freedom to act, to think and to love. Whatever we may do, we can and ought to do it in the (expansive and strengthening) awareness of laboring in some small way to realize an effort which (even in its tangible reality) is required, at least indirectly, by the Body of Christ. . . . Because you act and operate as best you can (even in failure), you are constituting yourself in the World and you are aiding the World to constitute itself around you. How could you fail, then, to feel yourself thrilled momentarily by the immense joy of Creation?[24]

Note what Teilhard says about euphoria: when a man whose mind and spirit are oriented to a Christian way of living finds a spontaneous joy in his task, this signifies that this task is in harmony with his deep spiritual bent and with the bias of his very being. Thus his accomplishments have an authentically human and therefore ultimately Christian value.[25] But what is of special interest to us is the Teilhardian explanation here presented.

Even such a material and earthly thing as business life has as its goal and end the liberation of the reserve energy of mankind, giving men greater liberty, an enlarged power of acting and thinking, and finally of loving, as autonomous personalities. Think of the increase and expansion of prosperity, which deliver the mass of mankind from constant concern with the prime vital necessities of life and permit men to give more attention to things spiritual; which render child labor superfluous and can build up a valuable educational machinery permitting all to read, to make contact and enrich themselves with the thinking of others; which make travel abroad available to all, enlarging and broadening the horizons of each and all. . . . But this conviction does not rest primarily upon facts of experience, nor can it be refuted by other facts of experience, such as that the new prosperity has involved a new slavery or that the mass of mankind is incapable of making truly human use of its new freedom. We have here a general principle, philosophical in nature and resting on the image of man as sketched by Teilhard. All activity and operation in conformity with man's nature makes man more truly man. Being more truly and more fully man means that each personality is more strongly centered upon itself, that all persons are brought closer one to another, become more and more convinced that they are members of a single humanity. Man grows in freedom in proportion as he becomes more himself, can dispose more consciously and deliberately of himself, think for himself, act in the strength of his own inner riches. And his capacity for loving grows likewise, for true freedom consists in the fact of being free for the not-self. Economic work indisputably pertains to truly human operations, quite in accord with man's nature, for it aims at bringing to light the wealth of the earth and putting it at the disposal of all.

Teilhard's remarks in this letter on the subject of economic and business operations hold true equally for all the other realms of human action and operation: for science, which causes man to grow in the knowledge of the world and of himself; for technology, which puts the forces of nature at his service; for art, in which he expresses himself and makes available to others the wealth of his own inner life; for social and juridical organization, which gives a more concrete and universal form to human solidarity.[26] By its very nature, all conspires to enrich the personalities of all, to cause the unity of the human family to be lived more intensely. These are the higher and exclusively human values. If a new technological or scientific discovery does not ultimately serve these values, the conclusion must be that man has abused the potentialities prevailing in his world. He has given a bad steer to the thrust of progress.

It might be objected that mankind's progress from the moral point of view is very debatable. Is the modern technocrat better than the Ice Age reindeer hunter? Does modern mankind number among it any greater geniuses than a Plato or a Euripides, any more ardent hearts than a Paul or an Augustine? These questions must remain unanswered. But it can be supposed without the slightest doubt that the faculty of human thought has grown because the opportunity for exchange of thoughts and experience has grown, because there have come into being forms of world-wide collective thinking of which our fathers could not have dreamed.

In each human element, the individual power of feeling and thinking may well have levelled off (at least for the time being) for 30,000 to 40,000 years. But the fantastic spectacle, right before our eyes, of a *collective Reflection*, rapidly mounting in step with a more and more unitary organization, to my mind, is a formal disproof of the contention that Hominization in its essence (that is, the concentration upon itself of the global Mental Life of the earth) has already been halted.[27]

It can and must be asserted, in this conception of the meaning of history, that the capacity for loving is growing in mankind, since the ultimate consummation of mankind, and thus the sole truly definitive human value, consists in the love-union of all men among themselves and of mankind with God. Thus the true and real progress of mankind must ultimately be in the service of this value. There can be no question of a true progress of mankind unless it is accompanied by a progress in the faculty for loving. It is this toward which, as we have said,[28] the great impulse of life is pushing mankind; this is the line of conduct against which man must measure his activity. The true ideal of mankind can be stated as follows: "To grow in stature and strength so as to be able to give more of oneself and clasp in a tighter embrace . . . this is the true and noble manner of interpreting and canalising the impulse which urges us upward."[29]

Or to use the wording of an earlier Teilhardian essay, true human progress resides in the awakening of *the spirit*.[30] Spirit does not signify in the first instance any negation of physical nature, but rather the conscious and free possession of each and every person and of mankind as a whole; it includes, thus, as an essential element the progressive integration, in this human self-possession, of all the possibilities and all the values contained in the material world. Nor can it be lost sight of that this *spirit*, conscious and free possession of self, is nothing other than an opening to love. The man who says a conscious and free *Yes* to himself, is also saying a *Yes* to his unity with other men and to the collective orientation of all men to God.

The growth in the faculty of loving is still less susceptible to measurement even than the growth in the faculty of thinking. This faculty is so intangible that it can justifiably be doubted whether it is susceptible to growth. But the thesis can also be defended that, for example, technological, economic or organizational development can in fact lead to a growth of this faculty of loving. In this connection it would have to be understood that love is on the one hand the voluntary *Amen* to the solidarity of all men while on the other hand it pertains to the plenitude of love, as of all human virtues, to exteriorize itself in acts. Modern communications media allow man better to conceive of the universal solidarity of mankind; foreign peoples are becoming less foreign to us, every human being can witness the joy and the distress of all the others and "sym-pathize" with them. And man has the opportunity for transforming this sympathy into acts, thanks to the development and expansion of medical science and economics. He can organize a world-wide assistance campaign in times of disasters, efficaciously combat epidemics on a large scale, put an end to famine. Finally, the development of law is affording to every human being upon earth, even to the weakest, a chance for social equality and security. In the light of all this, it is not mere foolishness to assert that mankind today disposes of greater opportunities than ever for actualizing the solidarity of all by acts and in a truly universal manner. For the first time in history, the unity of all men is not just a tenet but a daily and personal mission of every member of the human family.

But even when granted in principle, the growth of the faculty of loving still has one great obstacle remaining in force against it, namely, the hard fact that man still remains egotistical, cruel, and insensible toward his fellows. Not only does modern man have at his disposal new opportunities for sympathizing with others and assuaging their needs; he has, likewise and equally at his disposal, means, and these not the least, for making others suffer and increasing their miseries. The fact is undeniable. The discovery of new possibilities is, in all appearance, constantly being exploited in a bad sense. The nineteenth-century development of the industrial economy produced in the first instance a new pauperism and a new slavery; atomic science's first step was the creation of the atomic weapon; the civil state, expression of juridical equality, first served for Napoleonic enrollment and later for the extermination of the Jews. This fact must be looked squarely in the face in order to avoid slipping into a naïve optimism about progress. This fact will also aid us better to clarify the heart of the Teilhardian design.

It would be an error, we have said, to identify the progress of science, technology, organization, etc., with the actualization and realization of the Kingdom of God. The Kingdom of God is actualized by the love-union of all men among themselves in a common love of the Father. But progress in these realms does involve a growth of "spirit," i.e., of conscious domination and mastery of self and of the world and, accordingly, of the faculty of loving, though not as yet of love itself. Love always remains a personal commitment, the supremely personal commitment of the heart of each individual. It remains voluntary; it implies a choice. While on earth, man can always refuse to love or to be loved. With the power of loving the power of shutting the heart to love grows equally.

Progress in this world whose value Teilhard so extols always carries within it a profound ambivalence. With the new faculty provided by the free domination of self and of the world, the opportunity to consecrate oneself and all that one has to one's fellows and to God, there grows equally and simultaneously the capacity for perverting this consecration into an ever-greater self-sufficiency and egotism, of transforming the instrument of community into an instrument of isolation. The growing faculty seems even to augment the temptation to perversion: "This crisis of human action is, by its nature, as old as Man. . . . Coming into being together with the intellect, the temptation to revolt must constantly vary and *grow* with that intellect."[31]

The growing capacity includes in fact a heavier task and demands a more total dedication. Thus, the confrontation in urgent immediacy with the distress of millions of human beings, as that distress is revealed to us by press, radio, films and television, is an invitation to broadened generosity and devotion. But it is also and equally a temptation to hardheartedness; man fears that by opening himself to a limitless misery, he will end by losing himself. Likewise the new mastery and domination of the world, which offers the possibility and opportunity for worshiping God with prouder gratitude, also increases the temptation to a Promethean worship of self.[32]

This holds true for each personal life and also, it seems, for the life of a people or for that of mankind as a whole. We may here have the kernel of truth in the cyclic notion of history. Every time a human being enters into a new phase of his life, every time that a new dimension of his existence opens up, he finds himself placed before the alternative of putting these new riches at the service of his fellows or of enjoying them egotistically and to the detriment of the community. Each time the same old struggle is resumed at a new level. A similar phenomenon prevails in the progress of mankind. Each and every new discovery increasing man's power over the world or his influence over his fellows involves the temptation to exploit this power in the partisan service of a group or a nation and to turn it against the community. Each and every technological, economic, or organizational development threatens to become a weapon to subjugate or tyrannize other men. Each and every advance in science or philosophy has brought on a religious crisis with a new temptation to emancipation from God. Each time mankind has to fight to put its new acquisitions to the service of the human community, to the service of the love of neighbor and the love of God. The old fight must be taken up again and again, each time on a higher plane. Man's progress, the progress of mankind, is therefore, as Teilhard quite clearly saw, a rectilinear one. It bears more resemblance to a screw or a spiral. The same cycle is ceaselessly repeating itself, each time at a little higher level than the time before. The new crisis seems each time to be produced by the very conclusion of the preceding crisis "one turn of the spiral higher."[33]

Such a view of the ambivalence of progress does not call in question the value of the progress.[34] On the contrary, each new step increases the temptation precisely because it does have a value. Man is not tempted by evil as such but by good. Sin does not consist in the use of evil things but in the evil use of good things. It consists in man raising a relative value to the rank of an absolute, placing it in practice above the only true absolute value, the love-union of all men in the love of God. This is why the temptation becomes stronger in proportion as the relative value shows more likeness with the absolute value. The power of sin lies in the fascination of a partial good which makes man forget the absolute good and causes him to be unfaithful to that absolute good.

Two conclusions can be drawn from all this which are of exceptional importance for the spirituality presented by Teilhard. In the first place, the human being and the Christian cannot recoil from a new step toward progress under pretext that this step is dangerous. It is dangerous only because it is good. Man, and more precisely the Christian man, must experiment with every new capacity of his world and of his being: "We must try everything for Christ; we must hope everything for Christ. *Nihil intentatum*."[35]

In the second place, every man personally, and the whole of mankind collectively, must be at pains, with an ever-greater endeavor and ever more intense awareness, to put each and every new acquisition into the service of love. They must keep ever more vigilant watch against the danger accompanying every new step, so as to direct progress into its true and proper channel, not using it against the community of men which is to be promoted or against their union with God. Ever more consciously, more generously and more totally must man place his knowledge and his power at the service of the true human community. Since this community is a person-to-person union, man must place progress at the service of the inner enrichment of each and every person and of his outgoing movement to other persons. He must also tend ever more consciously and generously to put the enrichment and interiorization of the human community at the service of the edification of the Body of Christ. And since the ultimate consummation of this Body can only be attained if the whole human family loses itself in God by virtue of the sacrifice of Christ and in union with him, mankind must ultimately, after having established its dominion over the world and unfolded all the capacities of its own nature, fortify and strengthen within itself the disposition to sacrifice all this glory in a final holocaust.

In all his consecration to the earth and to mankind, in all his enthusiasm for progress and the actualization of the human community, the Christian must realize that human activity must in the end lead to the final love union with God, realized by an ultimate union to the sacrifice of the death and resurrection of

Christ. By his preaching and by his cross, the Lord has taught us "that the term of creation is not to be sought in the temporal zones of our visible world, but that the effort required of our fidelity must be consummated *beyond a total metamorphosis* of ourselves and of everything surrounding us."[36]

It is only athwart the mystery of death and resurrection that man and mankind attain the final fulfillment they have been pursuing throughout their whole evolution. For this reason the ultimate meaning of progress and human history cannot be reduced to a clear and logical formula but only to words of mystery. And this is no cause for astonishment; logic is not even capable of expressing the love between human beings; how much less capable is it, then, of expressing love toward God! But Teilhard did nonetheless succeed in finding a formulation, coining an image which expresses felicitously the ultimate meaning of our human activity. It is a formula or image which merits to be meditated, which may well find a place in the treasury of the great inspirational sayings wherein Christianity has stored up its experience of life and relations with God:

The effort of mankind, even in realms inaccurately called profane, must, in the Christian life, assume the role of a holy and unifying operation. *It is the collaboration,* trembling with love, which we give to the hands of God, concerned to attire and prepare us (and the World) for the final *union through sacrifice.*[37]

In ancient liturgical practice, the victim was chosen from among the strongest and most thoroughbred of the flock, adorned with garlands and flowers; Jesus was sacrificed in the fullness of his maturity. Humanity, mankind must likewise adorn and spread itself in all its wealth to allow itself to be sacrificed to the Father by the one and only High Priest in an ultimate holocaust. Its endeavor to develop and actualize itself is holy service in the measure in which it opens progress, even secular progress, to the mysterious and ultimate horizon of God's creative and redemptive operation upon it.

INCARNATION, CHURCH, EUCHARIST

To the Christian's sensitised vision, it is true, the Creator, and more specifically, the Redeemer (as we shall see) have steeped themselves in all things to such a degree that . . . "The World is full of God." But this aggrandisement is only valuable in his eyes insofar as the light, in which everything seems to him bathed, radiates from an his-torical center and is transmitted along a traditional and solidly defined axis. The immense enchantment of the divine milieu ultimately owes all its value in the long run to the human-divine contact which was revealed at the Epiphany of Jesus. . . . Thence forward, however dazzling the expansions which we shall try . . . to discern in the resurrected Christ, their beauty and their stuff of reality will always remain inseparable from the tangible and verifiable truth of the Gospel event. The mystical Christ, the universal Christ of St. Paul, has neither meaning nor value in our eyes except as an expansion of the Christ who was born of Mary and who died on the Cross. . . . However far we may be drawn into the divine spaces opened up to us by Christian mysticism, we never depart from the Jesus of the Gospels. On the contrary, we feel a growing need to enfold ourselves ever more firmly within this human Truth.[1]

CHAPTER 11

The expositions and discussions of the foregoing Chapters might tend to obscure the fact that in the Teilhardian spirituality it is not a question of theses or theories but rather of the encounter with the living person of Jesus. In the great laws of the cosmos, the Christian can recognize the creative word of God. In the enormous and varied wealth of the real and possible beings of which the cosmos is made up, he can see and serve a divine reality. But the creative word is nothing other than the person of Jesus of Nazareth, the divine reality, his Body, his fullness and his consummation. It might appear for a moment that the new view of the world is too large for the Christian compass. "Is the Christ of the Gospels, imagined and loved within the dimensions of a Mediterranean world, capable of still embracing and still forming the center of our prodigiously enlarged Universe?"[2] The familiar and beloved figure of our Savior would seem to dissolve and vanish into the infinite contours of the cosmos.

The prologue to St. John's Gospel and the Epistles of St. Paul, especially those to the Ephesians and the Colossians, teach us the contrary. The Jesus of the Gospels, with his entirely human countenance and personality, concrete and well delimited, is himself the Word which was with God, through whom everything came into being and by whom everything is sustained. He is the Risen Lord who is directing and guiding history, the history of the world and of mankind, a history whose immeasurable grandeur we are even now beginning to perceive, and who is building up for himself a Body by the efforts and the sufferings of the world. The universal and cosmic Christ, as Teilhard sometimes calls him, is none other than the Jesus of the Gospel, the Jesus who came down from heaven and who went up again to the Father athwart death and resurrection. This Jesus is an entity encompassing the world and mankind. In the great laws impelling the cosmos to its human consummation and mankind to its fulfillment, we can hear and follow the familiar voice of the Gospel. In the great Body at whose building mankind is laboring, we can serve him, converse with him and, so to speak, touch him. Even while remaining concrete and personal, he is present mysteriously everywhere, in all things, active in all realities, builder in the whole of history.

This awareness, this faith, was for Teilhard the great liberating discovery of his life. The whole world of things and men became, for him, transparent, showing him the figure of Jesus whom he had learned to love in the school of Ignatius, the Sacred Heart, focus of love divine and human, venerated by Teilhard since his childhood. Everywhere, into the deepest recesses of the material world, the Christian can find this burning heart whose flame of love gives to all things existence and life, drawing them to itself in all their movement and in all their activity. The devotion to the Sacred Heart, which at first had seemed petty and narrow, because addressed to one limited aspect of the human nature of Jesus, discloses the symbol of the broad and powerful love that embraces the world and history and penetrates them in all their fibers, of the universal and penetrating love that is yet concrete and personal.[3]

Thus, in the light of faith, the whole world that surrounds us and the whole world that we ourselves are can cause the beloved and familiar figure of Jesus to shine through. In obeying the law of life and collaborating in the flowering forth of mankind, we are obeying his voice, we are submitting to the power of attraction of his love. In the alienation of death, wherein man loses the world and himself, he can drink the cup of which Jesus himself drank and which affords the perfect and most specifically Christian communion with him.[4] In things and events, in labor and disappointments, in life and death, the Christian can encounter the living person of the Lord and serve him. To the extent to which man believes, the whole world becomes for him the phenotype, the "body" of the Christ who can be seen and touched in all things.[5] Such is the enthralling mystery of this "prodigious identification between the Son of Man and the divine Environment."[6]

Anyone confining his reading of Teilhard to his expositions concerning the march of evolution and the development of mankind may well carry away the impression that in this ascent there are no other peaks than the origin of man, the entry of humanity, mankind, into its convergent phase, and finally the consummation. The Incarnation of the Son of God, his life in Palestine, and his death under Pontius Pilate seem to disappear entirely into the great ascent. If God is everywhere active and if we can encounter him in all things, if the entire human family is the Body of the Son of God *in fieri*, what further meaning can there be in this limited event? Some of Teilhard's readers have in fact posed to themselves this question.

They are forgetting that the Incarnation of the Son of God is precisely the summit and the focus of God's operation in his creation; that we can encounter God in all things only because he has become man and part of the world; that the human family can become the Body of the Son of God only because this Son became a child of the human family. The passage above, cited from *Le Milieu divin*, stresses that the divine presence radiates from this historical focus and owes its very consistency to it.[7] In one of his very first writings, Teilhard had said:

The single Business of the World is the physical incorporation of the faithful into Christ who is from God. . . . At the outset of its developmental processes, there was need of an operation of a transcendent order which would graft (following mysterious but physically regulated conditions) the Person of a God into the human Cosmos. . . . *"Et Verbum caro factum est."* It was the Incarnation. Out of this first and basic contact of God with our race, in view of the very penetration of the Divine into our nature, a new life was born, an unexpected enlargement and "obediential" prolongation of our natural capacities: Grace. Now, grace is the single sap mounting in the branches from the same trunk, the Blood running in the veins under the impulsion of one and the same Heart, the neural influx passing through the members at the good pleasure of the one Head—and the radiant Head and the mighty Heart and the fertile Stalk, are inevitably Christ. . . .

The Incarnation is a renovation of *all* the Forces and Powers of the Universe; Christ is the instrument, the Center, the End of the whole of the animate and material Creation; through Him all is created, sanctified, vivified.[8]

More strongly than current classical theology but in conformity with Scripture and the teaching of the Fathers, which is again coming into its own in present-day theologizing, Teilhard insists that the whole of creation was directed to the Incarnation of the Son of God and that the whole of the subsequent history of mankind can be regarded as a prolongation of this Incarnation:

> Everything was moving toward the Infant born of the Woman. And since Jesus' birth, his coming to man's estate, his dying and his rising again, *everything has continued to move, because Christ has not finished forming himself*. He has not caught up to himself the last folds of the Robe of flesh and the love formed for him by his faithful. *The mystical Christ has not attained his full growth*. And in the prolongation of this begetting is located the mainspring of all created activity.[9]

That unique event which is the Incarnation cannot be isolated from what precedes and from what follows it. There is continuity in the whole of the development of mankind and of the world, from the primordial atom to the ultimate consummation. The Incarnation of Christ is no mere break in this continuity; rather it is the fulfillment and consummation of all that lay before it. Not yet consummated under all aspects by the Resurrection, it must become a reality in and for the whole of mankind. But it does constitute the absolute summit of the history of the earth, the center of all the forces, the focus toward which and from which all things and all events are directed. And so, when we read such an exclamation as the following from Teilhard: "the great mystery of Christianity is not exactly the appearance but rather the transparence of God in the universe . . . not only Your Epiphany, Jesus, but Your diaphany,"[10] it must not be forgotten here that the source of the diaphany is the Epiphany.[11] The whole of the divinization of the world can be but an emanation of this unique act of God's grace by which the Father makes of a man his divine Son.

At the very heart of the social phenomenon, a kind of *ultra-socialization* is in progress: that whereby the "Church" is being formed little by little, vivifying by its influence and collecting under their sublimest form all the energies of the Noosphere; the Church, reflectively Christified portion of the world; the Church, main focus of inter-human affinities via super-charity; the Church, central axis of universal convergence and exact point of encounter flashing between Universe and Omega Point.[12]

A question similar to that posed concerning the Incarnation in Teilhard's spirituality also arises with regard to the Church. If the whole human community is, as we have seen, the Body of Christ *in fieri*, what then is the place of the Body of Christ which is the Church? The reply to this question is given in the passage just cited above.

Just as the point of development is constituted in the world by mankind, so it is constituted in mankind by the Church. In the Church, there has been already realized and actualized in a sense the ultimate ideal of human development, the love-union of all men in the common love of God and in the common desire for union with him. The Church is the community of men to the extent to which that community is already gathered together upon earth and united by love, the love of God which, as such, encompasses all men and all mankind. That is why the Church can reunite all men beyond the oppositions of race, nationality, class and condition. In the Church the essential and universal unity of the human family is already being lived. The love of God is placed above all else in the Church and is there directed to what is at once the deepest and the most deeply personal trait in every fellow man, his relation to God and his divine vocation.[13]

Since the unity of all men is freely accepted and voluntarily lived in the Church, the solidarity of all human beings there ceases to be an anguish and a cause of suffering; it there precedes, prepares, and commences already the eschatological freedom of the children of God. The central marrow of the human community in the Church is formed by the love of each member of the Church for Christ and the Father, poured forth in the heart of each by the Holy Spirit. The presence of a generous and expansive love opens up the narrowness of each and every heart, causing an increase in interest and openness for others. Even outside the visible walls of the Church there can exist an authentic genuine fraternal charity. For no man is a stranger to the impulse of the Holy Spirit and the force of attraction of the Heart of Christ. It is even possible for a non-Christian to respond with greater generosity to this grace than do many Catholics. Yet only in the Church can fraternal charity entirely unfold its expansive action upon the human heart. Every man truly loving his neighbor is obeying a voice holier than himself, something that merits total devotion and unreserved surrender. But only the Christian recognizes this voice and this absolute, seeing Christ in his neighbor. The Christian believes that the community that unites him to his fellows has been founded by Christ. He believes that in his neighbor he can serve and love the Lord. For the Christian, fraternal love, even where it demands onerous sacrifices, is a personal encounter with him whom the Christian knows to love him with an eternal faithfulness and a divine intimacy. Though it is impossible to love Christ without loving one's neighbor or to love that neighbor in a spirit of generous communion without loving him in Christ,[14] this source and deep bias of all fraternal love becomes conscious and, therefore, fully human only in Christianity. The Church is the reflectively and consciously Christified sector of mankind.

In the Church there is already occurring, beneath the veil of faith but nonetheless in a mysterious immediacy, that encounter which will be the rapturous delight of the Omega Point, the encounter of each and every individual person, in communion with other persons, with his Lord and God. In the Church is being stockpiled the tension of the expectation of love which will one day cause the spark to leap between heaven and earth. Although the ultimate meaning of all things and all the potentialities of creation consist in aiding mankind to ripen against the second coming of Christ, this meaning is actualized in the measure in which these things and potentialities are assumed in and by the Church. By the Church, all the forces constructing the Noosphere are purified, joined, and liberated for the service of the true unity of the human family. Even if non-Christians do dedicate themselves to the building of this unity, this is an imperfect and provisional phase, for these non-Christians are aware neither of the work at which they are laboring nor of the master to whom they are devoting themselves. The hour must come when all men of good will shall awake to the awareness that their service of the human community is serving the construction of the Body of Christ, when they shall recognize and admit Christ as the central humano-divine center point of the cosmos.[15] Within the Church there is already manifesting itself this ultimate and expansive sense of the human community.

For this reason all Christians must exert themselves to be "present" everywhere where work is in progress upon the inner unity of men.[16] Upon Christians devolves the holy and apostolic task of witnessing, by their word and by their action, to the way that the most *profane* values in which human society is seeking its progress can be placed at the service of a sacred love; of showing how precisely the service of men unfolds in all its expansive power when inspired by this service of God. This is why, likewise, all the members of the Church, from the humblest to the most exalted, must continually be at pains to purify and to maintain in that purity the ecclesiastical forms of human community, so that they really appear as the figure and witness of love.

The whole world can be considered as the scaffolding of the ultimate Body of Christ, because it is the scaffolding of the human community. This in no way infringes upon the unique place of the Church, even now in an earthly manner the Body of Christ. On the contrary, the Church has a crucial place and function in this undertaking. To such an extent that Teilhard, with all his esteem for what is being realized and actualized by the non-Christians and the unbelievers, can nonetheless write in all truth:

"The closer I approach to the end of my life, the more I feel myself indissolubly linked to a Christian current, outside of which I do not see any complete valorization (nor, above all, any possibility of amorization) for what we call evolution."[17]

Since the Church is in fact the community of love founded by Christ, authentic and in principle universal, the "sacrament," the form and the operative presence of the redemptive grace which saves mankind from the division that besets it when it is not in love, no human effort can contribute to the real unification of the human family except to the extent to which that effort is oriented, consciously or unconsciously, to the Church and allows itself to be inspired by the grace present in the Church.

Since I, your priest, O Lord, have this day neither bread nor wine nor altar, I am going to spread out my hands over the whole of the Universe, and take its immensity as the matter of my sacrifice.

Is not the infinite circle of things the ultimate Host that you will to transform?

Is not the seething crucible, wherein mingle and boil up the operations of all living and cosmic substance, the chalice of pain that you desire to sanctify? . . .

Let there be repeated again today and tomorrow and forever, until the transformation shall have been exhaustively effected, the Divine Words "This is my Body."[18]

This reflection and this prayer of the priest stretcher-bearer at the front, prevented from celebrating Mass but confronted with the extremes of the misery and grandeur of suffering, with death and with heroic courage, expresses one of the favorite thoughts of Teilhard's spirituality. The same thought recurs five years later, in *La messe sur le monde,* when once again, this time in the immense Chinese desert, the bread and wine for the Eucharist were not available to Teilhard. The thought is further developed in *Le Milieu divin.*[19]

Catholic doctrine holds that the bread and the wine are really changed into the Body and Blood of Christ by the words of the priest as he repeats Christ's own words at the Last Supper, and that they become the holy offering for the salvation of the whole world. In receiving this Body and this Blood under the species of bread and of wine, the faithful Catholic is receiving communion with his Lord and becoming himself an offering within this one and only offering; he is receiving participation in Christ's Risen Life. For Teilhard's cosmos-girdling gaze, the bread and the wine assume cosmic dimensions. The whole life of the world and especially the aspiration of mankind to progress surely become the edifice of the Body of Christ. Every suffering, every pain and affliction, every renunciation and every death, by which man loses himself, surely become the only acceptable offering, the Blood shed by Christ. The whole world and our entire existence, with its enrichment and its loss of self, can surely become a community with Christ, one single great "communion." These are certainly arresting and thrilling thoughts! Yet they may also be disquieting. For here again it may appear that this universal and cosmic extension is throwing overboard that which is distinctively Christian and detaching itself from the strictly eucharistic sacramental celebration, from the consecration and the communion.

This is certainly not Teilhard's intention. His reflections are inspired precisely by the painful deprivation of the daily summit of his priestly life, the celebration of Mass. He is led to extend the notion of the sacramental celebration and to expand upon it, not by any lack of esteem but rather by his esteem and love for it. It is the prototype, the source, and the focus rendering possible the cosmic consecration and communion. Teilhard indicates this quite clearly: "In a secondary and generalized sense, but in a true sense, the sacramental Species are formed by the totality of the world, and the duration of the creation, is the time needed for its consecration."[20]

Therefore one can speak of cosmic consecration and communion in a derivative and secondary sense. The reality of these latter rests thus upon the sacrament in the strict sense. As Boros remarks, Teilhard is not attempting an essay in theological justification; he does not say to what level of the Eucharistic structure this dimension can be attached.[21] We shall now try to show its possible place, both in the light of the *de fide* doctrine on the Eucharist and in the whole of Teilhard's design. This will, let us hope, cast some light on the relations between the strictly sacramental experience of our unity with Christ and a possible universal cosmic extension of this experience and this unity. It may also help to prevent some of the misunderstandings that might be provoked by a rapid cursory reading of Teilhard's poetic outbursts.

There are several ways of approaching the meaning of the eucharistic celebration for the ultimate sanctification of the cosmos, in order to grasp the real meaning of the figurative language used by Teilhard. Recourse can be had to the teaching of several theologians, St. Thomas Aquinas apparently among them, to the effect that every grace is accorded in a sense in virtue of the Eucharist.[22] And since the sanctification of the cosmos is indubitably a work of grace because it is an aspect of the Redemption,[23] the eucharistic celebration is likewise the principle of this sanctification. Or again, the symbolism of the Eucharist can be taken as point of departure. The bread and the wine can be regarded as the prototypes of the products of nature and culture, the repast as the prototype of the human community. In the Eucharist, these realities are sanctified and become the symbols and the instruments of the community with God and of the new community of men. Or, in a third approach, it can be considered that, according to a generic law of Christian existence, the sanctification of a prototype constitutes the principle or the earnest of the sanctification of everything which is represented by the prototype. Thus, the celebration of the Eucharist as a consecration and a communion can be regarded as the principle and the promise of the sanctification of all the values which are enclosed within nature, culture, and the human community.[24] We prefer still another way, more in conformity with the categories of Teilhardian thinking. It is more complex but also lends itself better to conceptual analysis.

This way can be summarized as follows: The Eucharist is not only the sacrament which consecrates the bread and the wine into the "physical" Body and Blood of Christ; it is also the sacrament which consecrates the human community into his Mystical Body. This consecration into the Mystical Body includes the fact that the sacrifice of Christ is also actualized and accomplished in the community, so that this community becomes a community offering itself to God in virtue of its unity with the sacrifice of Christ. The actualization and the accomplishment of this sacrifice, which is the Church, includes in its turn the fact that the entire world becomes the offering. By the virtue and power of the eucharistic consecration, there thus occurs a true consecration of mankind and of mankind's world.

The axis of this consideration is constituted by the eucharistic consecration and by its aspect of sacrifice. In this fashion, the line of our exposition will better mesh with that of Teilhard's reflections. But we have no intention of taking sides in the controverted question concerning whether the essence of the eucharistic celebration is sacrifice or repast.[25] There is a strict and essential relation and nexus between the sacrificial aspect and the communion aspect; the realization of the sacrifice of Christ likewise accords participation in his new life; the communion can thus be included, without any difficulty, in this consideration.

The present picture of the Eucharistic faith presents a certain narrowness, in the wake of the continual controversies in which eucharistic theology has had to become involved for nearly nine centuries. In connection with the consecration, almost the only object of consideration is transubstantiation, i.e., the changing of the bread and the wine into the Body and Blood of Christ, and the consequent Real Presence of Christ. Our contemporaries in the twentieth century scarcely realize that, according to St. Thomas Aquinas, this transubstantiation and Real Presence are not the ultimate reality of the Eucharist, that they refer beyond to a reality which is the Church.[26] The matter is usually presented as if the consecration were distinct from the offering of the sacrifice of Christ. Though there is generally a clear understanding of the fact that in the Mass the Church is offering the sacrifice of Christ, it is too often forgotten that, in offering Christ, the Church is offering herself and that the Church therefore herself becomes an offering to the Father in virtue and by the power of the Eucharist.

Yet Pius XII on several occasions drew attention to the fact that, in the Mass, the Church herself becomes an offering, which Christ offers in offering himself and which she offers together with Christ:

Thus, in this pure offering, not only does Christ offer himself as the Head of the Church to the heavenly Father; he also offers in himself His mystical members.[27]

If the people offer at the same time with the priest, this is . . . but because the people unite their votive offerings of praise, intercession, expiation and thanksgivings to the mental votive offerings or intentions of the priest and indeed of the Great High Priest, in order to present them to God the Father in the very external rite of the priest offering the Victim. The external rite of the Sacrifice must in truth necessarily, by its nature, be a manifestation of the interior cult; now the Sacrifice of the New Law signifies the supreme homage by which the chief celebrant, who is Christ, and with him and through him all his mystical members, render to God the honors that are his due.[28]

. . . they must immolate themselves as victims.[29]

. . . they cannot but offer themselves with him and through the Great High Priest, as a spiritual host.[30]

The theological meaning and significance of these texts may well have been lost sight of by seeing in them nothing but pious exhortations. This they are without a doubt. But the exhortation rests upon the sacramental reality produced in the sacrifice of the Mass and in virtue of it. In the same spirit does Paul exhort the baptized to die with Christ because they have died with him by baptism.[31] It is worthwhile to develop the theological significance of this doctrine a little at this point.

By the eucharistic consecration, the bread and the wine are changed into the Body and Blood of Christ, so that Christ himself becomes present under the sacramental species. But we must not consider this Real Presence "as an *inert presence;* it is a *personal presence,* in the strictest sense. The Christ present under the Sacred Species is the Christ *who is offering Himself.*"[32] Christ makes himself present since he is to be offered by the priests of the Church to the Father. He has offered himself once for all, by losing himself voluntarily in death and receiving himself anew from the hand of the Father in the Resurrection. He gives the same one sacrifice to the Church so that it may be offered by her as her own sacrifice. By the ministry of the Church and of her priests, Christ offers himself, making present the sacrifice of the cross in an ecclesiastical and sacramental manner. The Council of Trent teaches that:

In order to leave and bequeath to his beloved spouse, the Church, a visible sacrifice . . . whereby would be represented the bloody sacrifice about to be accomplished once only upon the cross . . . he instituted a New Passover, that is, himself, to be offered in the Church by his priests under visible signs. In this divine sacrifice of the Mass, Christ is rendered present and immolated in an unbloody fashion, he who did offer himself once in bloody fashion upon the altar of the cross. . . . It is one and the same offering, offering himself now by the ministry of the priests.[33]

Christ is giving himself to the Church in giving her the sacrifice that she offers to God. Christ so arranges it that the Church is offering him himself. This very important fact is often neglected. It is admitted that the Church offers Christ as her own sacrifice. There is discussion concerning the nexus between the one sacrifice of Christ and the ecclesiastical renewal of this sacrifice. But it tends to be forgotten that the Church is able to offer Christ only because Christ did and does give and grant it to the Church to offer him.

Yet this is very important for a right understanding of the sacramental nature of the sacrifice of the Mass. If in each and every Mass, Christ gives himself to the Church to be *her* sacrifice, if he so arranges things that the Church is offering him to the Father, he also so arranges things that she is offering herself in him and through him. He so arranges things that the Mass is, as a sacrifice of the Church, a real and sincere sacrifice. Christ effects in the Church the Christian sense of sacrifice which makes this sacrifice sincere. Usually, theology sets the sacraments over against the acts of worship, especially the supreme act of worship which is the sacrifice of the Mass, in a sort of spatial context and framework. In the sacraments, the movement comes from above, God is giving his grace to man. In the acts of worship, the movement comes from below, man is offering something of himself to God. This may be satisfactory as a phenomenological presentation of the situation, but it renders only imperfectly the real heart and core of Christian worship. In Christian worship, mankind can approach God only because God grants that mankind should approach him. Christian worship, a sign whereby mankind offers itself to God, has a deeper meaning; it is the sign that God himself is presenting himself as a God who can be approached. This worship is itself a sign of grace, a sacrament.[34] The Mass is not exclusively a prayer to obtain grace; it is a sign of grace and it confers the grace in virtue of this sign. In the celebration of the Mass, and especially in the consecration, there is visibly expressed the fact that Christ is giving himself to the Church as the sacrifice of that Church, that he is granting to her the favor of approaching the Father in him and with him, that he is making of her an offering to the Father, therefore that he is "consecrating" her.

If the Church commemorates the sacrifice of Christ and offers that sacrifice to God as her own sacrifice, then she is offering herself. Christ has in fact offered himself as mankind's Chief Priest and Head; therefore he has offered himself for all. And it must be borne in mind that, in the language of the Bible, the preposition "for" signifies both "on behalf of" as well as "in the place of," i.e., as replacement or as representative, and that most often the two meanings overlap.[35] Christ has offered himself on our behalf, but also in our stead and in our name. In dying, he offers his life; in rising again he received a new life, to the end that, by the strength of his sacrifice and in union with him, we should sacrifice our life to receive it anew from the hand of God. When the Church offers this sacrifice to Christ in the Mass by commemorating it, she is permitting it to become potent in her and she is offering herself to the Father. Such is the meaning of the ecclesiastical sacramental "remembrance" (*anamnesis*); not only does it simply recall a past event, it renders that event immediately presently operative.[36] In offering the sacrifice of the Mass, the Church is saying *Amen, Yes,* to the sacrifice Christ has accomplished in her name. She is accepting the efficacy of this sacrament upon her. She is offering herself to the Father so as to lose herself with her Head in death and to receive the new life from the hand of God.

It must be recalled here that Christ is the "chief celebrant and priest" and that he is causing the Church to offer sacrifice. The sacrificial activity of the Church in the Mass consists in allowing herself to be offered and sacrificed by Christ. She allows herself to be caught up into his act of offering, she allows herself to be transformed by him into a true sacrifice, i.e., into the Body of the Lord who is offering himself.[37] In the sacrifice of the Mass there occurs a real, if derivative, consecration of the Mystical Body.

This City, redeemed whole and entire, that is to say the assembly of the company of the saints, is offered to God as a universal sacrifice by the High Priest who, under the guise of a slave, went so far as to offer himself for us in his passion, in order to make of us the body of so great a Head. . . . The sacrifice in its totality is we ourselves. . . . And this sacrifice the Church does not cease to celebrate in the Sacrament of the Altar, right well known to the faithful, in which it is shown unto her that in this which she is offering she is herself being offered.[37ᵃ]

249

But Teilhard was speaking of a consecration, not only of the Church, but of the cosmos. In order to determine to what extent such language is justified, two apparently opposed aspects of the sacrifice of the Mass must be taken into consideration. As sacrifice it connotes totality, but as sacramental sacrifice it connotes imperfection and therefore limitation. All true sacrifice connotes totality. Sacrifice is the pre-eminent act of worship which can only be offered to a real or presumed divinity,[38] because man is here expressing the fact that God is for him *God*, that is, everything. Offering a sacrifice signifies recognizing God as the source of all that we have and of all that we are and recognizing him as the one and only destiny and end toward which we are oriented with all that we possess.[39] Sacrifice is a total and absolute consecration of self. A total consecration, for man, of himself, includes a consecration of the whole of his world. Man is in fact himself enmeshed in a web of relations with his fellows and of bonds with the material world. When man is consecrating himself entirely to God, recognizing him as man's first origin and last end, he likewise sees the whole world of his fellows and of things as coming from God and leading back to God. He accepts in gratitude all the good as a gift of God and he submits in patience to suffering as a cross sent him by God. All the faculties and all the potentialities that are his and those of his world become for him so many divine missions and assignments; he seeks to please God in all his relations with his fellows and with the world. Every circumstance, every thing becomes for him a site on which he can encounter God and his good pleasure. Everything becomes precious and holy for man, divine gift and divine task. And at the same time, all the other values pale in the light of Him who appears behind every value. Such is Teilhard's frame of mind when he is speaking of the consecration of the world for the believer:

To reach those priceless layers is to experience, with equal truth, that one has need of everything and that one has need of nothing. Everything is needed because the world will never be large enough to provide our taste for action with the means of grasping God, or our thirst for undergoing with the possibility of being invaded by Him. And yet nothing is needed; for as the only reality which can satisfy us lies beyond the transparencies in which it is mirrored, everything that fades away and dies between us and it will only serve to give reality back to us with greater purity. Everything means both everything and nothing to me; everything is God to me and everything is dust to me.[40]

Attachment to the earth and detachment from the earth, the willingness to enjoy its beauty in gratitude and to sacrifice this beauty, the inclination to develop oneself entirely and to the limit and to lose oneself entirely and unreservedly—all of this is included in the spirit of Christian sacrifice. All of these attitudes and all of these acts can bring us closer to God.[41] And since, through the sacrament of the sacrifice of the Mass, Christ is giving to the Church the spirit of sincere sacrifice, he is operating in her all these dispositions. He thus grants to her to seek and to see, to serve and to encounter the Father in everything. *He consecrates the whole world for her.*

But this is accomplished sacramentally and therefore imperfectly and so the manner of its accomplishment is still to be perfected. This observation will prevent a misunderstanding that could be provoked by Teilhard's words and defines more precisely the nexus between the eucharistic consecration and the cosmic consecration. None of the spiritual attitudes enumerated above forms an actual definitive sacrifice which would consecrate man entirely to God. None of them expresses the totality of this consecration as such. The totality can be expressed and actualized only by an act which encompasses the whole of life. Our personal existence, our human community, our relationship to the world remain tainted by sin, by the revolt against God and by defection from God; so the ultimate act consists in death and resurrection, the death in which man loses himself entirely together with his world, and the resurrection in which he accepts everything from God as a renewed gift.

Christ has accomplished this act of ultimate offering. For the human community and for the Church, the sacrifice will not be accomplished until the end of time.[42] The Church is living in an interlude, a time between the past accomplishment of the sacrifice of Christ and the ultimate accomplishment and consummation of this sacrifice. In that time between, the Church celebrates the sacraments and especially the sacrifice of the Mass, in which she "shows forth the Lord's death, until he come."[43] On the one hand, she shows forth the death and Resurrection of the Lord, commemorating the sacrifice which he himself accomplished once for all and looking to the Lamb immolated before the altar of God.[44] On the other hand, she lives in the expectation of his return, wherein the sacrifice of the Head will be perfected in the Body. By and in the power of the sacrifice accomplished by the Lord, she advances toward the accomplishment of her own sacrifice. The point of intersection of the two lines is always the sacrifice of the Mass. In the Mass, the Lord renders present in the heart of the Church his sacrifice already accomplished; in the Mass, he consecrates the Church and the world to the sacrifice that will be achieved in that Church. In the Mass, the sacrifice of Christ becomes the sacrifice of the Church; in the Mass, the totality of the gift made to God, which pertains to the essence of the sacrificial act, is expressed as already actualized and realized in Christ and as still to be actualized and realized in the Church.

In the Mass, as we have seen, Christ consecrates the Church as an offering to the Father. He does this not in the sense that the ultimate sacrifice is already accomplished in the Church, but rather in the sense that he is preparing that sacrifice there. The consecration of the Church and of her world is therefore not yet accorded to the Church in the Mass as a perfect gift. The gift is still a task and assignment. In the power of the sacrifice accomplished by Christ, the Church must advance along the path of the ultimate accomplishment of this sacrifice within herself. The Mass is not an actualization of the ultimate consecration of the Church and of the world; it is only an initial consecration, in the power of which mankind can and must consecrate itself and the world in ever-increasing extent and intensity, in preparation for the hour at which the Lord himself will accomplish in mankind the final and ultimate consecration. André Cruiziat, writing from a slightly different point of view, quite rightly remarks: "The Eucharist is a sign in time of a reality that will be fulfilled and accomplished outside of time. . . . It is a dynamic call to the deepest human unity. . . .

But it is not yet that unity fully accomplished. It is but a bread of wayfarers who are making the Church."[45]

The consecration will never be complete during the terrestrial existence of the Church nor during the personal life of the individual Christian. In every man, in the human community and in the world, there still lives the power of sin. Pleasure, sloth, ambition, and all the forms of egotism are constantly swerving the values and the potentialities of man and of the world from their orientation to God and to the true community of love among men on earth. They are continually muddying and obscuring the divine transparency of things. In order to seek and find God in all things, in order to serve the edification of the Body of Christ, every Christian personally and the Church as a whole must make a constant effort and fight a constant battle. The effort must be constantly renewed to keep the values of the earth and of human existence, and especially the progress of mankind in the fields of technology, economics and organization, steadily directed to the one and only goal and end, the true community of men in the common love of God. Never on earth will there be perfect peace; never will the consecration of the world be fully accomplished.

If, therefore, Teilhard's poetic outbursts on the cosmic consecration leave the impression that this is definitively accomplished by the words of the consecration pronounced by the priest, even as the bread and the wine are definitively transubstantiated by these words, this is due to a faulty or a false understanding. In the first place, the cosmic consecration is the task of all the priestly Christian people and not exclusively of the hierarchical priests. Furthermore and even more important, this consecration will never be completely accomplished so long as the Christian is a pilgrim on this earth. We may here again have an instance of that deliberate and forced optimism that we have already recognized in the thinking of Teilhard.[46] This optimism has a large portion of truth in it; the Church and Christians must in fact tend to this definitive and complete consecration of the whole world and of all the potentialities and values of things and of men. They must tend toward it, work and struggle for it. The perfect consecration must be the final end and goal. The Christian cannot set his sights any lower.

But he must also know that he will never enter into the Promised Land so long as he is upon this earth. He will constantly be finding his holiest endeavors ending in disappointment. What he had thought to be victories will change into defeats. The final victory will be given only by the Lord when he comes again.

Clearly the central place held by the eucharistic celebration in this consecration of the world comes out. In this celebration, we commemorate the fact that the sacrifice has been accomplished and that the consecration has been consummated in Christ for us and for all men of good will. In that celebration, we hear the words spoken into the very midst of our anguished disillusionments and our trials: "Be of good cheer; I have overcome the world."[47] The eucharistic consecration renders present, in the life of the Church Militant of today, the consummated consecration and the final victory. In this celebration, the victorious Lord comes in power into the midst of his own, his faithful ones. In this celebration, Christians receive the pledge that the resistances in the world and in the heart of each and every one of them, opposed to the kingdom of love, have been overcome by Christ. In the Eucharist are renewed the faith and the hope which enable the Christian to persevere in the good fight. In the Eucharist is nurtured the charity which deploys all things in the service of the future Kingdom and which is ready to lose all things in exchange for this pearl of great price. In the Eucharist, we have the Body and the Blood that have been delivered over unto death and have been resurrected again unto life, the focus and the home from which all Christians are sent forth consecrated and strengthened to go their way through the changing times toward the final accomplishment and consummation of the cosmic sacrifice. In the Eucharist, they are consecrated and nourished by Christ to fulfill to the end their task and assignment within mankind and in the world. In the Eucharist, which imparts the definitive and complete consecration to the first fruits of the old earth, there lies the point of departure for the consecration of mankind and of his world, a consecration which progresses slowly, painfully, more often than not imperceptibly but nonetheless irresistibly; for "the kingdom of God cometh not with observation."[48]

If Teilhard's words on the cosmic consecration be considered from this point of view, they in no way involve any depreciation of the sacramental celebration of the Eucharist. On the contrary, it is seen to be the ultimate gift that makes Christendom able to fulfill the task that remains. The broad vistas of a consecration of the whole world will bring Christians back with still greater fervor to the Eucharist in which the Lord of the World is consecrating them to a task and giving them their wayfarers' bread.

In each of the three great theological and spiritual motifs we find an analogous structure: a universal diaphany of Christ, resting upon the concrete form of the Gospel epiphany; a cosmic edifice of the Body of Christ, built round an axis which is the body of the Church; a consecration of the entire world, radiating out from the sacramental consecration of the bread and the wine in the Mass. And in each of these motifs we find a clear-cut eschatological perspective. This homogeneity of structure, which Teilhard did not highlight and indeed may not himself have suspected, favors the genuinity of his spiritual vision. We must note that he had scarcely any contact with contemporary theologizing; yet his central ideas in his spirituality are in perfect harmony with the favorite motifs of this theology of our day. His spirituality is eucharistic, ecclesiological, oriented both to the earthly values and to the final transcendent consummation; above all, it is pronouncedly Christo-centric. The speculations which he sometimes risked in the realm of theological "metaphysic" have proven quite insubstantial and may be considered to be completely outmoded. But the theology implicitly contained in his spiritual vision is at once authentically modern and traditional in the best sense of the word; it reflects the eternal youth of the ancient Catholic truth.

In conclusion, we would underscore still another particular aspect of the Teilhardian spirituality. The three motifs round which it is grouped, namely the Incarnation, the Church and the Eucharist, are the three mysteries which pre-eminently reveal to us the divine initiative in salvation, the redemptive intervention in the life of mankind; in these mysteries, therefore, mankind takes cognizance of his own basic impotence.[49] Can Teilhard's marked preference for these motifs be said to have been purely accidental?

Do not his spirituality, his Christian experience, and his reflection provide instead a spontaneous corrective to the somewhat unilateral and slanted nature of his theoretical view of the world as we have felt that view could be explained on the basis of the polemical and apologetic content of his work? There Teilhard seemed to be underestimating the power of evil and thus derogating the joy of the Redemption. There also he seemed to be presenting the great overall lines of the human ascent as straight lines, as realizing or at least approaching their final terminus by their own immanent power. Now, the crucial components and forces of this ascent proved to have been formed and molded by a re-creative intervention of the divine love taking pity upon the culpable impotence of men. By the Incarnation, the Father actually is engendering himself a Son within the human family, a Son through whom he restores forever and in more glorious fashion the original divine image. This man constituted by God is the only way by which humanity can approach God. The Church is the human community gathered together by God in and out of all tongues and all races. The outpouring of the Holy Spirit breaks down the walls of separation erected by a hard and aggressive egotism between races, nations, cliques, and social categories. In this community gathered together by God and animated by the Spirit of God, the solidarity of the human family is freed from the threatening anguish and from fatal destruction by redemptive love. In the Eucharist, finally, we have the point of insertion where the word of God sanctifies the material world. In it, man recognizes and admits his true life, his real strength, his finest endeavor and his noblest love to come from God and to be nurtured by God. In these three mysteries, which inwardly sustain the ascent of mankind, the grace of God passes through the immanent powers of man, to convince man of his own impotence. Anyone who recognizes in these mysteries the hidden axis of mankind's progress can commit all his human powers to the realization of the final destiny; his optimism is, in the final analysis, the optimism of the Redemption.

LIST OF ABBREVIATIONS

Cahiers   –*Cahiers Pierre Teilhard de Chardin*, Seuil, Paris, 1958 ff.

CT   –*Construire la terre* (*Cahiers*, I), extracts from unpublished works, Seuil, Paris, 1958.

Cuénot   –C. Cuénot, *Pierre Teilhard de Chardin, les grandes étapes de son évolution,* Plon, Paris, 1958.

Dz   –H. Denzinger, *Enchiridion symbolorum* . . . , ed. K. Rahner, Herder, Freiburg, 1953.

Genèse   –Pierre Teilhard de Chardin, *Genèse d'une pensée: lettres* (*1914–1919*), presented by A. Teillard-Chambon and M. H. Begouën, Grasset, Paris, 1961.

GZ   –*Le Groupe zoologique humain*, Albin Michel, Paris, 1956 (written in 1949).

Hymne   –*Hymne de l'univers*, Seuil, Paris, 1961 (under this title were published a series of "mystical" texts, including *La Messe sur le monde*).

LV   –*Lettres de voyage* (1923–1939), collected by C. Aragonnès, Grasset, Paris, 1956.

MD   –*Le Milieu divin* (*Oeuvres*, IV), Seuil, Paris, 1957 (composed in 1926–1927).

257

NLV   –*Nouvelles lettres de voyage (1939–1955)*, collected by C. Aragonnès, Grasset, Paris, 1957.

Oeuvres   –*Oeuvres de Pierre Teilhard de Chardin*, 7 vols., Seuil, Paris, 1955–1963. *PH* and *MD* constitute Vols. I and IV. The other volumes include *L'Apparition de l'homme, La vision du passé, L'Avenir de l'homme, L'Énergie humaine, L'Activation de l'énergie*, being various published and unpublished essays from different periods. It is therefore preferable to avoid these global titles.

PH   –*Le Phénomène humain (Oeuvres, I)*, Seuil, Paris, 1955 (composed in 1938–1940, revised in 1947–1948).

Revue   –*Revue Teilhard de Chardin*, ed. *Société Pierre Teilhard de Chardin*, Brussels, 1960 ff.

Tresmontant–C. Tresmontant, *Introduction à la pensée de Teilhard de Chardin*, Seuil, Paris, 1956.

Italics in the quotations are those of Teilhard himself, unless otherwise indicated.

NOTES

PREFACE

[1] *La Messe sur le Monde* (1923), *Le Milieu divin* (1926–27), *Le Phénomène humain* (1938–40), *Le Groupe zoologique humain* (1949).

[2] Cf. I Pet. 3: 15.

CHAPTER 1

[1] *Le Coeur de la matière*, 1950.

[2] C. Cuénot, *Pierre Teilhard de Chardin, les grandes étapes de son évolution* (Paris: Plon, 1958); Eng. trans., *Teilhard de Chardin: A Biographical Study*, tr. by V. Colimore (Baltimore: Helicon, 1965). Cf. also: P. Leroy, *Pierre Teilhard de Chardin tel que je l'ai connu* (Paris: Plon, 1958); G. Magliore and H. Cuypers, *Présence de Pierre Teilhard de Chardin: L'Homme, la pensée* (Paris: Éd. Univ., 1961); J. V. Kopp, *Teilhard de Chardin* (Tielt: Lannoo, 1961).

[3] H. Bremond, *Le Charme d'Athènes* (Paris: Bloud et Gay), pp. 29–30, cited in Cuénot, p. 16, Eng. trans., p. 4.

[4] *Gènese*, p. 37. The English translation of this volume appeared under the title *The Making of a Mind: Letters from a Soldier-Priest, 1914–1919* (New York: Harper & Row, 1961).

[5] Teilhard wrote to her in 1914–19, several times a week; the letters have been published under the title *Genése d'une pensée* (Paris: Grasset, 1961). Marguerite's letters have unfortunately not been preserved, so it cannot be decided to what extent she may have inspired the ideas of Teilhard. She had for a long time been playing an active part in the renewal of secondary Christian teaching in France; later, under the pseudonym of Claude Aragonnès, she was to win a place in French literature.

[6] *Genèse*, p. 115: "to reflect a little on my own self." Eng. trans., p. 101.

[7] Most of these essays, numbering sixteen between 1916 and 1919, were not written for publication (*Genèse*, p. 52). One of them, *La nostalgie du front*, was published in an abridgement in the *Études* of November, 1917. Recently there have been published: *Le Christ dans la matière, trois histoires comme Benson* (1916), and *La puissance spirituelle de la matière* (1919), in *Hymne*, pp. 39–58 and 59–75. The *histoires comme Benson* pose a problem which may be of great importance for a definitive evaluation of Teilhard's spirituality. An imaginary friend here reports three visions in which he sees the Sacred Heart spread itself over the entire world. The general inclination is to see in this the mystical experiences of Teilhard. There seems little doubt that the protagonist is indeed

Teilhard himself. But I do doubt that we here have to do with mystical experiences properly speaking. The reference to Benson and the subtle and elegant literary form indicate rather theoretical reflections clothed in the mantle of a vision. This impression is strengthened by Teilhard's own words (*Genèse*, pp. 166, 173; Eng. trans., pp. 150, 160).

[8] P. Leroy, *Pierre Teilhard de Chardin* (Paris, 1958), p. 28.

[9] Cf. below, p. 255. The text has been published in *Hymne*, pp. 17–37 (Eng. trans., pp. 19–37). On the dating, cf. Cuénot, p. 71, n. 2; Eng. trans., p. 50, n. 4; Wildiers, in *Hymne*, p. 13; Eng. trans., *Hymn of the Universe* (New York: Harper & Row, 1961), p. 13.

[10] Cf. Cuénot, p. 85; Eng. trans., p. 61.

[11] Cf. Cuénot, p. 81 f.; Eng. trans., p. 58.

[12] G. B. Barbour, "At Work in the Field," in *The World of Teilhard* (Baltimore: Helicon, 1961), p. 26.

[13] *Lettres de voyage 1923–1939* and *Nouvelles lettres de voyage 1939–1955* (Paris: Grasset, 1956–57).

[14] Published in *Oeuvres* IV (Paris: Seuil, 1957); below, pp. 200 f. Eng. trans., *The Divine Milieu* (New York: Harper & Row, 1960).

[15] This is difficult to harmonize with the fragments from letters cited by Cuénot, p. 150; Eng. trans., p. 143.

[16] Published in *Oeuvres* I (Paris: Seuil, 1955); Eng. trans., *The Phenomenon of Man* (New York: Harper & Row, 1959).

[17] *NLV*, 97, note 1. Eng. trans., *Letters from a Traveller*, p. 301.

[18] Paris: Albin Michel, 1956.

[19] Letter of October 13, 1933, in Cuénot, p. 264; Eng. trans., p. 213.

[20] Cf. below, pp. 118 f.

[21] Letter of July 4, *Genèse*, p. 72; Eng. trans. *The Making of a Mind* (New York: Harper & Row, 1961), p. 59.

[22] Letter of October 12, 1951, in P. Leroy, *Pierre Teilhard de Chardin tel que je l'ai connu* (Paris: Plon, 1958), p. 57 f.

[23] Letters of August–September, 1929, in Cuénot, p. 149 f.; Eng. trans., p. 118.

[24] Letter of July 31, 1930, in P. Grenet, *Teilhard de Chardin, un évolutionniste chrétien* (Paris: Seghers, 1961), p. 26: "I am indeed fortunate to be involved in this business. Such unexpected developments serve merely to intensify and accentuate my love for the Divine Influence guiding the world."

[25] J. Lafarge, in *The World of Teilhard*, ed. R. T. Francoeur (Baltimore: Helicon, 1961) pp. 4 f.

[26] Letter of October 12, 1951, in P. Leroy, *op. cit.*, p. 58.

[27] *Cahiers*, II, 35.

[28] *NLV*, 97 f., October 28, 1948; Eng. trans., *Letters from a Traveller*, p. 301.

[29] Cf. below, p. 42.

[30] *Genèse*, p. 158.

[31] Letter of October 15, 1926, in Cuénot, pp. 95 f.; Eng. trans., p. 70.

[32] *Oeuvres*, III, 265. For other similar remarks, sometimes more drastically worded, cf. *Oeuvres*, V, 11; Cuénot, pp. 263, 339 f., 392.

[33] *Oeuvres*, II, 362.

³⁴ Letter of May 16, 1936, in P. Grenet, *op. cit.*, p. 145.

³⁵ On several occasions in Cuénot, pp. 264 f.; Eng. trans., p. 213 f.

³⁶ C. d'Armagnac, "Philosophy of Nature and Method in Father Teilhard de Chardin," (French) in *Archives de philosophie*, XX (1957), 16. On the Teilhardian method, cf. also: G. Crespy, *La Pensée théologique de Teilhard de Chardin* (Paris: Editions Universitaires, 1961), pp. 25–26. Also in *Recherches et Débats*, 40 (October, 1962), "Essais sur Teilhard de Chardin," F. Russo, "La Méthode du P. Teilhard de Chardin"; Cl. Soucy, "Teilhard de Chardin est-il un philosophe?"—Cf. especially M. Barthélemy-Madaule, *Bergson et Teilhard de Chardin* (Paris: Editions du Seuil, 1963), pp. 564–631.

³⁷ Cf. d'Armagnac, *loc. cit.*

³⁸ In his last years, Teilhard took notice of the divergent meanings of the term *phenomenology*, as witness his letter of April 11, 1953: "I admit that my 'phenomenology' is not that of Husserl and of Merleau-Ponty. But how to find another word to define a *Weltanschauung* based on the study of the development of the phenomenon? . . . In fact, if I understand their theory aright, the 'phenomenologists' right to that title is vitiated to the extent that they seem to ignore one of the most essential dimensions of the phenomenon, which is that it shall not only be perceived by an individual knower but shall also signify (additionally and simultaneously) to this individual particular knower that that knower is a part of a universal process of *noogenesis*. I do not understand how anyone can call himself a 'phenomenologist' and yet write whole books without a single mention of Cosmogenesis, of "Evolution"! Sartre and Merleau-Ponty (and the other Sorbonne philosophers) are surely still operating in a pre-Galilean universe" (Cited by d'Armagnac, *op. cit.*, p. 17). Clearly Teilhard had not an accurate grasp of the spirit animating these phenomenologists.

³⁹ *PH*, 21; Eng. trans., *The Phenomenon of Man*, p. 29.

⁴⁰ *PH*, 21; Eng. trans., p. 29; cf. below, pp. 40 f.

⁴¹ Cf. below, Chapter II.

⁴² Letter of October 13, 1933; cf. above, n. 19 to Chapter 1.

⁴³ Letter of October 11, 1936; "an ultraphysics (the true *phusiké* of the Greeks, I imagine) where matter and spirit would be embraced in one single coherent and *homogeneous* explanation of the World" (in Cuénot, p. 264 f.; Eng. trans., p. 213). For the parallel between the *Physics* of Aristotle and this Phenomenology of Teilhard, cf. D. Dubarle, "A propos du phénomène humain du Pére Teilhard de Chardin," in *La vie intellectuelle*, XXVII (March, 1956), 6–25.

⁴⁴ Cf. below, p. 41.

⁴⁵ *Oeuvres*, III (1930), 242 f.

⁴⁶ Excellent studies on the thought of Teilhard from this point of view are: C. d'Armagnac, "Philosophie de la nature et méthode chez le Père Teilhard de Chardin," in *Archives de philosophie*, XX (1957), 5–41; O. A. Rabut, O.P., *Dialogue avec Teilhard de Chardin* (Paris: Cerf, 1958). English translation, *Teilhard de Chardin: A Critical Study* (New York: Sheed and Ward, 1961). In P. Grenet's *Pierre Teilhard de Chardin ou le philosophe malgré lui* (Paris: Beauchesne, 1960), criticism is also concentrated mainly on this point of the Teilhardian method. Grenet's later brief work, *Teilhard de Chardin, un évolutionniste chrétien*, shows many earmarks of an apology for the earlier drastic criticism.

[47] O. A. Rabut, O.P., *Dialogue avec Teilhard de Chardin* (Paris: Cerf, 1958), p. 204: "To the scientist and scholar, this method is suspect, partial, and annoying. The philosopher is distressed by the lack of detail, which seems to him almost irresponsible. To the ordinary layman, the results are striking, astonishingly expressive and (partly) true. Beyond all the uncertainties of science, beyond all the cautious procedure of rational method, there is doubtless scope for the penetrating gaze which discovers before it can prove. This is Teilhard's aim: to coincide with what is, in fact, the intelligible movement of the universe." (English trans., *Teilhard de Chardin: A Critical Study*, p. 241.)

[48] Cf. below, pp. 61 ff.

[49] *PH*, 22; Eng. trans., p. 30.

[50] Cf. below, n. 20 to Chapter 4.

[51] Cf. below, p. 110.

[52] Cf. text cited above, pp. 8 f.

[53] Cf. below, Chapter 5.

[54] Cf. below, n. 35 to Chapter 6.

[55] An example of concordism on the first point: "The Bible . . . describes the gradual development of life on earth, the separation of the water from the dry land, the creation of plants, fishes, birds, reptiles, four-footed animals and finally man. The progressive development signalled by this biblical narrative of creation . . . has been confirmed by science" (H. Kuhn, *Het ontwaken der mensheid*, tr. H. Meijer-von Arnim [Het Spectrum, undated but later than 1954], p. 9). An example of concordism on the second point: "One (theory on the origin of the universe) proposed by Lemaître and seconded by Gamow, Herman and Alpher, envisages a universe beginning five thousand million years ago with the explosion of a single primordial atom. . . . If eventually, as could well happen, the first of these two theories should prove to be scientifically demonstrable, we should be faced with an example of Nature's telling us something that had previously been known only through Revelation" (J. E. Bruns, "Cosmogenesis and Theology," in *The World of Teilhard*, ed. R. T. Francoeur [Baltimore: Helicon, 1961], p. 168). A primordial explosion is not the same thing as creation!

[56] A. Brunner, in *Stimmen der Zeit*, 165 (1960), 211. P. Grenet even goes so far as to speak of "ultra-concordism" (in *Pierre Teilhard de Chardin ou le philosophe malgré lui* [Paris, Beauchesne, 1960], p. 14). It is a curious thing to note how certain Catholic champions of evolution are suspect of a new form of concordism. Thus the first account of creation is held to provide a confirmation of the polygenetic origin of the human race; cf. a remark of M. Pouget, cited in J. Renie, *Les Origines de l'humanité* (Paris: Vitte, 1950), p. 102.

[57] *PH*, 22; Eng. trans., p. 30.

[58] Letter of August 4, 1916, *Genèse*, p. 148; Eng. trans., p. 116.

[59] Pope Pius XII, in his allocution to the members of the Pontifical Academy of Sciences on November 30, 1941, spoke of "the deep-seated inclination of your intellect to achieve an ambitious synthesis of the sciences . . . in conformity with the order of creation" and noted that "our soul ardently desires to mount toward God by the ladder of the knowledge of this world" (AAS 33 [1914], 509, 512).

This would indicate that the deepest motivating force of scientific research is the longing for the one Light, fully realized only in the beatific vision, to which corresponds on this earth the revelation of faith "through a glass darkly."

60 *Comment je vois* (1948), p. 1: "We must be careful not to confuse 'concordism' with 'coherence.' We are all familiar with certain childish efforts at overhasty harmonizations which confounded the levels and sources of knowledge and, because of their artificiality, resulted only in unstable accommodations. But these caricatures of harmonization should not blind us to the fact that the essential criterion . . . of truth is the ability to sustain an indefinite enucleation, not only consistently free of any internal contradiction but also productive of a positively structured totality whose components become steadily more mutually compatible and complementary." (Cf. the letter of April 14, 1953, in Cuénot, p. 477; Eng. trans., pp. 395–396).

61 *PH*, 316; Eng. trans., pp. 283–284.

62 C. d'Armagnac, "Philosophie de la nature et méthode chez le Père Teilhard de Chardin," *Archives de philosophie* XX (1957), 34: "The Universe of phenomena plays an equivocal role, being *simultaneously token and cloak* of a transcendent Presence.

63 *PH*, 348; Eng. trans., p. 313: "The findings and suggestions—*always ambiguous* beyond a certain point—furnished by experience" (*Italics* ours—Author's Note).

64 Cf. below, pp. 231 ff.

65 Cf. above, p. 15, note 7 to Chapter 1, and *Hymne de l'Univers*, pp. 39 f.

66 *Cahiers*, 2, p. 35.

CHAPTER 2

1 *Un phénomène de contre-evolution en biologie ou la peur de l'existence* (1940) cited in *Cahiers*, II, 153.

2 A report on the conference on "Biological Evolution," probably from the pen of Teilhard, has this summing-up: "Obstinate and fruitful rivalry between the two complementary attitudes represented, the one by Neo-Darwinism (purely external forces moulding living matter into various arrangements: chance combinations by natural selection), the other by Neo-Lamarckism (forces moulding biological composition ultimately interior and psychic: random interplay utilized or dominated by choice and invention)" (in *Études*, 263 [1949], 392; cf. *PH*, 111; Eng. trans., p. 120).

3 Note that an increasing number of competent scientists consider synthetic Neo-Darwinism a valid theory of the mechanisms of evolution: cf. M. Lamotte, "La théorie actuelle des mécanismes de l'évolution," in *L'Evolution et ses Mécanismes* (*Archives de Philosophie*, I [1960]). This article is one of the best expositions of Neo-Darwinism in French for the non-specialist.

4 Letter of September 28, 1950, in Cuénot, p. 352, n. 3.

5 *Oeuvres*, II (1956), 298, n. 2; cf. *PH*, 152, 242; *Oeuvres*, III, 214 f., 348.

6 Teilhard declared in 1950, in the course of a discussion on faith and evolution: "The idea of evolution . . . is no longer being presented by science except as a genuine phenomenology, entirely devoted to the study of a process

(chain of antecedents and consequents), with no intrusion into the realm of 'natures' and 'causes.' . . . A process is not a philosophical explanation" (*Oeuvres*, III, 347 f.). Teilhard's ideas exercised an undeniable influence on H. Breuil, "Soixante ans de découvertes de fossibles humains et préhumains," in *Bull. de litt. eccl.*, LVIII (1957), 104; and on M. M. Labourdette, who says on p. 147 of *Le Péché original et les origines de l'homme* (Paris: Alsatia, 1953): "Duration, time, *preparation* are always of crucial importance in this world. This seems to us to be the great law highlighted by the theory of evolution; and it is this which makes that theory fruitful."

[7] M. Allessandri, "Il pensiero di Pierre Teilhard de Chardin," in *Divinitas*, III (1959), 355: "There is nothing to prevent the Creator from imparting existence to animals of similar or divergent structure and constitution, wherever and whenever it pleases him."

[8] L. Monden, *Le Miracle signe de Salut* (*Museum Lessianum*, Theology Section 54), (Bruges: Desclée De Brouwer, 1960), p. 29: "In the hypothesis of a purely natural disposition and regulation of the universe, miracle would have no justification in good theology." Miracle is in fact nothing else than the translation into the sensibly *extra*ordinary of the *extra*ordinary love of God (p. 30).

[9] *Oeuvres*, III (1930), 215.

[10] This obviously does not mean that the believer and the philosopher (and every man and every scientist and scholar is a latent philosopher!) should not recognize that all the intracosmic causes are ultimately sustained by the single First Cause, the Creator of all being and of all operation.

In this connection, we might mention Sertillanges' reflections on the appearance of new forms of being and life in the course of the earth's history: "It may be questioned whether the first of these theories, 'creationism,' the traditional theory, undoubtedly most in line with the popular and anthropomorphic idea of creation, is not . . . the least satisfying.

"Abrupt implosions, with no nexus of continuity with the past . . . is an idea which no naturalist will ever find it easy to swallow. And what of the philosopher? He knows that an act of creation is not a becoming and must therefore suppose, on the grounds of this 'creationist' theory, that there is something new in the world *without anything having happened*, and further that, if the physical universe is in fact a universally solidary complex, then this irruption from outside is equivalent, every time and no matter how tiny the effect produced, to *the creation of another universe* [italics ours—Author]. It can readily be seen therefore that for him the hypothesis involves much that is bizarre." (A. D. Seritillanges, *Dieu ou rien?* [Paris: Flammarion, 1931], I, 98 f.).

[11] St. Thomas, *Summa Theologica*, I, q. 47, a. 3.

[12] *Oeuvres*, III (1925), pp. 141, 147; cf. pp. 36–39.

[13] *GZ*, 9.

[14] *PH*, 43; Eng. trans., p. 48.

[15] Teilhard speaks of the "*étoffe de l'Univers*," and also incorporates into his own vocabulary the German term "*Weltstoff*." These words designate the concrete reality comprising the universe, a reality at once corporeal and endowed with interiority: it is considered in its most generic common traits, but together with its energies and potentialities which are reduced to act in the form of life and mental operation. Thus the notion is much richer than the old sense

of the word *matter*. Teilhard coined the expression deliberately to avoid the dualism and oversimplified dichotomy of matter and thought. —(Author's Note.)

[We have, for equally weighty reasons, deliberately chosen in this translation the English term *fabric*. We wished to avoid the excessively material and somewhat foreign sound of *stuff*. But there is a deeper reason for our choice. Unless "*Weltstoff*" is to revert to nothing more helpful than precisely "material to be worked up in manufacture or out of which anything is to be or may be formed," it must be made to mean something more generic. Now Webster, from whom the above definition of *stuff* has been taken, defines *fabric* as "a structure; . . . cloth woven or knit from fibers," thus clearly highlighting the notion of structuring and of an advance over the primordial stuff. Note precisely that in Teilhard's enucleation, the "*Weltstoff*" *itself* proceeds in a way that constitutes "a 'convolution' of the fabric about itself"; now, either this is an improper simile or else the "*Weltstoff*" is *ab initio* more than *mere* primordial stuff, contains *within itself* in potency the very convolutions it later assumes. *Fabric* incidentally is given as Webster's fifth definition of *Stuff;* hence it cannot be maintained that our choice tips the scales too heavily on the side of manufacture! —(Translator's Note.)]

16 *Oeuvres*, V (1945), 137; Eng. trans., *The Future of Man* (New York: Harper & Row, 1964), p. 105.

17 *Oeuvres*, III (1942), 312–313.

18 In the case of the tobacco virus, 17×10^6; *Oeuvres*, III, 314.

19 Cf. eg., *Oeuvres*, V, 138 f. (Eng. trans., p. 106 f.); *GZ*, 18 f. Cf. also the graphic demonstration of the truly astronomical magnitude of these numbers; the diameter of the Milky Way, measured in *centimeters* (!), is approximately of the order of 10^{21}.

20 V. J. Koningsberger, "Una quaelibet vita," in *De evolutieleer na honderd jaar* (Haarlem: Bohn, 1959), p. 249.

21 E.g., *PH*, 62 f.; Eng. trans., p. 64–65. The translation by "centripetal" and "centrifugal" in the Dutch translation seems to me somewhat deceptive. Teilhard seems to have borrowed the notion of the "interior" of things from the philosopher M. Blondel (cf. C. d'Armagnac, "De Blondel à Teilhard, nature et intériorité," in *Archives de philosophie*, XXI [1958], 302 f.). Teilhard often uses such terms as "consciousness" or "mental operation" (e.g., *PH*, 53, 334 [Eng. trans., 57, 308]; *GZ*, 36, n. 1) to designate this "interior" even in the inorganic world. Such a use of terms borrowed from the animal and human world does not seem advisable (C. d'Armagnac, "Philosophie de la nature et méthode chez le Père Teilhard de Chardin," in *Archives de philosophie*, XX [1957], 23 f.; B. Delfgaauw, *Het vraagstuk van het materialisme* [Baarn: Wereldvenster, 1961], p. 11 f.). In the first place, even if it be admitted that every material being is in some senses analogical to the human being (cf. below in this same note), there are nonetheless certain notions and terms which ought to be retained exclusively for the specific definition of living and human beings. Indeed Teilhard himself admits that the term *life* is inapplicable below a certain definite degree of interiority (*GZ*, 22 f.). It is a ticklish business to talk of "consciousness" among the animals, even the higher animals, or of a "psychic" life in the case of plants. *A fortiori*, then, in the case of a hydrogen molecule, such predication would involve "losing contact with the whole of experience"

(d'Armagnac, *loc. cit.*). This is a weak point, at least in vocabulary, in Teilhard's phenomenology. And Teilhard attempts to justify it by an appeal to a philosophical argument. Moreover, any surreptitious introduction of these notions into the inanimate world entails the danger of the penetration of other uncritical notions. Teilhard himself eviscerates in this way the category of finality (*Oeuvres*, III, 134–136), a category which his phenomenology could have brought to the fore and really highlighted, but which in fact that phenomenology only half acknowledges in a fashion so enigmatic as to smack of awkwardness.

This psychological terminology does, however, contain elements of truth. In the first place, it points up the fact that man necessarily conceives everything material on analogy with himself, that man is "the measure of all things." Human thought has its origin in the perception which is man's empirical experience of individual unity, even in the nonhuman world, on an analogy with his experience of his own unity. All human language dealing with the infra-human world uses notions and words whose full meaning emerges only at the human level.

In the second place, this terminology expresses the fact that there exists in matter as such a potency and an aptitude to become living, conscious, even human matter. Did not this aptitude exist, then life, and human life, would not be the highest form of existence of matter itself. And it is one of the dogmas of Christian philosophy, on which Teilhard insists with good right, that human life is precisely that.

[The French translator notes that he is, throughout the preceding paragraph, translating by "matter" the Dutch word "*stof.*" We have preferred, in the interests of a completely faithful rendering and also in deference to the more familiar terms of the English philosophico-cosmological vocabulary, to use "matter" also above. But a more faithfully Teilhardian rendering would substitute for "matter" throughout in the preceding paragraph the expression "fabric of the universe." —(Translator's Note.)]

[22] *GZ*, 18.

[23] *GZ*, 35.

[24] *GZ*, 34; *Oeuvres*, V, 327 f.

[25] *Oeuvres*, III (1942), 313.

[26] *Ibid.*, p. 315.

[27] Miller, USA, 1955.

[28] *GZ*, 26–30.

[29] *GZ*, 30–32.

[30] *GZ*, 42–45.

[31] *GZ*, 56–58; *Oeuvres*, V (1945), 144.

[32] *GZ*, 58–68.

[33] *GZ*, 68–73; *Oeuvres*, II (1951), 200–202.

[34] *GZ*, 79.

[35] *GZ*, 79.

[36] "*Reflexions sur l'Ultrahumain*," in Tresmontant, p. 52; this is not only the first time, it is also the only time this threshold has been crossed: *GZ*, 79, n. 1.

[37] *Oeuvres*, V (1942),115; Eng. trans., p. 67.

[38] *GZ*, 116.

[39] *GZ*, 117; cf. *PH*, 276 f.

[40] *GZ*, 23.

[41] *GZ*, 13.

[42] *PH*, 30; Eng. trans., *The Phenomenon of Man*, p. 36.

[43] *Oeuvres*, II (1954), 319.

[44] Cf. below, p. 61.

[45] *Oeuvres*, III (1928), 209.

[46] *PH*, 22; Eng. trans., p. 30.

[47] Against those who are not prepared to see in consciousness anything other than an epiphenomenon of no significance, Sertillanges quite rightly says: "The man who would speak seriously in this fashion would be a madman; any sane man talking this way is not serious. In short, the real author of such a remark is not the man making it but the system." (A. D. Sertillanges, *Dieu ou rien?* [Paris: Flammarion, 1933], I, 113).

[48] *GZ*, 4.

CHAPTER 3

[1] *Oeuvres*, III (1925), 142.

[2] *Oeuvres*, III (1942), 323 f.

[3] For what follows, we refer the reader to H. Renckens, *Israels visie op het verleden* (Tielt: Lannoo; 6th ed., 1960); G. Lindeskog, *Studien zum neutestamentlichen Schöpfungsgedanken* (Uppsala: Lundequist, 1952).

[4] Gen. 1: 1–2, 4.

[5] *Op. cit.*, p. 42.

[6] *Schöpfungsglaube und Evolutionstheorie* (Stuttgart: Kröner, 1955), p. 29.

[7] Eccles. 18: 1.

[8] Cf. "De evolutieleer en hat geloof," in *Nederlandse Katholieke Stemmen*, XLVI (1950), 271 f.; E. Mangenot, "Hexameron," in *Dict. de théol. cath.*, VI, col. 2335 ff.

[9] St. Thomas, *In II Sent.*, d. 12, q. 1, a. 2; cf. *Summa Theologica*, I, q. 74, a. 2.

[10] von Rad, *op. cit.*, p. 28.

[11] Renckens, *op. cit.*, p. 54.

[12] von Rad, *op. cit.*, p. 34.

[13] Deut. 4: 15–20.

[14] Isa. 55: 11.

[15] II Kings 22: 19 f.

[16] Gen. 1: 3 f.

[17] Diogenes Laertius, *Vita philosophorum*, III, 49, 61: on Plato.

[18] E.g., Isa. 51: 9 f.

[19] Lindeskog, *op. cit.*, p. 22.

[20] Renckens, *op. cit.*, pp. 68–70.

[21] H. Gunkel, *Genesis*, 3rd ed., p. 103; Renckens, *op. cit.*, pp. 71 f. Thus in placing the dualist cosmogonies, as belief in creation, on the same level as the biblical conception, G. Mensching ("Die Schöpfungs vorstellungen der alten Re-

ligionen," in *Schöpfungsglauben und Evolutionstheorie* [Stuttgart: Kröner, 1955], pp. 14–17) is forgetting this intention of the creation narrative. Yet nothing is more evident in that narrative.

[22] Renckens, *op. cit.*, p. 56.

[23] Lindeskog, *op. cit.*, p. 28; St. Thomas, *Summa Theologica*, I, q. 104, a. 1, ad 4.

[24] Lindeskog writes: "The drama of the celebration of the New Year did more than simply recall the original creation of the world by Yahweh; it further affirmed that Yahweh created the world anew at the beginning of the new year. Creation is not simply presented as a *creatio originalis;* there is also a *creatio continua* to be seen anew each year in the liturgical office" (p. 35). This involves some exaggeration in the matter of the religious feelings of Oriental antiquity: for the Israelite, the exodus and the creation were not myths; they were the beginning of history.

[25] St. Thomas, *Summa Theologica*, I, q. 104, a. 1, ad 4: "The conservation of things by God is accomplished not by a new operation on the part of God but because the operation by which he imparts being is sustained. This operation is accomplished extrinsically to motion and to time, even as the conservation of light in the atmosphere is accomplished by the sustained action of the sun." (Cf. S. T., I, q. 45, a. 3, ad 3; *De potentia*, q. 3, a. 3, ad 6.)

[26] A. D. Sertillanges, *L'Idée de création et ses retentissements en philosophie* (Paris: Aubier, 1945), pp. 67 f.: "In ordinary speech, we do not say that the universe is created at this moment, but rather that it has been created, that our soul has been created, etc. Yet in actual fact, the universe and every individual being is indeed suspended from God at every moment by this relation of dependence which is creation itself. Or, to put it better, each creature is suspended from God at once in respect of its being and in respect of its moments which are but the immanent measure of that being."

[27] As Lindeskog (*op. cit.*, pp. 28 ff.) rightly points out, the act of creation also has an eschatological aspect. But a detailed treatment of this point would lead us too far afield at this point.

[28] In Cuénot, p. 114; Eng. trans., p. 89.

[29] *Oeuvres*, III (1921), 39: "Rather than 'making' things, God 'makes them make themselves.' " Cf. (1930), p. 217.

[30] A. D. Sertillanges, *Dieu ou rien?* (Paris: Flammarion, 1933), I, 96.

[31] *Oeuvres*, III (1926), 188.

[32] See pp. 214 f. The principle cited holds also for the finality of creation. Since the being of things is entirely dependent on God, things are ordered to an end and seek this end in all their operations. This finality is included in the very nature of things; and this nature actualizes its effect only in accord with the laws of statistical probability. The fact that "chance" plays such a great part in evolution is no argument against the finality of evolution. On this point, cf. C. d'Armagnac, "Épistémologie et philosophie et de l'évolution," in *Archives de Philosophie*, I (1960), 158–161; Neo-Darwinism and finality. Cf. also O. A. Rabut, *Le Problème de Dieu inscrit dans l'évolution* (Paris: Cerf, 1963), e.g., pp. 43–44, 78 f. In this connection, Teilhard warns us that the perceptible phenomenon of the orientation evident in evolution should not be confused with finality in the strict sense of the word (*Oeuvres*, II [1954], 304, 8 note 1). Elsewhere he is less

cautious and shows a marked preference for a Neo-Lamarckian opinion (*Oeuvres*, III [1959] 360): he introduces into the biosphere a sort of "psychic force," "desire," "inventiveness" (*Oeuvres*, III [1925], 134–139), and posits "an 'innate' (and therefore scientifically inexplicable) preference on the part of the fabric of the universe for higher states of complexity and consciousness" (*Oeuvres*, III [1952], 369).

33 *Oeuvres*, V (1941), 104; Eng. trans., *The Future of Man*, p. 79.

34 "La messe sur le monde," in *Hymne*, p. 19: "Creation pulled by your magnetic power." *Oeuvres*, III, 323: "We now realize that this paradoxical movement is sustained by a Prime Mover who is in front. The branch mounts, not supported by its root below, but rather suspended from the future."

35 Apoc. 1: 8.

36 Cf. Chapter 10.

37 "Du Cosmos a la cosmogenèse" (1951), in Cuénot, pp. 354 f. (Eng. trans., p. 293) and *LV*, p. 107.

37ª And this misunderstanding is fostered and compounded by the pusillanimity of translators in hesitating to imitate Teilhard's own uninhibited inclination to coin new words. Evidently a translation of "Dieu évoluteur" as the "evolving God" renders incomparably more difficult for the English reader the transitive understanding of the appellation than does the word "Evolver" which we have here coined. —[Translator's Note.]

38 Cf. below, p. 238.

39 Perhaps Teilhard borrowed this expression from Sertillanges who writes: "We attain God in the proof from final causality to the point where his creative operation reveals itself by the ordering and progressive tendency of things which he directs inasmuch as he animates them and animates inasmuch as he creates them." (A. D. Sertillanges, *Dieu ou rien?* [Paris: Flammarion, 1933], p. 79.)

40 *Oeuvres*, III (1925), 142.

41 Cf. Appendix I, pp. 77 ff.

CHAPTER 4

1 *Oeuvres*, V (1942), pp. 122 f.; Eng. trans. *The Future of Man*, p. 93. For the subject matter of this Chapter and its positioning in the history of philosophy, cf. E. Borne's article, "Matière et esprit dans la philosophie de Teilhard," in *Recherches et Débats*, No. 40 (1962), 45–65.

2 *Dz.*, n. 1783.

3 Fourth Lateran Council, *ibid.*, n. 428.

4 When Teilhard speaks in this context of the "spirit," he has in mind exclusively the spiritual soul of man. He states this explicitly in a note in *Le Coeur de la matière* (1950). In 1934, he writes at the outset of *Comment je crois*: "I believe that the Universe is an Evolution! I believe that the Evolution proceeds toward Spirit! I believe that Spirit is consummated in the Personal! I believe that the supremely Personal is the Christ-Universal!" To this text we shall recur later (p. 120). In 1950, he was at pains to specify more precisely the third axiom: "I believe that Spirit, in Man, culminates in the Personal." This makes

it clear that it is a question not of a metaphysical definition of "Spirit," but rather of the historical and biological place of the spirit in our world. This intention had, moreover, been clearly apparent in the whole of *Comment je crois*. Therefore, when Teilhard writes: "the mind, seen from our side, is essentially the power of synthesis and organization" (*PH*, 288, Eng. trans., p. 259–260), we must not look in these words for a direct metaphysical definition of what "spirit" is, as such, but solely for a phenomenological approximation to the form in which the spiritual (=human) appears in the world. He thus corrects, if not the idea, at least the formulation of his essay *Esquisse d'un Univers personnel* (1935), in which he had written: "The purely spiritual is as unthinkable as the purely material. . . . Every spirit owes its reality and its nature to a particular type of universal synthesis. However 'pure' it be (indeed the purer, the better) it is expression and consummation of a genesis" (*Oeuvres*, VI, 75). But the context here showed clearly enough that Teilhard intended only to speak of the "spirit" insofar as it belongs to this terrestrial world.

⁵ *PH*, 22; Eng. trans., p. 30 refers to "basic assumptions." And *Oeuvres*, VII, 133: "The notion of centrocomplexity furnishes us with a criterion . . . to establish objectively the primacy of the Spirit."

⁶ Cf. above, pp. 42 ff.

⁷ *Comment je crois* (1934).

⁸ Cited in *Cahiers*, II, 144 f. Teilhard's review of his own spiritual development in *Le Coeur de la matière* (1950) presents us with a more turbulent picture: "As trained by my education and religion, I had always docilely admitted . . . a fundamental heterogeneity between Matter and Spirit, Body and Soul, Conscious and Unconscious: two 'substances' of different nature, two 'species' of Being, incomprehensibly associated in the living Composite, and with the first having to be maintained . . . at all costs to be but the servant, the slave (not to say the adversary) of the second, while the second (that is, the Spirit) was reduced, from that moment, in my eyes, to being nothing more than a Shadow. . . . Judge, therefore, what was my inner feeling of liberation and expansive glow, when my first step into an 'evolutive' Universe showed me that the dualism in which I had been till then immured was dissipating like fog at sunrise. Matter and Spirit, not two things, rather two *states*, two faces, of an identical cosmic fabric, depending on whether you look at it, or protract it, along the line . . . of its 'self-fabrication' or, on the contrary, along the line of its 'self-defabrication.' " See also *PH*, 327 f.; Eng. trans., p. 291 f.

⁹ *PH*, 343; Eng. trans., p. 307–308.

¹⁰ Cf. below, Chapter 10.

¹¹ M. L. Guérard des Lauriers, "La démarche de P. Teilhard de Chardin," in *Divinitas*, III (1959), 257.

¹² *Comment je crois* (1934).

¹³ 1933; in Cuénot, p. 268; Eng. trans., p. 217.

¹⁴ St. Thomas, *In librum de causis*, lect. 15: "Quod redeat ad essentiam suam reditione completa." Cf. *Summa Theologica*, I, q. 14, a. 2, ad 1: "*Redire ad essentiam suam nihil aliud est quam res subsistere in seipsa.*" On this Thomistic conception, cf. J. Webert, "Reflexio,' in *Mélanges Mandonnet* (Paris: Vrin, 1930), I, 285–325.

¹⁵ J. Mouroux, *Sens chretien de l'homme* (Paris: Aubier, 1945), pp. 108,

109; Eng. trans., *The Meaning of Man* (New York: Sheed & Ward, Inc., 1948), p. 116.

[16] St. Thomas, *Summa Theologica*, I, q. 14, a. 2, ad 3: "In knowing something as knowable (our intellect) knows the knowing itself"; II–II, q. 25, a. 2: "Love returns by nature upon itself. For it is the spontaneous movement of the lover to the beloved. Therefore if someone loves, he loves to love."

[17] Council of Vienne, 1311; Dz., n. 480 f.

[18] St. Thomas, *De potentia*, q. 3, a. 10: "Without the body, the soul does not have the perfection of its own nature, because it is not in itself a perfectly specific nature, but rather a part of human nature." Cf. *Comp. theol.*, c. 152.

[19] St. Thomas, *De spiritualibus creaturis*, a. 2, ad 8; cf. F. Malmberg, *Eén lichaam en één geest* (Utrecht: Het Spectrum, 1958), p. 211. Teilhard, *Oeuvres*, III, 188–189: "Precisely because he is spirit, his appearance necessarily assumed the form of a crowning consummation."

[20] St. Thomas, *Summa contra Gentiles*, III, c. 22: Cum vero; cf. *Comp. theol.*, c. 149. It is almost incredible that St. Thomas should here be speaking of all the processes of material production. Is he perhaps referring solely to the process of human generation? The entire structure of the chapter precludes any such limitation. The process of human generation is indeed cited, but solely as an illustration. The principle and the conclusion are posited in an entirely generic fashion. Here is the conclusion: "If, then, the movement of the heavens is ordered to generation and generation to man as the final end of this generation, it is clear that the end of the celestial motion is ordained to man as to the final end in the order of realities subject to generation and motion. Therefore it is written that God made the celestial bodies to serve all peoples." (Cf. J. Legrand, *L' Univers et l'homme dans la philosophie de S. Thomas* [Bruges: Desclée de Brouwer, 1946], I, 236–238).

It is important to compare this opinion with another thesis of St. Thomas on the relation between tendency and end: "In everything acting for an end, there must be a tendency to this end and, so to speak, a certain rudimentary beginning of that end (*'quasi quamdam incohationem finis'*). Otherwise it would not act for this end" (*III Sent.*, dist. 23, q. 1, a. 4, sol. 3). Juxtaposing these two theses, the reasoning might be as follows: the tendency to an end supposes a certain 'rudimentary beginning' of the end to which the tendency is tending. Now in every process of material development there is an active tendency of matter toward the human soul as its highest substantial form and its last end. Therefore every process of material becoming and production supposes a sort of 'rudimentary beginning' of the end, i.e., of the material-spiritual existence as realized and actualized in man. This 'rudimentary beginning' may be more or less (even immeasurably) remote from actualization. It is not itself the actualization, the realization of the end, but rather a real 'rudimentary beginning' of it. Otherwise the tendency to the end could not exist. To define this 'rudimentary beginning,' this pre-existence of the end in the tendency, Thomas borrows from Aristotle the category of *potentia:* "potency." This term indicates a positive tendency which can be characterized (in a figurative but nonetheless meaningful sense) as an appetite or an aspiration (*"appetitus," "tendit"*) and as a "beginning."

Is this not a very close approach to an expression of Teilhard to which we have already alluded (p. 17) and which provoked violent indignation in some readers? *"In the world, nothing could ever burst forth as final across the different thresholds successively traversed by evolution (however critical they be) which has not already existed in an obscure and primordial way."* (PH, p. 69 f.; Eng. trans., p. 71.)

A good part of P. Grenet's book is devoted to the refutation of this opinion (P. Grenet, *Pierre Teilhard de Chardin ou le philosophe malgré lui* (Paris: Beauchesne, 1960), pp. 124–165. According to Grenet, it would follow from this that there is no essential distinction between matter and spirit; man as spiritual being would have been actualized in primordial matter, even though in a hidden fashion as yet. The first origin of man would signify solely that this hidden reality appears in a clear light: "It is only his manifestation which makes him burst forth one fine day" (p. 146). Grenet quite rightly rejects such a "larval pre-existence" (p. 164).

On the basis of what texts does Grenet attribute to his adversary the notion of an actual, though still hidden, pre-existence? Is it because Teilhard says that the final actualization is "obscurely primordial"? Or because Teilhard speaks of the possibility of "seeing" the destination even in the beginning when looking from the point of view of man? The chief reason seems to lie in the very curious notion which Grenet himself holds concerning "pre-existence in potency." He describes this as "the power residing in the old to be one day the new" (p. 160). We agree, even though "become" would here be a better word than "be." But Grenet immediately subjoins this comment: "Which means precisely that the old was not *at all* the new." So potency would be nothing other than the negation of actualization! If that is the opinion one holds of "pre-existence in potency," then obviously any expression which speaks of a positive tendency of matter to man, of a foreshadowing of man in the animal, etc., will obviously seem to have too much "actualization" in it.

Now, St. Thomas describes "pre-existence in potency" as an inclination, a sort of "rudimentary beginning." Teilhard may indeed use the principle in a fashion lacking in subtlety, but in this notion as such, the "philosopher in spite of himself" is more of a Thomist and a better philosopher than several of his adversaries.

It is very astonishing to hear P. Grenet insinuate in this context that, according to Teilhard, there would be a larval pre-existence of the supernatural even in nature itself. Nowhere does Teilhard even indicate any such thing. There is no reason to suppose that Teilhard neglected the classical distinction between the *potentia naturalis,* which determines the relation between the disposition and the actualization within nature, and the *potentia oboedientialis,* which expresses the mystery of the relation between nature and supernature, grace. Teilhard expresses this distinction in several texts: cf. those cited by H. de Lubac, *La Pensée Religieuse du P. Pierre Teilhard de Chardin,* pp. 169–183, and by C. d'Armagnac, in the revue *Etudes,* I (1963), 63, n. 1. And Teilhard obviously admits, with all theologians, that the whole of nature has in fact been elevated to the supernatural order.

[21] In reading Teilhard, it must always be borne in mind that for him the term *biological* has a special meaning. It does not signify merely what belongs to the fields of anatomy, physiology, etc., which constitute biology as commonly

understood. A global objective knowledge of life, *bios,* is what Teilhard understands by biology and precisely this is supposed to broaden biology as a science. This Teilhardian terminology is a deliberate protest against the shifting and narrowing of the notion of life in the materialist sense.

22 This point is so central in Teilhard's works that the quotations could be multiplied *ad infinitum.* Aside from *Le Phénomène humain* and *Le Groupe zoologique humain,* we refer the reader to several passages from writings going back to various periods of Teilhard's life and writings, viz.: *Oeuvres,* III (1923), 91–95; (1930), 233–234; (1952), 372–373; II, (1954), 313–315. This paragraph of our own text is entirely borrowed from these four passages.

23 Cf. Sertillanges' commentary: "Fr. Teilhard de Chardin's formula seems to me tolerably felicitous: 'Thought succeeds to life by crossing a threshold.' Crossing a threshold does not involve an interruption of the forward course. But because there is a threshold, there is the necessity here of speaking of continuity and novelty, of evolution *de plano* and of transcendence" (Sertillanges, *L'Idée de création et ses retentissements en philosophie* [Paris: Aubier, 1945], p. 152, n. 1).

24 *Oeuvres,* III, 95. Cf. *Oeuvres,* V (1921): 43 f. (1921): "the 'human' could not exist if it did not contain, *transfigured in terms of mind,* a property common to all animals, of which the beginnings are to be detected as they vanish into the past." Eng. trans., *The Future of Man,* p. 27–28.

25 *PH,* 188; Eng. trans., p. 171.

25ª "le monde de l'Universel *pensé.*"

26 E.g., *GZ,* 77–80.

27 *Oeuvres,* III (1923), 92.

28 *GZ,* 79.

29 *Oeuvres,* III (1952), 372; II, 314.

30 *Oeuvres,* V (1947), 205; Eng. trans., p. 158.

31 *Oeuvres,* II (1954), 314.

32 Cf. below, pp. 114 f.

33 Cf. above, p. 64. This agreement of expressions is probably not accidental. Teilhard, who had been seeking, since his first years as a thinker, for the distinctive feature of man in the reflection of his own consciousness, may have found in Mouroux a felicitous formulation of his own personal intuitions.

Let us hope that it is a mere oversight that has led Grenet, in his critique of Teilhard's notion of the human spirit, not to mention these texts of Teilhard or of St. Thomas (P. Grenet, *Pierre Teilhard de Chardin ou le philosophe malgré lui* [Paris: Beauchesne, 1960], pp. 175–184).

34 I find it impossible to understand how anyone who had read any appreciable number of Teilhard's works could write: "As to the fashion in which this categorical monism opens up matter to spirit, P. Teilhard provides no other explanation than the distinction between two forms of energy: 'material and axial,' 'tangential and radial' (M. L. Guérard des Lauriers, "La démarche du P. Teilhard de Chardin," in *Divinitas,* III [1959], 227). To define the continuity and the discontinuity between the material and the spiritual on this earth, Teilhard continually uses the fundamental category of "interiority," that is, of the "very being" of consciousness. Sometimes the very being of the material thing is explained, with reference to its auto-alienation, by the figures of radial and tangential

energy (cf. above, pp. 35 f). But can these auxiliary notions be thought to take the place of the fundamental category and so justify the accusation of monism? Also, it would be desirable for the accuser to define better what he understands by Teilhard's monism (*art. cit.*, 222, has this: "a monism, that is a view of the world resting upon a *single* principle, to the *exclusion* of any other").

35 Pius XII, Encyclical *Humani generis, Dz,* n. 3027. The word *commands* may here signify that it is a question of a genuine doctrine of faith or of a conclusion not belonging to the object of faith as such. The doctrines of this last category are usually called "theologically certain." The latest theological manual lists among them the creation of the soul (M. Flick Z. Alsezghy, *Il Creatore* [Florence: Ed. Fiorentina, 1959], pp. 238 f.).

36 *PH,* 186; Eng. trans., p. 169.

37 *Oeuvres,* III (1926), 188 f.

38 Cf. above, p. 60.

39 Cf. above, pp. 57 f and n. 34 to Chapter 3.

40 A. Hulsbosch, "De Kosmogenese van Teilhard de Chardin," in *Annalen van het Thijmgenootschap,* XLVII (1959), 317. Cf. also J. Galot, "Le Phénomène humain," in *Nouvelle revue théologique,* LXXVIII (1956), p. 178.

41 St. Thomas, *De potentia,* q. 3, a. 9; *Summa contra Gentiles,* II, c. 87–89; *Summa Theologica,* I, q. 118, a. 2; A. D. Sertillanges, *L'idée de création et ses retentissements en philosophie* (Paris: Aubier, 1945), pp. 145–160.

42 Sertillanges, *op. cit.,* p. 120.

43 *De potentia,* q. 3, a. 9, ad 21.

44 *Ibid.,* ad 20.

45 *Loc. cit.*

46 *Ibid.,* ad 19.

47 Sertillanges, *op. cit.,* p. 121. Cf. his statement of the case on p. 20: "There must be no anticipation of two actions constitutive of man's being, as an ontological composite essentially one, even though there is well-nigh a dual principle. There is not an action of nature on the one hand and an action of God on the other. There is not generation of the body, creation of the soul, infusion of the soul into the body. Such a way of speaking, which is indeed common, even in St. Thomas, is a concession to anthropomorphic language. Or else it is poetry, like

>   For the one who took you, young soul, in heaven
>   And put you into the world . . . (V. Hugo).

In reality, there is generation of the composite, and the term of this generation is the composite itself, not merely the body, *Homo generat hominem.* The soul? It is not the fruit of generation, properly speaking, but it is quite really the term, to wit, the conjoined term." Cf. also A. M. Henry, in *Initiation théologique* (Paris: Cerf, 1952), II, 386: "What comes into existence is neither the body alone nor the soul alone, but the individual or, at least, the person."

48 Cf. St. Thomas, *De potentia,* q. 3, a. 10, obi. 4: "The various species pertain to the substantial perfection of the world, because they are willed for their own sake by God. But the individuals which are not permanent pertain to an accidental perfection of the world; for they are not willed for their own sake but for the preservation of the species. Rational souls, on the contrary, have a permanent existence, not only in reference to their species but also in reference

to the particular individuals." Which therefore means that each particular soul "is willed by God for its own sake"; cf. *Summa contra Gentiles,* III, c. 112.

⁴⁹ J. Mouroux, *Sens chrétien de l'homme* (Paris: Aubier, 1945), p. 118; Eng. trans., *The Meaning of Man,* p. 125.

⁵⁰ After we had already written these lines, we found a similar thought in L. Richard: "If man is created 'specially' . . . this means that he is willed for his own sake . . . Willed for his own sake, man is also willed for God, that is, for his relation to God." (L. Richard, *Le Mystère de la rédemption* [Tournai: Desclée et cie, 1959], p. 229).

⁵¹ Cf. P. de Haes, "Het goddelijk moederschap," in *Verbum,* XXI (1954), p. 54: "Therefore the mother does not play an exclusively biological role in the generation of the child. . . . We are here, in fact, in the *order of persons,* which transcends the purely cosmic. This order cannot be simply positioned on or reduced to the level of the preponderant species of which the individuals would be nothing but the links or fugitive elements, barely appearing only in order to disappear forthwith. The complete term of the maternal activity is the child, that is, a new person. As person, this term possesses an irreducible originality and an ultimate value. Though born into the continuing line of the species, this term is at the same time an original value directly created by God."

APPENDIX I

¹ Fragments in Tresmontant, *Introduction à la pensée de Teilhard de Chardin* (Paris: Seuil, 1956), pp. 110–116.

² § 25.

³ *Comment je vois,* § 26. Cf. *La lutte contre la multitude,* 1917: Plus esse = plus, et a pluribus uniri" (To be more = to be united more, and by more [agencies]).

⁴ *Comment je vois,* § 27.

⁵ In a somewhat different context, that of the opening outward to the not-self on which rests the human community, Malmberg makes the distinction between "the individual exposure of indigence" and "the personal exposure of riches." Inasmuch as man is an individual, only partially realizing and actualizing the perfection of human nature, he seeks, in his relations with others, the complement of his own deficiency. Inasmuch as he is a person, totally realizing and actualizing the perfection of human nature, and thus bearing his fellows within himself by perichoresis and being present to all his fellows, he forms a community of union with the others. It is only under this latter aspect that the human community can be considered a reflection of the divine Community. (F. Malmberg, *Één lichaam en één geest* [Utrecht: Het Spectrum, 1958], pp. 171 f.)

⁶ *Comment je vois,* § 28. Other passages from the earlier period are less clear in their assertion that the absolute Multitude is Nothingness; one such passage asserts that "its essence was to be infinitely divided in itself, that is to be tethered full length upon Nothingness" (In Tresmontant, *op. cit.,* p. 112).

[7] Tresmontant, *op. cit.*, pp. 113, 115. "Prime Matter," which is not existence but the principle of multiplicity and determinability.

[8] In Tresmontant, *op. cit.*, p. 112.

[9] St. Augustine, *De fide et symbolo*, 7: "Nihil ergo habet Deus contrarium."

[10] *Comment je vois,* § 29.

[11] Cf. e.g., St. Thomas, *Summa Theologica*, I, q. 93, a. 1–2, on man, the image of God; q. 45, a. 7, on the "vestigium Trinitatis" in every creature; q. 45, a. 6, on the intratrinitarian origin of Son and Holy Spirit as the fundamental motif (and therefore the basic image) of creation.

[12] L. B. Geiger, *La participation dans la philosophie de S. Thomas d'Aquin* (Paris: Vrin, 1942), p. 381: "There is no *outside of* God, as there is nothing, save evil, which is radically foreign to God."

[13] Vatican I, *Dz.,* n. 1783.

[14] In an earlier work, Teilhard indicates that he is aware of the danger latent in such a line of thought: "I take full cognizance of the fact that this conception of a kind of *positive Nothingness,* subject of Creation, raises serious objections. No matter how tethered full length upon non-being it may be supposed to be, the Thing, dissociated by nature, required for the action of creative union, does inevitably signify that the Creator found, outside of Himself, a kind of purchase, or at least a reaction. It thus insinuates that the Creation was not absolutely gratuitous but rather represents a Work of almost absolute self-interest. All of this 'redolet manichaeismum.' But, really now, in all sincerity, can we avoid these risky reefs (or rather these paradoxes) without falling into purely *verbal* explanations?" (*L'Union créatrice* [1917], in Tresmontant, *op. cit.*, pp. 113 f.). Teilhard's own effort at explanation is an imaginative exposition and would certainly lead to dualism.

[15] *MD*, 19; Eng. trans., *The Divine Milieu* (New York: Harper & Row, 1960), p. 12.

[16] Cf. below, pp. 147 ff.

[17] "Let us now see how, in another sense, he [God] consummates himself only in uniting." (*Comment je vois,* § 27).

Tresmontant (*op. cit.*, p. 115) cites a very patent passage of this sort from *Le Coeur de la matière* (1950): "In the world viewed as the object of the 'Creation,' classical metaphysics had accustomed us to see a kind of extrinsic production, issuing . . . from the supreme *efficiency* of God. Irresistibly . . . I am now impelled to see in it . . . a mysterious product of *completion and fulfillment* [italics ours—Author] for the absolute Being himself." Here the dual difficulty attaching to the interpretation of Teilhard's ideas is clearly evident. Another (later?) edition of this essay has replaced the phrase, in which we underlined the crucial three words, with the following phrase: "a mysterious product of *satisfaction* for the absolute Being himself." This is certainly less shocking, especially upon reflection on the words of Proverbs 8: 31: "finding my delights among the children of men." But above all, and this is more important still, the passage figures in an explicitly Christological context; it is immediately followed by these words: "And in the same vision I see Christ . . . 'absolutizing' himself in a certain sense." In other words, it is only in Christ that creation finds this opportunity of serving as "fulfillment" to God. As we shall point out directly, this thesis is theologically acceptable. But even as fine and sympathetic an expert on Teilhard as Tresmontant failed to see the extent to which he was pushing this passage by taking it out of its Christological context.

18 Cf. below, pp. 218 ff.

19 "God wants it because he has willed to have need of it" (*MD*, 61 f.). Cf. Pius XII, Encyclical *Mystici corporis:* "But Christ must likewise be held, however astonishing this may appear, to have need of his members. . . . The reason for this is not to be found in any insufficiency or weakness of Christ, but rather in the fact that He Himself . . . has so disposed it." (AAS 35 [1943], 213.)

20 Tresmontant, pp. 110 f.

21 *Comment je vois,* § 25.

22 In Cuénot, p. 264.

23 Letter of March 24, 1917; *Genèse*, p. 245; Eng. trans., *The Making of a Mind*, p. 189.

24 *Comment je vois,* § 25.

25 Tresmontant, p. 129.

CHAPTER 5

1 *Oeuvres*, V, 341 f. (1949).

2 *Oeuvres*, III, 285–287 (1939).

3 *Oeuvres*, III, 358 (1951).

4 *GZ*, 122; cf. *PH*, 308.

5 *GZ.*, 46; *Oeuvres*, V, 58 (1939).

6 *PH*, 268.

7 *GZ*, 116; *Oeuvres*, V, 209 f. (1947); we find something resembling education even among the higher animals, *ibid.*, and 43 f. (1921).

8 *GZ*, 114–117.

9 *Oeuvres*, V (1952), 391; Eng. trans., *The Future of Man*, p. 300.

10 *Oeuvres*, II (1954), 324 f.

11 C. S. Lewis.

12 *GZ*, 125 f.

13 *GZ*, 132.

14 *Oeuvres*, V (1945), 146; Eng. trans., pp. 113–114.

15 *Oeuvres*, III (1923), 87 f.

16 *Oeuvres*, V (1945), 147; Eng. trans., p. 114.

17 *GZ*, 133.

18 *GZ*, 134; *Oeuvres*, V (1949), 322.

19 *Hymne*, p. 29 f.; Eng. trans., *Hymn of the Universe*, p. 30.

20 *MD*, 198; Eng. trans., *The Divine Milieu*, p. 135.

21 *Cahiers*, II, 153. And *Oeuvres*, VII, 189 f.: "existential fear."

22 *Oeuvres*, V (1949), 323 f.

23 *Oeuvres*, V (1949), 325 f.

24 *GZ*, 135.

25 *PH*, 244.

26 *Oeuvres*, III (1923), 107.

27 *PH*, 327.

[28] *Oeuvres*, V (1947), 259 f.; Eng. trans., p. 201.

[29] *PH*, 255 f.

[30] *Oeuvres*, V (1947), 260; Eng. trans., p. 202.

[31] *PH*, 254; Eng. trans., *The Phenomenon of Man*, p. 229.

[32] Cf. above, p. 12.

[33] *PH*, 30; Eng. trans., p. 36; cf. *GZ*, 22.

[34] *Oeuvres*, III (1951), 361.

[35] *GZ*, 139; italics ours—Author.

[36] *Oeuvres*, III, 223.

[37] *PH*, 259; Eng. trans., pp. 233–234.

[38] *GZ*, 136.

[39] *Oeuvres*, V (1939), 70.

[40] On socialization as an evolutionary process, cf. especially: *Oeuvres*, V, 75, 325–330; *GZ*, 105–123. Cf. also: F. Russo, "La socialisation selon Teilhard de Chardin," in *Revue de l'Action populaire* (December, 1962). This notion has, we know, been adopted in the Encylical *Mater et Magistra*.

[41] *GZ*, 136 f.; first italics ours—Author.

[42] "La grande option," in *Oeuvres*, V, 57–81.

[43] *PH*, 258; Eng. trans., p. 233; cf. 310.

[44] *Comment je vois*, § 20 (1948).

[45] Cf. below, pp. 124 f.

[46] "And so exactly, so perfectly, does this coincide with the Omega Point that doubtless I should never have ventured to envisage the latter or formulate the hypothesis rationally if, in my consciousness as a believer, I had not found not only its speculative model but also its living reality." (*PH*, 328; Eng. trans., p. 294).

[47] *GZ*, 136.

[48] *Oeuvres*, V (1947), 255; Eng. trans., p. 222.

[49] *Oeuvres*, V (1939), 60; Eng. trans., p. 38.

[50] *Oeuvres*, V (1947), 255; Eng. trans., p. 222.

[51] *GZ*, 137.

[52] *Oeuvres*, V (1949), 342.

[53] *Cahiers*, II (1943), 62.

[54] *Oeuvres*, III (1942), 326.

[55] *PH*, 271; Eng. trans., p. 244.

[56] "La crise présente," in *Études*, 123 (1937), 147.

[57] *PH*, 273.

[58] *Cahiers*, I (1939), 23 f.

[59] *GZ*, 153.

[60] *Oeuvres*, V (1952), 393 f.

[61] *Cahiers*, I (1937), 26; Eng. trans., *Building the Earth* (Wilkes-Barre, Pa.: Dimension Books, 1965), pp. 90–92.

[62] *Oeuvres*, II (1942), 321.

[63] "La crise présente," in *Études*, 233 (1937), 155.

[64] *Oeuvres*, V (1950), 362, 373.

[65] *PH*, 297.

[66] *Oeuvres*, V (1949), 343.

[67] *L'Apport spirituel de l'Extrême-Orient* (1947).

68 *Oeuvres*, V (1949), 333; Eng. trans., p. 257.

69 *GZ*, 161; cf. *PH*, 256. On Human Power Engineering, cf. *Oeuvres*, VI, "L'Énergie Humaine," especially 172–198.

70 Cf. below, pp. 209 ff.

71 *Oeuvres*, III (1942), 322.

72 *Oeuvres*, V (1947), 264 f.; Eng. trans., pp. 206–207.

73 *Ibid.*

74 *Oeuvres*, III (1952), 377 f.

75 *PH*, 295; Eng. trans., p. 265.

76 *GZ*, 154. This principle "union differentiates" recurs constantly in this sense in Teilhard's writings: *Oeuvres*, III (1939), 292; 152 (1945); *PH*, 291, etc. It is unjust and indicative of a great lack of discernment to combat this principle by making Teilhard seem to say "unity differentiates," as does Guérard des Lauriers, in his article "La démarche de Teilhard de Chardin," in *Divinitas* III (1959), 259, n. 79). Far from saying what des Lauriers attributes to him, Teilhard explicitly warns against Indian pantheism: "identification is not union"; where there is identity, there is no room for love. (*L'Apport spirituel de l'Extrême-Orient*, 1947).

77 *Oeuvres*, V (1945), 152.

78 *Oeuvres*, V (1941), 99; cf. (1939), 74 f.; *Cahiers* I (1937), 24. This central idea of the primacy of love is certainly expressed in *Le Phénomène humain* (p. 295, cf. pp. 290 f.; Eng. trans., pp. 264 ff.); but it has been somewhat obscured by the desire to find prefigurations of this love in animate and even in inanimate nature. This work lends color to the reproach levelled by A. Hulsbosch that Teilhard overestimates the role of the mere "questing" and underestimates that of freedom and of love, in the unification of mankind (A. Hulsbosch, "De kosmogenese van Teilhard de Chardin," in *Annalen van het Thijmgenootschap*, XLVII [1959], 318 f.). But a correction is made to this restriction of the presentation, not only in the later writings, but even in the essays cited which are contemporary with *Le Phénomène humain* (Cf. *Oeuvres*, VI, 180–198).

As will become apparent in the sequel, the category of free and love-impelled evolution does indeed constitute a capital element in Teilhard's thought. And to the extent to which this category is not fully developed in *Le Phénomène humain*, this work cannot be regarded as the best summary of Teilhard's views.

79 Cf. below, pp. 232 f.

80 *Cahiers*, II (1943), 69.

81 *PH*, 297; Eng. trans., p. 267.

82 *Comment je vois*, § 20 (1948).

83 *Oeuvres*, V (1950), 363; Eng. trans., p. 75; III, 301 (1930).

84 *Oeuvres*, V (1950), 373; Eng. trans., p. 287.

85 *GZ*, 162.

86 In a somewhat different fashion in *Comment je vois*, § 20 (1948).

87 *CT*, 23 f.

88 *Oeuvres*, V (1942), 121 f.; Eng. trans., p. 92.

89 *PH*, 299 f.; Eng. trans., p. 269; cf. *PH*, 344.

90 *PH*, 301, Eng. trans., pp. 270–271; cf. *Oeuvres*, VI, 175–180,

91 *PH*, 324 f.

[92] *PH*, 327.

[93] *Oeuvres*, V (1947), 262; VI, 180–195.

[94] *Oeuvres*, V (1941), 100: "This mammoth development will attain its goal only by becoming Christianized"; p. 271 (1947): "In Man, Evolution . . . becomes moralized and 'mysticized.'" Cf. *PH*, 315–317.

CHAPTER 6

[1] *Oeuvres*, V (1949); 347 f.; Eng. trans., *The Future of Man*, pp. 267–268. This edition has "Incarnation" instead of "Parousia"; "Incarnation" is certainly a typist's or printer's error. As we have already pointed out, terms like "physical," "biological," or "organic" have no other purpose, in this context, than the exclusion of an exclusively "moral" or "juridical" bond, such as the Suarezian notion of merit or of the sacraments would hold. In the Suarezian system, in which Teilhard was trained and against which he is reacting, there is no internal nexus or bond between the human act and the divine gift of grace; this nexus is but an arbitrary decree of God. These terms, therefore, as used by Teilhard, have no more materialist overtones than the "physical" causality of the sacraments defended by the Thomists.

[2] On the apologetic cast of Teilhard's works, cf. the important article of C. d'Armagnac, "La pensée du Père Teilhard de Chardin comme apologétique moderne," in *Nouv. rev. théol.* XCIV (1962), 598–621.

[3] "La messe sur le Monde," *Hymne*, p. 24.

[4] E.g., in Cuénot, pp. 327 f., or in Guérard des Lauriers, "La démarche du P. Teilhard de Chardin," in *Divinitas*, III (1959), 260, n. 81; the former has the most infelicitous comment: "Father Teilhard means a 'transcending of Christianity.'" (Cuénot, p. 328, n. 1; Eng. trans., p. 271, n. 1).

[5] *Oeuvres*, III (1942), 324.

[6] Letter of April 15, 1953, in Cuénot, p. 477 f.; Eng. trans., p. 396; cf. *Oeuvres*, V, 267 (1947); *PH*, 331, etc.

[7] Letter of January 21, 1936, *LV*, 197.

[8] *Oeuvres*, III (1942), 324; cf. *GZ*, 162, above, pp. 113 f.

[9] Cf. below, pp. 220 f.

[10] Cf. above, pp. 109 ff.

[11] Cf. above, n. 4 to Chapter 4. H. Cuyper cites the third phrase as if Teilhard had written "in the personal God" instead of "in the Personal" (G. Magiore and H. Cuyper, *Présence de Pierre Teilhard de Chardin* [Paris: Éd. univ., 1961], p. 160). Our own reading is borne out by *Comment je crois* and in *Le Coeur de la matière*, and therefore certainly the right one.

[12] *Oeuvres*, V (1942), 118; (1945), 169.

[13] *Cahiers*, II (1943), 63.

[14] Cf. Pius XII, Encyclical *Humani generis*, Dz., n. 3006.

[15] *PH*, 302; Eng. trans., p. 272.

[16] Thus in "Esquisse d'un univers personnel" (*Oeuvres*, VI), and *Le Coeur de la matière*.

[17] E.g., *MD*, 139.

[18] *Oeuvres*, V (1939), 66; *PH*, 327.

¹⁹ Cf. below, p. 238.

²⁰ *GZ*, 162, cf. *PH*, 332; Cuénot, p. 291, n. 3, Cf. *Oeuvres*, VII, 156–158.

²¹ *MD*, 139; Eng. trans., 93–94.

²² Cf. above, p. 113.

²³ Anyone really believing that, according to Teilhard, "the Transcendent Himself is destitute of the personal character by which he could encounter the created subject" (M. L. Guérard des Lauriers, "La démarche du Père Teilhard de Chardin," in *Divinitas*, III [1959], 260), would of course have to hold Teilhard to be a heretic. But this is a palpable failure to grasp anything of the heart of Teilhard's thinking. With what color of spectacles has it been read to yield to such statements?

²⁴ "La messe sur le monde," in *Hymne*, p. 26: "Like the monist, I plunge into the all-inclusive One, but the One is so perfect as it receives me and I lose myself in it I can find in it the ultimate perfection of my own individuality." (Eng. trans., *Hymn of the Universe* [New York: Harper and Row, 1961] p. 26).

Teilhard sometimes calls his design a "monism," but he adds that he is taking the word in its purely etymological sense. As opposed to a pluralism which sees mankind dispersed into a multitude of individuals with no mutual tie, this "monism" consists in the consummation of mankind in a real "communion," a union of human persons (*Oeuvres*, V [1939], 66). Elsewhere he rejects "monism" out of hand (*MD*, p. 140).

²⁵ I Cor. 15: 29.

²⁶ *MD*, 139; Eng. trans., p. 93–94.

²⁷ *PH*, 244.

²⁸ *PH*, 344.

²⁹ *MD*, 139; Eng. trans., p. 93–94; cf. *PH*, 344.

³⁰ Looking back, he writes in 1950: "I have never, at any moment of my life, felt the slightest difficulty in addressing God as a supreme *someone*" (cited by Lubac, "Maurice Blondel et le Père Teilhard de Chardin," in *Archives de philosophie*, XXIV [1961], 142, n. 16). Cf. here a great number of passages cited marking the development of Teilhard's personalism from 1917 on; cf. *NLV*, p. 99, n. 1.

³¹ *Cahiers*, I (1937), 23 f. Another very strongly worded passage is in "Introduction à la Vie chrétienne," *Oeuvres*, VI (1944), 86–87, n. 2.

³² Cf. above, pp. 102 f.

³³ *Dz.*, n. 1795. The Council does not define the elements of the doctrine of faith which are such *mysteria stricte dicta* nor yet those which are accessible to human reason (e.g., the existence of God, the spiritual nature and immortality of the human soul). But it would be excessively absurd to class the doctrine of the Mystical Body of Christ in this latter category.

³⁴ "Christ is not, of course, the center that all things here below could by their natural powers aspire to wed. Destination to Christ is an unexpected and gratuitous gift and grace of the Creator. But it is still true that the Incarnation has so thoroughly recentered the universe within the supernatural that, in the concrete, we can no longer seek to imagine toward what center the elements of this world would have gravitated, had they not been elevated to the order of grace." ("L'Union créatrice" [1917], cited in *Études*, 316 [1963], 63, note).

[35] *Le Coeur de la matière,* part 3; cf. *Comment je vois,* § 24 (1948): "Apart from any deposit and corroboration of revelation, the only thing we would be able to conclude with certitude concerning the existence of Omega, once admitted, is that the tide of consciousness of which we form part is not due simply to some thrust coming from ourselves but is rather being raised by a star, upon which little by little, one by one, and all together, we are consummating, by union, our own consummation." Cf. very clear statements to the same effect in "Esquisse d'une dialectique de l'Esprit," *Oeuvres,* VII, 154–158. Cf. below, note 65 to this Chapter.

[36] So there is no reason to take offense at phrases like the following: "The Christogenesis (I mean, the growth of the Mystical Body) spoken of by St. Paul and St. John is nothing else and nothing less than the extension, both *awaited and unhoped for,* of that Noogenesis!" (*PH,* 331; Eng. trans. p. 297; italics ours— Author), as does C. Journet ("La vision teilhardienne du monde," in *Divinitas,* III [1959], 340). Even for St. Thomas, eternal supernatural beatitude is the object of a desire of nature as such (e.g., I–II, q. 3, a. 8), which is at the same time a real desire and nevertheless impotent. This is not far from the "prolongation, at once awaited and unhoped for."

Actually, Journet's objection seems directed against the notion that our natural activity efficaciously attains the supernatural end (and in this sense, wills it efficaciously). This emerges from Journet's own treatment of grace: "Grace surpasses absolutely every *power* and demand of every created nature, actual or possible . . . God is giving Himself in the operation of grace, whereas nothing other than Himself is worthy or *capable* of Him" (*ibid.,* p. 342). Journet is too familiar with St. Thomas and Thomism not to know that for both the distinctive property of the rational creature is to be "capax summi boni," (*De malo,* q. 5, a. 1; cf. *Summa Theologica,* I–II, q. 113, a. 10), and that Thomists have been debating for centuries the sense in which grace corresponds to the *powers* of nature. So there can be no out-and-out denial of any "power," or "capacity," of nature in relation to grace; the only thing that can be entirely denied is the "power" and the "capacity" of nature acquiring or attaining to the order of grace by natural forces and powers. And this is probably what Journet means.

His objection would therefore hold, with respect to Teilhard, only if the latter were maintaining that our natural operation and activity as such effects a supernatural reality. Teilhard does not say this; on the contrary, he insists on the distinction between the natural improvement and perfecting of man and the edification of the Body of Christ (*MD,* 128, n. 1; Eng. trans., 86, n. 1; cf. below, pp. 220 f.).

[37] Cf. below, Appendix II.

[38] Cf. below, pp. 222 ff.

[39] Diary Entry of December 12, 1919, in *Archives de philosophie,* XXIV (1961), 135.

[40] Diary Entry of December 29, 1919, in *Archives de philosophie,* XXIV (1961), 151 f.; *MD,* 195 f.

[41] *Comment je vois,* § 24 (1949).

[42] "Le christique" (1955).

[43] Col. 1: 16.

[44] On these two reasons for not the parousia alone as the end of the world but as a transition as well, cf. below, Chapter 10.

[45] *Oeuvres*, V, 347 f., cited above, p. 116. Cf. also *Oeuvres*, V (1948), 305: "[recognize] in the collective consummation of terrestrial Mankind, not an indifferent or even inimical event, but rather a preliminary condition (note: necessary but not sufficient condition) for the final, 'parousiac' establishment of the Kingdom of God."

[46] Luke 12: 37.

[47] Rom. 8: 21.

[48] H. Schiller, "Zum Verständnis der Geschicte nach der Offenbarung Johannes," in *Die Zeit der Kirche* (Freiburg: Herder, 1956), p. 268: "The Christian understanding of history differs essentially from that of the apocalyptic vision of the Jews, in that for Christianity, the "Advent" of God, which is, for Christianity as for Judaism, the meaning, end, and therefore fulfillment of history, has already ingressed into the course of events with Jesus Christ. This history is oriented to a future which is already present to it at every moment, and history itself is the actualization of this future which is henceforth present as of now in history."

[49] Cf. above, p. 103.

[50] Diary entry of December 12, 1919; cf. *MD*, 92 f. and "La lutte contre la multitude" (1917): "Once a man has resolved to be truly generous in the practice of the love of God and of neighbor, he realizes that he has done nothing by the mere fact of having righted his own interior unity by generous detachments. This unity must in its turn suffer an eclipse which will appear to annihilate it, before being reborn into Christ. Those will truly be saved who, in a bold transfer of their center of being outside of themselves, dare to love Another more than themselves, who became this Other in some sense, that is, go through death in search of life" (cited in *Archives de philosophie*, p. 141, n. 15).

[51] *MD*, 92 f.; Eng. trans., p. 50.

[52] *Comment je vois*, § 20 (1948).

[53] *PH*, 304.

[54] *Oeuvres*, V (1939), 77; Eng. trans., p. 56 (cf. p. 76).

[55] "In order to unify itself still further, Mankind, *taken as a whole*, will have . . . to reflect 'pointedly' [i.e., at a single point, in a thus sharpened awareness and concentration—Translator's Note] upon itself (which means, in this case, abandoning its organo-planetary foothold so as to pivot excentrically upon the transcendent Center of its concentration); then, for the Spirit of the Earth, the end and the consummation will have arrived.

"The end of the world: the wholesale internal introversion upon itself of the noosphere which has simultaneously reached the uttermost limit of its complexity and its centrality.

"The end of the world: the overthrow of equilibrium, detaching the mind, fulfilled at last, from its material matrix, so that it will henceforth rest with all its weight on God-Omega" (*PH*, 320; Eng. trans., p. 289).

Two points must be borne in mind for a good understanding of this text:

1. Mankind's perfect self-possession must, as has been shown above, be an eternal possession, abiding and everlasting, and therefore exempted from the auto-alienation involved in time and space.

2. The Spirit now no longer signifies negation of all physical nature or corporeity; it is man opening upon God; the body will also have its portion in the final resurrection, but this body will no longer be the matrix imparting its mold to the spirit, now that the human spirit has positioned its center of gravity in God; and so the human body will become a sheer expression of this spirit.

[56] Cf. below, pp. 214 f.

[57] "I do not think there is any better (nor in fact any other) form of adoration" (Letter of May 12, 1950 to Lucien Cuénot, in Cuénot, p. 331; Eng. trans., p. 273). Cf. other letters of 1924, 1931, and 1932, in Cuénot, pp. 78, 167, n. 1; *Cahiers*, I [1931] 27; *PH*, 317.

The exaggerated form of some of these passages is explained by the fact that Teilhard has to justify in his own eyes his own life, the life of a priest entirely absorbed in terrestrial science and in polemical writing against certain Christian circles who regard science and technology as valueless for the building up of the Body of Christ (cf. below, n. 34 to Chapter 10).

[58] *Cahiers*, I, 27 (1931).

[59] *Cahiers*, I, 44 (1941).

[60] *Oeuvres*, V, 348 (cf. above, p. 116); V, 305 (cf. above, n. 45 to Chapter 6). *Comment je vois*, § 24, n. 25.

[61] Cf. above, p. 116.

[62] Thus does P. Chauchard sum up the objections of those opposed to Teilhard on this point (*L'Être humain selon Teilhard de Chardin* [Paris: Lecoffre, 1959], p. 183).

[63] *LV*, 118.

[64] "Le Coeur de la matière" (1950).

[65] *Oeuvres*, V (1942), 121 f.; Eng. trans., p. 92. In "Esquisse d'une dialectique de l'esprit," [1944] *Oeuvres*, VII, 149–158. Teilhard makes some important specifications on: 1. the *distinction*, in our knowledge of Omega, between natural inferences, deposits of Revelation, and "points emerging under the action of *grace*, of *theological faith*" (p. 155); 2. the *distinction*, in Omega proper, between humano-cosmic (natural) elements, Christic (supernatural) elements and divine elements (pp. 156–157)—(Note by C. d'Armagnac).

[66] C. Journet, "La vision teilhardienne du monde," in *Divinitas*, III (1959), 341.

APPENDIX II

[1] Appendix I.

[2] *Comment je vois*, § 31. Related text from 1918, in Tresmontant, pp. 120 f.: "Are not Creation, Incarnation and Redemption each a higher degree in the gratuity of the divine operation? But are they not also three acts indissolubly linked in the epiphany of participated being?" ("L'Ame du monde," 1918).

Another text from 1945, in M. L. Guérard des Lauriers ("La démarche du P. Teilhard de Chardin," in *Divinitas*, III [1959], 246): "Creation, Incarnation, Redemption. Hitherto, these three fundamental mysteries of the Christian faith, indissolubly linked *de facto* in the history of the World, have always been considered as being *de jure* independent one of another for human reason. It seems to have been held that God could bypass the Universe with no restrictions. He could create without becoming incarnate. The Incarnation in its turn could have been free of all toil and suffering. When transposed from the Cosmos of antiquity . . . into the Universe of modern times . . . the three mysteries tend to form but one. Without creation, first of all, something would seem to be lacking absolutely to God considered in the fullness, not of his being, but of his act of Union. To create, therefore, is for God, by definition, to unite himself to his work, that is, to commit himself in one way or another *into* the world by the Incarnation. Now does not "to become incarnate" mean *ipso facto* to participate in the sufferings and evils inherent in the Manifold in process of laborious muster? Creation, Incarnation, Redemption: seen in this light, the three mysteries do in fact become, in modern Christology, but the three faces of a single and identical process, a *fourth* radical mystery (the only one that is its own justification and has value in itself, in the final analysis, from the viewpoint of thought), which ought to be called (in order to distinguish it explicitly from the other three): the Mystery of the Creative Union of the World in God, or Pleromization. . . . Simple and marvelous effect of hyper-orthodoxy" (in "Christianisme et évolution," 1945). Similar text from 1951, in Cuénot, p. 355: "In the context of convergent cosmogenesis, to create *is*, for God, *to unite;* and to unite with something is to become immersed in it. But to be immersed (in Purality) is to 'corpuscularize' oneself: and this, in a world whose organization statistically entails disorder (and mechanically, effort) means plunging (in order to overcome them) into imperfection and pain."

Thus, step by step, we find a remarkable and fruitful connection between Theo- and Christology. In spite of the spirit, and even the letters of St. Paul and St. John, we may say that until recent times the saving figure and function of Christ retain, in their usual dogmatic expression, something of the juridical and the accidental. Why the Incarnation? Why the Cross? Emotionally and pastorally, the Christian economy proved perfectly viable and effective. But intellectually speaking, it appeared more as an arbitrary series of fortuitous events than as an organically connected process. And mysticism suffered from this. . . . "Well, it is this lack of ontological coherence (and so of spiritual grip) that is rectified by the discovery of a type of Universe in which, on the one hand, as we have just seen, God cannot appear as the Prime Mover towards the future without becoming Incarnate and without redeeming, that is without *Christifying* Himself for us." ("Du cosmos à la cosmogénèse," 1951, *Oeuvres*, VII, 271–272; quoted by Cuénot, Eng. trans., p. 293.)

Cf. the several allusions to these ideas in *PH*, 327, "*Christologie et évolution*" (1933), "*Le Coeur de la matière*" (1948), and "*Le Christique*" (1955).

[3] *Comment je vois*, 24.

[4] Vatican I, *Dz.*, n. 1796.

[5] Cf. above, pp. 79 f.

[6] *Summa Theologica*, I–II, q. 1, a. 7–8; q. 2, a. 8.

[7] The discussion of this problem, on which Baius clashed with his predecessors and associates in Louvain in the sixteenth century (cf. "De oorsprong van de theorie der zuivere natuur," in *Bijdragen*, X [1949], 105–127; articles "Bajanismus," and "Bajus" in *Lexikon für Theologie und Kirche*, 2nd Ed.; I, col. 1197–1200) was violently reopened by H. de Lubac's work, *Surnaturel*

(Paris: Aubier, 1946). Cf. the important contributions of L. Malevez, "L'Esprit et le désir de Dieu," in *Nouvelle revue théologique*, LXIX (1947), 3–31; K. Rahner, "Ueber das Verhältnis von Natur und Gnade," in *Schriften zur Theologie*, I, 323–345 (French translation, *Écrits Théologiques* [Desclée De Brouwer, 1963], III, 9–33); H. U. von Balthasar, *Karl Barth* (Olten, 1951), pp. 278–335.

[8] It must, however, be noted that in an early passage Teilhard had stressed in clear-cut fashion the gratuity of the Incarnation and the grace of adoption with regard to the creation: "Christ is not, of course, the center that all things here below could by their natural powers aspire to wed. Destination to Christ is an unexpected and gratuitous gift and grace of the Creator" ("L'Union créatrice" [1917], cited in *Études*, 316 [1963], 63, note). Similar careful distinction between a natural destiny and the concrete supernatural destiny of mankind, in a note in *PH*, 332: "In deference to the theological concept of the 'Supernatural,' according to which the unitive contact *hic et nunc* between God and the World attains a super-intimacy and thus a super-gratuity, of which Man could not dream and to which he could not pretend, on the merits of his nature's needs alone."

But if Teilhard had been consequential in maintaining this distinction, he would have had to abandon the whole of his "metaphysical deduction." For he would have grasped the fact that the Incarnation belongs pre-eminently to the "super-intimacy" which surpasses every demand of nature as such.

[9] E.g., Gal. 4: 4–7.

[10] John 1: 16.

[11] *Tractatus in Johannem*, 110, 5; cf. 111, 6.

[12] Luke 3: 23–38.

[13] Hebrews 2: 11–17.

[14] Cf. e.g., F. Malmberg, *Ueber den Gottmenschen* (Freiburg, Herder, 1960), p. 23: "We feel that the essence of the 'human nature of Christ' must be understood as being the *becoming* human ('natura' comes from 'nasci') and the human fulfillment of the God-Man, a function of the redemptive operation."

[15] Cf. below, pp. 154 f.

[16] Cf. below, n. 43 to Chapter 7.

[17] In Cuénot, p. 484.

[18] John 3: 19.

[19] John 9: 40.

[20] John 11: 46–53.

[21] Rom. 5: 10.

[22] Cf. below, pp. 145 ff.

[23] Cuénot, p. 29; cf. p. 489.

CHAPTER 7

[1] *Oeuvres*, V (1924), 401 f.; Eng. trans., *The Future of Man*, pp. 306–307.

[2] Cf. above, pp. 99 f.

[3] *Oeuvres*, III (1939), 223.

[4] *PH*, 259; Eng. trans., pp. 233–234.

⁵ Phil. 1: 6.

⁶ John 16: 33.

⁷ Rom. 5: 20.

⁸ Cf. F. Malmberg, "Enige aspectien van de zonde als christologisch probleem," in *Jaarboek Werkgenootschap katholieke theologen in Nederland* (1956), pp. 5–19; Hans Küng, *Rechtfertigung* (Einsiedeln: Johannes-Verlag, 1957), pp. 150–169.

⁹ P. Fransen, "Hans Asmussens 'Via media,'" in *Bijdragen*, XII (1951), 360 f.

¹⁰ W. Grossouw, *Bijbelse vroomheid* (Utrecht: Het Spectrum, 1954), p. 71.

¹¹ Eph. 7: 10–17.

¹² Cf. below, p. 151.

¹³ *GZ*, 153.

¹⁴ *PH*, 281; Eng. trans., p. 253.

¹⁵ *PH*, 321; Eng. trans., p. 288.

¹⁶ *PH*, 321 f.; Eng. trans., p. 288 f.

¹⁷ *Oeuvres*, V (1924), 401 f.

¹⁸ *Oeuvres*, V (1947), 238; Eng. trans., p. 188.

¹⁹ *Ibid.*

²⁰ *Ibid.*, 229; Eng. trans., p. 188.

²¹ *PH*, 321; Eng. trans., p. 288.

²² *PH*, 321; Eng. trans., pp. 288–289.

²³ *Ibid.*; *MD*, 196.

²⁴ *MD*, 188; Eng. trans., p. 129.

²⁵ *Oeuvres*, III (1923), 106 f.

²⁶ But he does indicate one element, by adding, after his exposition of statistical certainty, that the ever-growing sum total of human freedom (growing "for good . . . or for ill") yet remains "always fallible," and concludes precisely from this to the indispensability of a personal Omega, attracting in love (*GZ*, 161).

²⁷ *Oeuvres*, V (1948), 304; Eng. trans., pp. 236–237; cf. (1939), 77 f.; (1947), 230 f.; *PH*, 342; *GZ*, 160.

²⁸ *PH*, 307; Eng. trans., p. 276; *Oeuvres*, V (1947), 231.

²⁹ *MD*, 173; Eng. trans., p. 118 (italics ours—Author's Note). Cf. *Oeuvres*, V (1948), 293: "In the wake of the continually growing emergence of the psychic (individual 'choices') overlaying the statistical, human evolution seems definitely to elude any possibility of exact calculations."

³⁰ P. Fransen, *Gods genade en de mens* (Antwerp: Patmos-Nelissen, 1959), p. 66.

³¹ Precisely for this reason, Teilhard will demonstrate that all forms of organizational, economic, cultural, and scientific unification of mankind are capable only of an indirect contribution to the realization and actualization of the Omega and of the sublime unity, insofar, namely, as these forms of unification enter in some fashion into the service of love, in which case they can make a real contribution (cf. below, pp. 229 f).

³² But note the limitations of the criticism we are here advancing. And remember that we are here envisaging only one of the two eventualities advanced

by Teilhard: "the possibility, mentioned above, of foreseeing accurately—*if all goes well*—certain precise trends of the future" (*PH*, 342). Remember further that, considering the apologetic character of these reflections, Teilhard probably is not claiming for them the force of an ultimate solution. He makes this reservation expressly in 1948: "I am very much less disposed to believe today that the tightening of the human mass will *of itself*, suffice to warm the human heart. . . . in the case, is it not apparent that success of anthropogenesis, ultimately dependent upon achieving contact with the supracosmic, must, despite the rigours of its external conditioning, essentially contain an irreducible element of indeterminacy and uncertainty?" (*Oeuvres*, V, 303–304; Eng. trans., pp. 235–236). Teilhard concludes that "for a Christian . . . the eventual biological success of Man on Earth is not merely a probability but a certainty: since Christ . . . is already risen. But this certainty, born as it is of a 'supernatural' act of faith, is of its nature supraphenomenal: which means, in one sense, that it leaves all the anxieties attendant upon the human condition, on their own level, still alive in the heart of the believer." (*Ibid.*, p. 305; Eng. trans., p. 237.)

On salvation deriving from Christ alone, cf. H. de Lubac, *La Pensée religieuse du P. Pierre Teilhard de Chardin*, pp. 169–183.

[33] It is to this that Tresmontant is alluding when he writes: "Teilhard made a practice of looking at the world somewhat like a mechanic and he did not direct his attention to the existential level of the phenomenon of man, to interiority and the problem of freedom" (p. 118). The last remark seems unjust to us and will probably seem so to the reader who has come thus far with us. It is not in the whole of his thought as such, but rather in his reflections on evil, that Teilhard neglects the personal existential aspect of interiority and freedom.

[34] *GZ*, 9; cf. in Cuénot, p. 473, n. 2.

[35] Aside from the section of *Comment je vois*, § 30 (1948), some fragments of which we cite in our text, we may refer the reader to the following passages: *MD*, 88 f., 188f., free of these defects; some lines of *Oeuvres*, V (1942), 119; an Appendix subjoined in 1948 to *Le Phénomène humain* (*PH*, 345–348); "Christologie et évolution" (1933).

[36] *PH*, 345; cf. *MD*, 188, Eng. trans., p. 129.

[37] A letter from 1952 speaks of "the greater importance which the explicit consideration of Evil is assuming in my thinking" (in Cuénot, p. 478). Might this mean that Teilhard was in 1952 no longer satisfied with his 1948 treatment of the problem?

[38] *Comment je vois*, § 30: "Out of stubborn habit, the Problem of Evil continues to be declared insoluble; this is a sort of reflex action and really one wonders what reason there is for it. In the Cosmos envisaged by antiquity as issuing ready-made from the hands of the Creator, it was but natural that it should appear difficult to reconcile the existence of a World partially evil and the existence of a God at once good and omnipotent. But from our modern standpoint, with its idea of a Universe in a state of *cosmogenesis*, . . . how can anyone fail to see that, intellectually speaking, the famous problem *no longer exists?*" (Cf. also *Oeuvres*, V, 119). Teilhard does explicitly admit that there remains a great emotional difficulty in accepting the existence of evil.

[39] *Comment je vois*, § 30 (1948); cf. *PH*, 346.

[40] Cf. above, pp. 79 ff. Tresmontant is to the point in writing: "It is

. . . illegitimate to assert that God 'could not' do otherwise than to allow Evil to eventuate if he willed to create: we cannot reason legitimately by putting ourselves at the point of view of God. We have no right to say either that God 'could have' or that he 'could not' create the World without Evil" (Tresmontant, p. 119).

41 *Contra Celsum*, VI, 55: "If we take the word in its strict sense, God has not made anything that is evil. But the things that are evil—and there are not many such in comparison with the harmonious order of the universe—were the consequence of the things that he did will. Thus shavings and sawdust are the consequence of the work of the joiner; and would anyone say that the masons are the cause of the piles of waste stone and plaster lying around the building site?"

42 P. Chauchard, *L'Être humain selon Teilhard de Chardin* (Paris: Lecoffre, 1959), p. 192. But Chauchard's efforts to excuse the lacunae in Teilhard's thinking in this realm are doomed to failure.

43 Cf. Appendix (1948) to *Le Phénomène humain*, pp. 346 f. Teilhard does not in the least intend to deny the culpability of sin by his consideration of it as inevitable and in this sense necessary, an accessory phenomenon of the upward thrust of man and in his final destiny. Even here sin is for Teilhard, in conformity with his understanding of freedom and love as determining forces of human development, "malice . . . of the Spirit . . . who is choosing" (*PH*, 346), and consequently a voluntary evil option, a fault.

It is difficult to conceive of sin being at once inevitable and really culpable. Catholic thought is, nevertheless, familiar with this notion: think of the bondage of sin spoken of by St. Paul and the Council of Trent (*Dz.*, n. 793), which is really a bondage yet does not, for all that, do away with the culpability. St. Thomas likewise teaches that the sinner "before being healed by justifying and sanctifying grace, can indeed avoid mortal sins in particular for a certain space of time, . . . but it is impossible for him to remain long free of mortal sin" (*Summa Theologica*, I–II, q. 109, a. 8). This paradox is essential for the Catholic doctrine of original sin (cf. below, p. 176, and n. 57 to Appendix III).

These texts are speaking of fallen man, whereas Teilhard is more or less abstracting from the fall. But the texts do prove that the inevitable is not necessarily the inculpable. There is, therefore, no justification for concluding that, for Teilhard, "sin is purged of culpability" (Guérard des Lauriers, *art. cit.*, in *Divinitas*, III [1959], 247). Teilhard does not say this nor does it follow logically from his premises. Not, that is, unless "inevitable" and "inculpable" be identified, in contradiction of St. Thomas.

44 E.g., *De veritate*, q. 24, a. 9.

45 The well-known remark of St. Augustine: "by the redemption, all that had been scattered in me is again gathered together" (*Confessions*, X, 40, 65) is the echo of an ancient tradition.

46 M. M. Labourdette, *Le Péché originel et les origines de l'homme* (Paris: Alsatia, 1953), p. 146: "Someone may perhaps be tempted . . . to add that, even on the human scene, there is need for thousands of defeats and reverses to score one success of salvation and of sanctity; but this would be to forget just the point, . . . that with man we enter into a different sort of 'history': a history guided by a special Providence that does not subordinate the individuals

to the species, but rather orders everything to persons, each one of whom has a value all his own, irreducible to the whole, not to be subordinated to any other finite common good, to be subordinated to God alone. Man does indeed seem, in his status as a corporeal living being, to be subject to this law of prodigality which squanders individuals without number . . . ; but man is more than a mere corporeal living being; he has a supernatural destiny and there has never been lacking, in any age of mankind, a condign rule of salvation."

[47] Tresmontant, p. 117 f.: "There is, in human evil, a *remainder* which cannot be explained either in terms of the multiple nature nor yet by the temporality of the genesis in progress. The perversity of the concentration camp butchers cannot be explained simply in terms of the Manifold! . . . Teilhard seems not to distinguish sufficiently between physical evil, which is susceptible of a natural explanation in terms of the unfinished state of creation, and the evil that springs from the sin of man."

[48] It could perhaps be said that for one canonized saint there must needs be a great number of mediocrities. For such sanctity and such mediocrity are also functions of factors such as disposition, character, etc., which are in part determined by corporeal magnitudes and are therefore quantitative. But the question at issue is whether the radical and exclusive option, the *yes* or *no* to love, can be quantitatively determined. Although, in fact, the *yes* and the *no* rarely attain the prodigious intensity that makes the saint or the human fiend.

[49] Cf. Appendix III, "Evolution and Original Sin."

[50] Matthew 12: 31 f.

[51] Titus 2: 11.

[52] Rom. 5: 8.

[53] In Cuénot, p. 484.

[54] *PH*, 347.

[55] Rom. 4: 5.

[56] Rom. 4: 17.

[57] Rom. 4: 25.

[58] II Pet. 3: 13.

[59] I Cor. 15: 54–57.

[60] II Cor. 1: 9–10.

[61] *PH*, 343, n. 1; Eng. trans., p. 308, n. 2; cf. *Oeuvres*, V (1948), 305.

[62] N. Corte, *La vie et l'âme de Teilhard de Chardin* (Paris: Fayard, 1957), p. 204.

[63] I Cor. 3: 11.

[64] Perhaps he does, all the same, indicate the insufficiency of the intra-cosmic optimism, when he writes that the final issue of evolution is "positively guaranteed" by the resurrection of Christ (*PH*, 343, n. 1; Eng. trans., p. 308, n. 2). But, he adds, this certitude rests upon supernatural faith, it is "of a supra-phenomenal order" and therefore allows the intracosmic anguish to subsist in a certain sense. Here, therefore, he is limiting himself deliberately to the apologetic aspect.

[65] *MD*, 19; Eng. trans., p. 12.

[66] Cf. below, p. 209.

[67] *MD*, 169; Eng. trans., p. 115.

[68] *MD*, 77; Eng. trans., p. 50; cf. 171.

[69] *PH*, 326.

[70] *GZ*, 162.

[71] *Oeuvres*, V (1941), 104.

[72] The passages cited above in note 64 to this Chapter seem to indicate this.

[73] Cf. above, p. 151.

[74] *Oeuvres*, III (1942), 323.

APPENDIX III

[1] *MD*, 89; Eng. trans., p. 58.

[2] Cf. above, pp. 152 f.

[3] *Christologie et évolution.*

[4] 1948.

[5] *Comment je vois*, note 32.

[6] *PH*, 332; *MD*, 117.

[7] P. Schoonenberg, "De erfzonde als situatie," in *Bijdragen* XXII (1961), 1.

[8] C. Dumont, "La prédication du péché originel," in *Nouvelle revue théologique*, XCIII (1916), 117; "What is primary is the disclosure of the vocation to salvation within the community of sinners."

[9] *Dz.*, n. 790 f.

[10] K. Rahner, "Das Dogma von der unbefleckten Empfängnis Mariens," in *Schriften zur Theologie* (Einsiedeln: Benzinger, 1956), III, 159.

[11] H. Küng, *Rechtfertigung* (Einsiedeln: Johannes Verlag, 1957), p. 150; cf. Küng's thinking on the place of the Incarnation and the Redemption in the Divine Plan, pp. 127–170.

[12] B. Willaert, "Aantekeningen bij de erfzondeleer," in *Collationes Brugenses Gandavenses*, VI (1960), 509.

[13] A. M. Dubarle, *Le péché originel dans l'Écriture* (Paris: Cerf, 1958), p. 127, n. 3; cf. pp. 130, 142.

[14] *Acta concilii Tridentini*, ed. Goerres, I, 75; for similar remarks by other bishops, cf. V, 178.

[15] Cf. an attempt to revive the notion of collective responsibility and guilt in L. Bouyer, "Les Deux Économies du gouvernement divin: Satan et le Christ," in *Initiation théologique* (Paris: Cerf, 1952), pp. 503–535; various studies by P. Schoonenberg, "Zonde en verlossing als grondsituaties," in *Annalen Thijmgenootschap*, XLVIII (1960), 136–151; "De erfzonde als situatie," in *Bijdragen*, XXII (1961), 1–30; *Het geloof van ons doopsel* ('s Hertogenbosch, Malmberg, 1962), IV, 73–200. There has been a revival of the original biblical notion via the concept of the "corporative personality," mentioned by J. de Fraine, among others, in his *Adam et son lignage* (Paris-Bruges: Desclée De Brouwer, 1959).

[16] This school of thought reduces concupiscence from a generic egotism to a merely sensual and sexual passion; cf. below, pp. 170 f.

[17] M. Flick and Z. Alszeghy, "L'opzione fondamentale," in *Gregorianum*, XLI (1960), 18. In his classical work, *Théologie de saint Paul* (33rd ed.; Paris: Beauchesne, 1912), I, 257, note. F. Prat was already writing that Röm. 5:12

referred to original sin, "on condition, however, that original sin be not considered *in isolation* but rather with its whole retinue of evils, among which is actual sin as well."

[18] An example would be B. Haering, *The Law of Christ* (Westminster: Newman, 1961), I. "Many shortcomings do not stem from any *personal* fault, present or past, but rather from the consequences of original sin, from the sin of our ancestors or from the 'burden' of an evil environment. For such shortcomings, we cannot elicit contrition in the strict sense."

[19] Col. 1: 15–17.

[20] Eph. 2: 20.

[21] H. Küng, *Rechtfertigung* (Einsiedeln: Johannes Verlag, 1957), p. 135. Cf. F. Malmberg, *Ueber den Gottmenschen* (Freiburg: Herder, 1960), pp. 9–26.

[22] Cf. below, p. 229.

[23] H. Renckens, *Israëls visie op het verleden* (4th ed.; Tielt: Lannoo), pp. 200 f.

[24] Cf. the commentary on Isaiah 2: 6–9, in H. Renckens, *De profeet van Gods nabijheid* (Tielt: Lannoo, 1961), p. 96.

[25] Rom. 10: 3.

[26] *Dz.*, n. 792.

[27] Thus St. Thomas Aquinas states against those who would see something despicable in marital relations: "The good use of the good things created by God is meritorious" (*In Sent.*, IV, dist. 26, q. 1, a. 4, ad 3).

[28] Cf. below, pp. 203 f. This whole complex of problems is treated with great thoroughness and incisiveness by Augustine in his sermons. Cf. "De pelgrim naar het Absolute, eeuwigheidsverlangen en tij delijke waarden bij Augustinus," in *Bijdragen*, XVI (1955), 136–155.

[29] St. Augustine, *De civitate Dei*, XIV, c. 28.

[30] One of the few post-Tridentine theologians to recognize and admit a concupiscence within the will itself ("*in mente*") was St. Robert Bellarmine (*Controv. de amissione gratiae*, V, c. 15, ed. Vivés, V, p. 441). In recent times, there has also been K. Rahner ("Zum theologischen Begriff der Konkupiszenz," in *Schriften zur Theologie* [Einsiedeln: Benzinger, 1954], I, 377–441). But Rahner's exposition is unsatisfactory: he does indeed demonstrate the metaphysical basis of the divided state of the will, but he does not make clear what is the inclination to evil.

[31] Rom. 7: 15.

[32] Cf. above, p. 154.

[33] I John 2: 6.

[34] I John 2: 15; James 4: 4.

[35] Rom. 8: 20.

[36] H. Renckens, *De profeet van Gods nabijheid* (Tielt: Lannoo, 1961), p. 86. Cf. James 4: 1–2, on the relationship between concupiscence and wars.

[37] Cf. Rom. 1: 28–32.

[38] Rom. 3: 3.

[39] Cf. Rom. 5: 8.

[40] P. Schoonenberg, *Het geloof van ons doopsel* (s' Hertogenbosch: Malmberg, 1962), p. 152.

41 V. Schurr, "Theologie der Umwelt," in *Theologie in Geschichte und Gegenwart, M. Schmaus dargebracht* (Munich: Zink, 1957), p. 164.

42 Eph. 2: 2.

43 H. Schlier, *Mächte und Gewalten im Neuen Testament* (Freiberg: Herder, 1958), p. 29.

44 This notion of a co-causality of the sins of the children of Adam with original sin is not absolutely contrary to the definitions of Trent, according to which sin is "*origine unum*" ("one in its origin" [*Dz.*, n. 790]). The Council's definition has another aim in view. Since these words likewise play a part in the monogenism controversy, we shall return to them later (cf. p. 192). The Council draft had the words "*quod unum est*," without "*origine*." Some wanted to delete this phrase entirely (*Conc. Trid.*, ed. Soc. Goerr., V, p. 173, 208, 218). The upshot was the submission on 14 June 1546 of the proposed reading "*quod origine unum est*."

Some days previously, there had been submitted to the bishops a list of errors to be condemned. Two of these related to the unity of original sin (*op. cit.*, V, pp. 212 f.): the fourth, the error of Albert Pighius and other nominalists, holding that original sin is not an interior reality in every child of Adam, but rather the act of Adam alone, imputed by God to Adam's children; and the last, mentioned and combatted by Peter Lombard as an opinion held by Augustine, to the effect that there was a hereditary transmission not only of the fault of Adam but also of that of the other ancestors to the fourth generation.

Some interpreters of the Tridentine decree assert, without further proof, that the formula is directed against this last "error" (W. Koch, "Das Trienter Konzilsdekret *de peccato originali*," in *Tübinger theologische Quartalschrift*, XCVI [1914], 104; M. Labourdette, *Le Péché originel et les origines de l'homme* [Paris: Alsatia, 1953], p. 42). This is highly improbable. The Council confined itself on principle to errors of contemporary interest; the "error" mentioned by Peter Lombard was certainly not one of these! The Council Fathers knew that it occurred in St. Augustine (e.g., *Enchiridion*, XIII, 47). It is unthinkable that they would have been willing to condemn an opinion of this Doctor of the Church without grave reasons and serious discussion. Undoubtedly the reason why several wanted to delete the first wording lay in their concern lest the Council take an unintentional sideswipe at Augustine. Moreover, the rest of the sentence is clearly aimed at Pighius' opinion. The noted expert on Trent, H. Jedin (*Geschichte des Konzils von Trient* [Freiburg: Herder, 1957], II, 135; cf. 128) is therefore correct in writing: "Only the doctrine of the numerical unity of original sin, as held by Pighius, . . . is clearly condemned in Canon 3."

It follows that the addition of "*origine*" aims at excluding any exaggerated and narrow notion of the unity of original sin. The formula says that original sin is not numerically one in all men but that its unity resides rather in its origin. The Council makes no pronouncement on the nature of this unity accruing from origin.

45 L. Bouyer, "Les deux Économies du gouvernement divin," in *Initiation théologique* (Paris: Cerf, 1952), II, 504.

46 Matt. 15: 11 10.

[47] James 1: 14.

[48] E.g. Jeremias 3: 17; 18: 12.

[49] Genesis 8: 21; cf. 6: 5.

[50] J. Freundorfer, *Erbsünde und Erbtod beim Apostel Paulus* (Münster: Axchendorf, 1927), pp. 82–84, 100 f.; O. Kuss, *Der Römerbrief* (Regensburg: Pustet, 1957), pp. 266, 270.

[51] Cf. e.g., the note to Rom. 7: 5, in the Dutch translation of the Bible (Willibrordvertaling). It often renders "*sarx*" as "egotism."

[52] Cf. Eph. 4: 17–19; Rom. 5: 12–21.

[53] Gal. 5: 17.

[54] Rom. 8: 7.

[55] St. Augustine in particular has stressed that "carnality" (*carnalitas*) has its seat, properly speaking, in the higher faculties, and that the revolt of the senses is but a consequence of it. He shows, for example, that "the carnal way of life stems not only from the vices of the body but also from those of the soul," so that a man who curbs and holds in check his sensible passions, out of pride, is still living carnally. Real carnal vice lies in the soul, where man chooses to live "his own way" and not God's. (*De civitate Dei*, XIV, cc. 2–3.)

[56] L. Bouyer, "Les Deux Économies du gouvernement divin," in *Initiation théologique* (Paris: Cerf, 1952), II, 507.

[57] Cf. Council of Trent, *Dz.* n. 793. To develop this paradox in all its details and ramifications would lead us too far afield. Theology speaks of a strict but "moral" impossibility (i.e., not explicitly stated to be "metaphysical") of observing the commandments for a protracted period, that is, of acting righteously, so as to merit the ascription of righteousness as a result of this course of action. Thomas Aquinas points out that this impotence has to do, in the first instance, with the loving of God; fallen man cannot love God without sanctifying grace (*Summa Theologica*, I–II, q. 109, a. 3). Every explanation of this doctrine must hold that the capacity and the incapacity to love God are both present at the same time in the will of the person. The incapacity, because otherwise man would be able to break the bonds of his servitude himself; the capacity, because the voluntary nature of every choice would vanish, and with it the culpability of vice, were the will no longer the faculty for *every* good and accordingly for God, the Infinite God, as well. In other words, the incapacity consists in the fact that the free will does not make use of its own faculty and therefore manifestly does not want to make use of it. This incapacity is at the same time a flaw and fault of will, a willing fault in more ways than one!

[58] St. Bonaventure, *In IV Sent.*, dist. 25, a. 1, q. 2, ad 6. The Council of Trent speaks of "*liberum arbitrium . . . inclinatum*" (*Dz.*, n. 792).

[59] *Dz.*, n. 788.

[60] Cf. the article "Esprit saint, Péres latines" in *Dict. de spiritualité*, IV (1960), col. 1280–1282.

[61] *Dz.*, n. 789.

[62] M. Oraison, "Psychologie et sens du péché," in *Le Péché* (Paris-Bruges: Desclée De Brouwer, 1959), p. 21.

[63] H Renckens, *Israëls visie op het verleden* (4th ed.; Tielt, Lannoo, 1960), p. 226.

[64] H. Renckens, *De profeet van de nabijheid Gods* (Tielt: Lannoo, 1961), p. 110.

[65] Cf. below, pp. 233 f.

[66] On the problem of whether Adam must be conceived necessarily as being an individual man or whether he can be taken to designate the ancestors of mankind, cf. the discussion of monogenism, below, Appendix IV.

[67] *Dz.*, n. 789.

[68] Rom. 5: 19.

[69] Adam means "man" and is usually used in the Bible to designate mankind, rarely as a proper name. Cf. J. de Fraine, *Adam et son lignage* (Paris-Bruges: Desclée De Brouwer, 1959), pp. 121–124.

[70] A. M. Dubarle, *Le Péché originel dans l'Écriture* (Paris: Cerf, 1958), p. 147: "The writer is delineating in the story of the ancestor the state of the race. Thus it is entirely in conformity with the intention inspiring this passage to see in the reflex of fear and flight before God immediately after the act of disobedience, not a purely individual occurrence, but rather the prototype of a gesture and of the feelings of sheer terror and the attempt to hide from contact with God, all of which are repeatedly described in Scripture."

[71] H. Renckens, *Israëls visie op het verleden* (4th ed.; Tielt, Lannoo, 1960), p. 199.

[72] G. von Rad, *Das erste Buch Mose: Genésis I–XII* (4th ed., Göttingen, 1960), p. 60.

[73] Cf. above, n. 44 to this Chapter.

[74] Rom. 1: 18–3:20.

[75] Ecclus. 25: 23.

[76] O. Kuss, *Der Römerbrief* (Regensburg: Pustet, 1957), pp. 227 f.: "This power of sin entered into the world as overlord . . . after Adam . . . had opened the way for it."

[77] A. M. Dubarle, *Le Péché originel dans l'Écriture* (Paris, Cerf, 1958), p. 72; cf. pp. 70 f.

[78] Rom. 5: 18.

[79] Rom. 6: 16.

[80] M. Flick and Z. Alszeghy, "L'opzione fondamentale," in *Gregorianum*, XLI (1960), 618.

[81] Cf. A. Feuillet, "Le verset 7 du 'Miserere' et le péché originel," in *Sciences religieuses* (*Recherches de science religieuse*, 1944), 5–26; J. Mehlmann, *Natura filii irae* (Rome: Pont. Instit. Bibl., 1957).

[82] Rom. 5: 12: "Therefore, even as by one man sin entered into the world and by sin death, and as thus death has passed into all men, in that all have sinned . . . " (Jerusalem Bible translation, S. Lyonnet; cf. the note by Lyonnet in *Les Eptires de saint Paul aux Galates et aux Romains* [2nd ed., Paris: Cerf, 1959], pp. 90–91). The translation and exegesis of the last phrase in the passage cited are highly controversial.

An ancient Greek tradition explained original sin by saying that all men were mysteriously included in Adam and had sinned in him (e.g., Irenaeus, *Adversus Haereses*, V, 16, 3, *PG*, VII, col. 1168; Origen, *In Rom.*, 5, i, *PG*, XIV, 1009 f.). It is probably this influence which impelled the Latin translation to render the words ἐφ' ᾧ (seeing that) as "in whom." In the case of Augustine and his disciples, this translation became the most poignant expression of our solidarity with Adam.

Presently, the majority of exegetes are persuaded that the Greek phrase is a causative particle: "because," "given that," "given the fact that" (thus, e.g., A. Hulsbosch, "Zonde en dood in Rom. V, 12–21," in *Tijdschrift voor theologie*, I [1961], 199 f.). P. Schoonenberg's suggested translation "inasmuch as" seems to us unacceptable, certainly when it is understood restrictively, i.e., in the sense of "to the extent that" (*Het geloof van ons doopsel* ['s Hertogenbosch: Malmberg, 1962], IV, 110 f., 196). But this causative translation involves a difficulty: Paul first says that by the sin of one man sin and death have asserted their domination; then he proceeds to say that all die because *all* have sinned. So the translation "all having become guilty" (guilty, that is, by the sin of the one Adam) has been suggested. (Cf. L. Ligier, " 'In quo omnes peccaverunt' Actes ou état?," in *Nouvelle revue théologique*, XCII [1960], 337–349, and *Péché d'Adam et péché du monde* [Paris: Aubier, 1961], II, 273–277). But this translation [which could only be rendered exactly in English by the neologistic barbarism "sinified," for Ligier precisely aims at suggesting something other than purely passive reception of a cachet of sin, much less active than "become sinful" (or guilty) really conveyed and evocative of the same kind of process as that suggested by "Christify" as used by Teilhard (though, of course, antipodal to it!)—Note to English Translation.] is scarcely plausible, the term "sin" always having an active meaning (S. Lyonnet, *De peccato originali* [Rome: Pont. Inst. Bibl., 1960], pp. 95–101).

Lyonnet provides an ingenious and elegant solution to this difficulty. He shows that the Greek expression ἐφ' ᾧ is consistently used in a special causative sense. In contracts, it indicates, not the principal reason but the secondary conditions: "on condition that," or retrospectively "given the fact that the condition has been fulfilled" or "it being the case that the condition has been fulfilled" (S. Lyonnet, 'Le Sens de ἐφ' ᾧ en Rom. V, 12, et l'exégése des pères grecs," in *Biblica*, XXXVI [1955], 436–456, and other articles). Paul would, on this reading, be saying: "the condition being fulfilled that *all* adults *have sinned* personally, ratifying in this way and making their own the revolt of Adam" ("Le Péché originel et l'exégèse de Rom. V, 12–14," in *Recherches de science religeuse*, XLIV [1956], 83 f.)

83 Cf. preceding note. Hulsbosch, *loc. cit.*, and G. Lafont, "Sur l'interprétation de Rom. V, 12–14," in *Recherches de science religieuse*, XLV (1957), 481–513, side substantially with Lyonnet.

84 Wisdom 2: 25.

85 S. Lyonnet, "Le Péché originel et l'exégèse de Rom. V, 12–14" in *Recherches de science religieuse*, XLIV (1956), 70.

86 Lafont, *loc. cit.*, p. 485.

87 Thus Lyonnet.

88 Thus Hulsbosch.

89 Cf. below, p. 188.

90 J. de Fraine, *Adam et son lignage* (Paris-Bruges: Desclée De Brouwer, 1959), p. 91.

91 *Dz.*, n. 790.

92 *Ibid.*, n. 791, 795.

93 J. de Fraine, *De Bijbel en het ontstaan van de mens* (Antwerp: Sheed & Ward, 1955), p. 60; *La Bible et l'origine de l'homme* (Bruges: Desclée De Brouwer, 1961), p. 109.

94 *Acta concilii tridentini*, ed. Soc. Goerres, V, pp. 201–203.

95 The Council Fathers were not envisaging a problem at the level of the question posed by St. Thomas (*Summa Theol.* I–II, q. 81, a. 4), as to whether a man formed of human matter without impregnation would incur original sin. The sanctity of Christ rests on the fact that he has God alone for Father, a fact of which the virginal conception is a sign; the Council did not examine the question of whether this sanctity depends also on the fact that he was "born not of the will of the flesh or of the will of man" (John 1: 13).

96 *Pensées*, n. 625.

97 C. Hauret, *Origines, Genèse I–III* (Paris: Gabalda, 1950), pp. 130–132; H. Renckens, *Israëls visie op het verleden* (4th ed.; Tielt: Lannoo, 1960), pp. 32–40. Cf. above, pp. 48 f.

98 A. M. Dubarle, *Le Péché originel dans l'Écriture* (Paris: Cerf, 1948), pp. 49 f.

99 H. Renckens, *Israëls visie op het verleden* (4th ed.; Tielt: Lannoo, 1960), pp. 129, 149.

100 G. von Rad, *Das erste Buch Mose: Genesis I–XII* (4th ed.; Göttingen), p. 81.

101 M. M. Labourdette, *Le Péché originel et les origines de l'homme* (Paris: Alsatia, 1953), p. 177.

102 A. M. Dubarle, *Le Péché originel dans l'Écriture* (Paris: Cerf, 1958), p. 60.

103 Philo, *De opificio mundi*, 140.

104 M. M. Labourdette, *Le Péché originel et les origines de l'homme* (Paris: Alsatia, 1953), p. 174.

105 Labourdette, *ibid.*, p. 173.

106 A. M. Dubarle, *Le Péché originel dans l'Écriture* (Paris: Cerf, 1958), p. 69.

107 Rom. 8: 20.

108 A. Dubarle, *op. cit.*, pp. 10 f. Cf. e.g., in Job 5: 26, and in Isaias 65: 19–23 a description of the Messianic Paradise.

109 Cf. e.g., K. Rahner, *Zur Theologie des Todes* (Freiburg: Herder, 1958), p. 33: "It is evident that man would have terminated and consummated his life when, while remaining in his body, he had matured and fulfilled his interior life to perfection . . . The end of the man of paradise, man in a state of primal innocence, this death without death, would have been a pure, manifest, active fulfillment of the whole man, a fulfillment originating in the inner man without passing through a death in the strict sense, i.e., a privation of concrete corporeity, physical nature, coming to smite him from outside." French translation: *Écrits Théologiques* (Desclée de Brouwer), III, 129.

110 Dz., 792.

111 Cf. above, pp. 169 ff.

112 The motif of nakedness having shame connected with it after the Fall but not before (Genesis 2: 25; 3: 7, 10 f., 21) has often been seen as being a direct witness to the preservation of the First Parents before the Fall from any

revolt of the sexual passion. Thus, e.g., J. van Dodewaard, "Bijbelse theologie van de kleding," in *Nederlandse katholieke stemmen*, XLIX (1953), 204. Later exegetes hold this to be extremely doubtful. Nakedness is almost never, in the Bible, the symbol of sexual seductiveness; it is the sign "of shame and humiliation, of weakness and powerlessness" (H. Renckens, *Israëls visie op het verleden* [4th ed.; Tielt: Lannoo, 1960], p. 211). The function of clothing is less to combat sexual desire than to manifest dignity. By his clothing, man gives himself a dignity that he would not perhaps have from his "naked" self. So that clothing is a "synecdoche . . . of all the dissembling that renders social life, life in society, possible" (A. M. Dubarle, *Le Péché originel dans l'Écriture* [Paris: Cerf, 1958], p. 64). The nakedness of the First Parents in Paradise would therefore signify rather that man then was fine and beautiful and impressive in himself and able to show himself without shame before his fellow human being(s) and before God; while the need for clothing after the Fall would signify that sin had raised a wall of hypocrisy, rendering even the man and the woman strangers to each other.

[113] Cf. Rom. 6: 13–19.

APPENDIX IV

[1] P. Overhage, *Das Problem der Hominisation* (Freiberg: Herder, 1961), p. 179; E. Boné, "Polygénisme et polyphylétisme," in *Archives de philosophie*, XXIII (1960), 102–106, n. 1.

[2] M. Labourdette, *Le Péché originel et les origines de l'homme* (Paris: Alsatia, 1953), p. 146.

[3] This is usually held to be the case from the moment they begin using tools (thus, e.g., Teilhard, *Oeuvres*, II [1955], 324). But recent years have seen considerable doubt cast on the fact that every use of tools is a proof of reason (V. Marcozzi, "Alla ricerca delle prime tracie sicure dell'uomo," in *Gregorianum*, XLI [1960], 688 f.; P. Overhage, *Das Problem der Hominisation* [Freiburg: Herder, 1961], p. 132–137).

[4] Pius XII, *Humani generis*, in *Dz.*, n. 3028. Cf. A. Bea, "Die Enzyklika 'Humani generis,' ihre Grundgedanken und ihre Bedeutung," in *Scholastik*, XXVI (1951), 54: "The question as to whether there are forms of polygenism which might be compatible with the known doctrine of the Church remains open."

[5] H. Renckens, *Israëls visie op het verleden* (4th ed.; Tielt: Lannoo, 1960), p. 186.

[6] Renckens, *loc. cit.*, p. 192.

[7] But attention must be paid to the fact that rabbinical exegesis used to interpret purely literary details as a prefiguration. Melchisedech is a prefiguration of the eternal priesthood of Christ because the Bible does not *mention* his father and his mother, his birth or his death (Hebrews 7: 3).

[8] Thus J. de Fraine, *La Bible et l'origine de l'homme* (Paris-Bruges: Desclée De Brouwer, 1961), p. 90. De Fraine does indeed desire to maintain the unicity of the first sin ("there is no doubt that the unity of the first sin is asserted; the state of sin of the whole of mankind is related to a single transgression"), but not that of one "individual transgressor." Since Paul insisted on

the one single sinner no less than on the one single sin, this distinction seems inspired by motives other than exegetical.

⁹ Renckens, *op. cit.*, p. 192.

¹⁰ If this is an accurate interpretation of the teaching of Scripture, the theologian should refrain from further specifications as to whether there was a single sin of which the first human group as a whole was guilty; as to whether it was the sin of a single individual of which a whole group was also guilty without any other member actually having personally committed it; as to whether various human groups which later merged into the one and only human race may have sinned separately. Incidentally, the contention that it would be improbable or even inconceivable that all the members of the first human group or of each one of these groups, supposing there to be several, would have sinned after having received grace, does not constitute a theological argument against such a polygenist interpretation (this argument is developed at length by H. Lennerz, "Quid dicendum theologo de polygenismo?" in *Gregorianum*, XXIX [1948], 419–423. M. Labourdette, *Le Péché originel et les origines de l'homme* [Paris: Alsatia, 1953], pp. 161 f.). If Scripture gave no details on original sin, it would be entirely pointless for theology to try to envision what might or might not have happened. This would be the purlieu of human curiosity, not of theological reflection.

Karl Rahner has attempted a major exercise, of imposing proportions, in philosophically based proof of monogenism (K. Rahner, "Theologische zum Monogenismus," in *Schriften zur Theologie* [Einsiedeln: Benzinger, 1954], I, 253–322). He contends that all participation in humanity must be based upon descent. He grounds this contention on the fact that no one becomes a member of the human family save by birth. But this argument neglects the difference between actual humanity and humanity *in fieri*, a difference which the polygenist view considers essential. In the world of our own experience no one can become a member of mankind save by birth; it is crystal clear that there can be no humanity without consanguinity. But polygenism supposes that, in the age of primitive primordial humanity, an age of biologically active evolution, a human being could be born of non-human parents.

¹¹ *Dz.*, n. 790.

¹² Cf. above, n. 44 to Appendix III.

¹³ It is certainly inaccurate to say, as does Lennerz ("Quid dicendum theologo de polygenismo" in *Gregorianum*, XXIX, 1948, p. 423) that Trent intended, with these words, an out-and-out teaching of the unity of the *peccatum originans*. The problem at issue had to do with the unity of original sin in men today, the *peccatum originale originatum*. By saying that this original sin was one in its origin, the Council was not making any pointblank, categorical definition on the nature of this single origin.

¹⁴ *Dz.*, n. 3028.

¹⁵ In an earlier study, we stated it as our opinion that monogenism was a doctrine of faith, its *de fide* note being based on the authority of the bishops taking part in Vatican I. They did indeed move to define that "the whole human race descends from the one Adam" (Mansi, LIII, col. 236), and not one of the sixty bishops giving an opinion on this proposition formulated any objection

to this clause, an impressive proof of the conviction of the bishops in council assembled (cf. "De evolutieleer en het geloof," in *Nederlandse katholieke stemmen*, XLVI [1950], 370 f.). But a closer look shows that a doubt still persists. The bishops were desirous of teaching that the human race is one, against those who considered the Negroes or the Indians as not being really human at all: "Tertium dogma, quod statuitur, est unitas generis humani" (col. 212; cf. *Dz.*, n. 2123). It was a reflex action for them to express this unity in the formula of the single ancestor. Perhaps a more thorough and minute discussion would have made the distinction between the doctrine and its presentation.

[16] *Oeuvres*, III, 131.

[17] *Oeuvres*, III (1925), 132; (1926), 177 f., *PH*, p. 205 f.; *GZ*, pp. 81–83.

[18] The very recent past has seen doubts appearing among the paleontologists concerning this explanation of the disappearance of intermediary forms. This disappearance could equally well be a sign of the small number of individuals actively involved in the evolutive process. Cf. P. Overhage, "Der 'leere Raum des Ursprungs' oder die 'Brüche' in der Evolution des Lebendigen," in *Stimmen der Zeit*, CLXIX (1961–1962), 339–351.

[19] *PH*, p. 206, n. 1; *GZ*, 83, n. 1.

[20] On the status of the question among the naturalists, on these points, cf. E. Boné, "Polygénisme et polyphylétisme," in *Archives de philosophie*, XXIII (1960), 99–141.

[21] *Courrier de l'Unesco*, July–August 1950. Teilhard writes: "The human social group—which no one can deny to be perfectly monophyletic, despite all the gaps . . ." (*GZ*, 119; cf. *PH*, 208, n. 1). Likewise Boné: "The family of the Hominidae, as we know it today in all the complexity of its present races and the sum total of the fossil types . . . which have preceded them, can be called *monophyletic* in this sense, that it constitutes a homogeneous group, genetically unitary, possessing a single original animal ancestral stock" (*loc. cit.*, p. 136).

[22] Boné, *op. cit.*, p. 136.

[23] *Oeuvres*, III (1923), 99: "Man appeared in very modest fashion, in a strictly and narrowly limited region of Life and of the Earth . . . in a very restricted zone of the ancient world . . ." *PH*, p. 208: "All the human lineages . . . would focalize generically, toward the base, at the very point-event of Reflection."

[24] *Oeuvres*, II (1953), 260; (1955), 286–288; (1955), 315, 322 f. Thus, when he envisages the possibility that "certain remains (such as some in Australia?) might represent the traces of a more or less transformed state of a phyletic verticil more ancient than Homo Sapiens" (*Oeuvres*, II, 323, n. 1), he probably has in mind the possibility that certain primitive races may owe their origin to a cross-breeding of Homo sapiens with the Neanderthal Hominidaes or other such.

[25] *Oeuvres*, III, 219.

[26] *Ibid.*, 220.

[27] A summary of this theory is presented by Boné, *loc. cit.*, pp. 133 f.

[28] It must, however, be noted that Neo-Darwinism is gaining ground in the minds of very eminent scientists. And it favors polygenism. Cf. M. Lamotte, "La théorie actuelle des mécanismes de l'évolution," in *Archives de Philosophie*, XXIII (I–1960), 8–56.

[29] Boné, *loc. cit.*, p. 130–132; P. Overhage, *Das Problem der Hominisation* (Freiburg: Herder, 1961), pp. 182–184.

[30] Boné, *ibid.*, p. 137; cf. *PH*, p. 209.

[31] Overhage, *loc. cit.*, p. 185.

CHAPTER 8

[1] "Le Christique" (1955).

[2] Those who have are: Fr. H. de Lubac, in his major work, *La Pensée religieuse du P. Pierre Teilhard de Chardin* (1962); P. N. M. Wildiers, in his *Teilhard de Chardin* (1960, pp. 110–126); Tresmontant (in a brief section, 97–107); and L. Boros, in his series of articles, "Evolutionismus und Spiritualität: ein Versuch über die 'geistliche Lehre' Teilhard de Chardin," in *Der grosse Entschluss*, XV (1959–1960), 254–259; 301–303; 346–350; and 398–403.

[3] *MD*, 18; Eng. trans., p. 12.

[4] Tresmontant, p. 100.

[5] Cf. above, pp. 62 f.

[6] Cuénot, p. 19.

[7] *LV*, 107 (1927).

[8] Letter of 22 July 1916, *Genèse*, p. 145; Eng. trans., *The Making of a Mind*, p. 114.

[9] E.g., *MD*, 33–36; Eng. trans., 18–21.

[10] The words *"heil"* (=salvation) and *"heel"* (=whole, intact) in the original Dutch are etymologically identical. The English translator has however felt justified in conveying the play on words by this slight variation, since the same *kind* of etymological nexus (a highly significant one) exists in English between "holiness" and "wholeness."—[Translator's Note.]

[11] I Tim. 4: 4–5.

[12] Cf. "De pelgrim naar het absolute: eeuwigheidsverlangen en tijdelijke waarden bij Augustinus," in *Bijdragen*, XVI (1955), 136–155.

[13] N. M. Wildiers, "Préface," in *Oeuvres*, V, 15 f.

[14] *MD*, 62; Eng. trans., p. 45.

[15] *MD*, 36; Eng. trans., p. 21; italics ours—Author.

[16] *MD*, 39; Eng. trans., p. 23.

[17] *Ibid.*

[18] Cf. a similar criticism in K. Rahner, "Ueber die gute Meinung," in *Schriften zur Theologie*, III (1956), 127–154.

[19] John 4: 37.

[20] *NLV*, 78.

[21] I Cor. 10: 31.

CHAPTER 9

[1] *MD*, 41 f.; Eng. trans. p. 25.

[2] *Exercises*, n. 23.

[3] Cf. above, pp. 49 f.

[4] Genesis 1; cf. Psalm 8.

[5] I Cor. 3: 21.

[6] *MD*, 77; Eng. trans., p. 50.

[7] *MD*, 79; Eng. trans., p. 51.

[8] *Ibid.* These lines are reminiscent of the "sacrament of the present moment," of Fr. de Caussade, S.J., proclaiming that nothing can better unite us to God than the conformity to his creative and sanctifying will at every instant of our life.

[9] Wisdom 2: 23.

[10] St. Augustine, *De Trinitate*, XIII, 4, 7.

[11] *MD*, 143 f.

[12] Thomas à Kempis himself, incidentally, inserts into the next chapter a rectification of a possible misunderstanding (*Imitation of Christ*, III, 54 and 55).

[13] "Réflexions sur le bonheur," in *Cahiers*, II, p. 61.

[14] *MD*, 64; Eng. trans., p. 41.

[15] "Réflexions sur le bonheur," p. 62.

[16] *MD*, 93; Eng. trans., p. 61.

[17] "Réflexions sur le bonheur," pp. 61 and 63.

[18] *MD*, 111, Eng. trans., p. 73. Cf. "La signification et la valeur constructrice de la souffrance," in *Oeuvres*, VI (1933), 59 f.

[19] *MD*, 112 f. Eng. trans., pp. 75, 176, Eng. trans., p. 117.

[20] *MD*, 86; Eng. trans., p. 56.

[21] Proverbs 3: 9. Cf. "The Mass of the World," in *Hymn of the Universe*, p. 20. Cf. also the meditations on the meaning of the religious vows, in Cuénot, p. 43 f., and the sentiments confided by Teilhard to a friend just prior to his taking of solemn vows in 1918: "I am about to take a vow of poverty: never have I had a better understanding of the extent to which money can be a powerful means for the service and glorification of God. I am about to take a vow of chastity: never have I had a better understanding of the extent to which man and woman can conspire to lift up a mutually perfected heart to God. I am about to take a vow of obedience: never have I had a better understanding to the extent to which God makes those who serve him free."

[22] E.g., Tresmontant, pp. 98–100.

[23] *MD*, 51; Eng. trans., p. 31.

CHAPTER 10

[1] Letter of 30 July 1918, *Genèse*, p. 290; Eng. trans., *The Making of a Mind*, p. 1.

[2] *Comment je vois*, 1934; cf. *MD*, 200.

[3] *MD*, 40; Eng. trans., p. 24.

[4] *MD*, 199; Eng. trans., pp. 133–134; fragment from 1955 in N. M. Wildiers, "God en het Universum," in *Revue Teilhard de Chardin*, n. 1–2 (1960), p. 15.

[5] "Le Christique" (1955) in Leroy, p. 54; cf. Wildiers, *loc. cit.*

[6] "Now was the moment when I became aware of something: and it was that, from the depths of the cosmic future even as from the heights of Heaven,

it was still God, it was *still the same God,* who was calling me. A God of the *Perge* (Forward!) suddenly come into view transversely to *the traditional God of the Sursum (Upward!)* . . . in such a way that henceforth we should never be able to offer *adequate worship* without superimposing the two images *into a single one* . . ." (*Le Coeur de la matière,* 1950). Related texts in *Oeuvres,* V, 342; "Le Christique." Elsewhere the same categories of the *Sursum* and the *Perge* are employed in a slightly different sense: *the Sursum* signifying the vertical line of the (supernatural) relation to God, the *Perge* signifying the horizontal line of (natural) human effort. Thus we read: "The Christian *Sursum* is incorporated with the human *Perge!* ('supernaturalizing' that *Perge* rather than being submerged in it!) . . . Salvation (deliverance) is at once heavenward and vanward." (*Oeuvres,* V [1949, p. 348 f.] Other passages in C. d'Armagnac, "La pensée du Père Teilhard de Chardin comme apologétique moderne," in *Nouv. Rev. Théol.* 94 [1964], 617 n. 46.)

[These two categories virtually defy translation into English and even Smulders seems to have allowed their drastically and consistently bidimensional Teilhardian significance to slither somewhat, hence precisely necessitating the explanatory note above about the "slightly different sense." In fact, Teilhard's use is consistently univocal: *L'En Avant* = the Forward (in the static locational and in the dynamic motional sense); *L'En Haut* = the Upward (in the static locational sense more punctiliously rendered in English by "On High," and in the dynamic motional sense precisely of "Upward!"). We have therefore elected to have recourse to Latin expletives: *Sursum* is fortunately entirely bidimensional (*Sursum corda!* is not simply, "Lift up your hearts!" but, "Have your hearts on high!"—a point rendered much more evident by the Slavonic rendering of the original Greek into *Gore imeem serdtsa:* "Let us *have* our hearts on high!"); *Perge* is the only parallel, though unfortunately incomparably less bidimensional, much more restrictively motional in evocation. Yet, precisely in the case of the "horizontal line of (natural) human effort," this stress is by no means undesirable. Yet *Perge* implies a destination. In the final sentence of the Teilhardian quotation above ("Salvation [deliverance] is at once . . .") we are however defeated, in the context of English, and have had to have recourse to two English terms "heavenward" and "vanward," though the Teilhardian terms remain the same, "*Le salut (l'issue) est à la fois en Haut et en Avant.*" But the most resilient English syntactical sense boggles at an imperative being converted into an adverb (bidimensional, at that!) and with this explanation we feel that justice has been done to the bidimensional subtlety of Teilhard's thought on this point. It should be specially and cautiously noted that our last "heavenward" is entirely inadequate, *strictly speaking,* in that it accents far too much the dynamic motional; but the difficulty could only have been resolved by the neologistic barbarism "heavenwardly" and such a semanteme belongs surely in an explanatory note, even when Teilhard is the subject of translation.—(Translator's Note.)]

[7] Cf., e.g., *MD,* 151–153.

[8] Cf. Col. 1: 16–17.

[9] *MD,* 150; Eng. trans., p. 101.

[10] *MD,* 149; Eng. trans., p. 101.

[11] Tertullian, *De anima* 33, 9; *De carnis resurrectione,* 6.

[12] Cf. Luke 3: 23–38

[13] St. Thomas, *De potentia*, q. 3, a. 10, ad 4: *"cum tota corporum mundi transmutatio ordinetur quodammodo ad animarum multiplicationem"*; cf. ad 3.

[14] *Oeuvres*, V, 342.

[15] H. Berkhof, *Christus de zin der geschiedenis* (Nijkerk: Callenbach, 1958), p. 17: "It is neither to Greece nor to Persia, but to Israel, that we owe the awareness of the finality of history and accordingly of history's meaning."

[16] *Oeuvres*, V (1947), 236; Eng. trans., p. 186.

[17] *Oeuvres*, V (1952), 394.

[18] *Oeuvres*, V (1947), 269; Eng. trans., p. 210.

[19] *MD*, 150; Eng. trans., p. 101; italics ours—Author. The use of the word *physically* is not in contradiction with the explanation given; it is opposed to a purely "moral" or "juridical" influence, such as there would be, for Teilhard the Suarezian, in the notion of merit; thus, *physically* here signifies *really*.

[20] *MD*, 56.

[21] Letter of January 9, 1917 (*Genèse*, p. 213): "What I appreciate in the earth is obviously not its lower part, now outstripped and decrepit. . . . For me the real earth is that part of the universe, still almost universally dispersed and in the course of gradual segregation, but which little by little is taking on body and form in Christ" (Eng. trans., p. 165).

[22] *MD*, 152; Eng. trans., p. 103.

[23] *MD*, 128, n. 1; Eng. trans., p. 86.

[24] *LV*, 129 f. (1930). Cf. a talk given by Teilhard in 1930 on money, which "represents to human beings material energy in an easily handled form. . . . And yet the more it can do, the more wonderful it is, the more, too, . . . does it require caution. Gold, which is blameless so long as it is busy in service and so long as it helps along the current of humanity, becomes corrupt as soon as it stands still . . ." (in Cuénot, p. 44; Eng. trans., p. 28).

[25] A very concrete application of the Ignatian principle: "In the case of those who are mounting from the good to the better in the service of the Lord, it is typical of the good spirit to give courage and strength . . . and to make everything easier" (*Exercises*, n. 315). Cf. letter of October 20, 1916 (*Genèse*, p. 172; Eng. trans., p. 134).

[26] Cf. the allocution of Pope Pius XII before the Pontifical Academy of Sciences, November 30, 1941: "The stature of man is imposing. Yet what but the dominion he exercises . . . upon the infra-human world can explain the advances he is scoring and developing in the physical, natural, mathematical and industrial sciences, in his eager thirst and yearning for ever better, broader and surer advances?" (ASS, 33 [1941], 507).

[27] *Le Coeur de la matière*, 1950; cf. *Oeuvres*, V (1920), 28 f.

[28] Cf. above, p. 110.

[29] *Oeuvres*, V (1947), 238; Eng. trans., pp. 187–188.

[30] *Le Prêtre* (1918).

[31] *Oeuvres*, III (1923), 106 f. A later essay (*Oeuvres*, V [1947], 238) again alludes to this equivocal nature of terrestrial progress but presents it as constituting but a transient phase. The old notion of persistent temptation and growing danger seems to me theoretically better founded. The danger seems

to me to have been exorcised only when a certain definite step in human progress is envisaged. This seems to be the way Teilhard is looking at the matter in the later essay. Romano Guardini reaches a similar conclusion: "This means that there is a constant increase in the possibility that man will use power badly" (*Das Ende der Neuzeit*, 1950, p. 99).

[32] In this connection, Berkhof's ideas are specially valuable. According to him, the Judeo-Christian doctrine of creation frees man from the servitude of the cosmos and affords him, on the contrary, the opportunity and the mission of subjecting the cosmos to his own service. But it also affords him the opportunity of exalting himself into a god: "The new Lord dispenses man, by obedience to Himself, from being a mere part of nature and of the social institutions revered as powers of nature. Christ brings with him the humanization of man and the subjection of nature." (H. Berkhof, *Christus de zin der geschiedenis* [Nijkerk: Callenbach, 1958] p. 84). "The prisoner of nature can emancipate himself and become child of God, but of course he can also monopolize the role of idol. This second possibility is also a derivative of the preaching of the Gospel!" (*ibid.*, p. 85).

[33] *Oeuvres*, V (1949), 334.

[34] Gabriel Marcel seems to be among those who succumb to this temptation to condemn the thing itself because of the danger it involves, when he writes: "I would be inclined to wonder today whether the hypertrophy of the technical sciences . . . would not tend toward the constitution of what would have to be called a *body of sin*, in opposition to the *body of light*, whose sole principle is charity" (G. Marcel, *Les Hommes contre l'humain* [Paris: La Colombe, 1951], p. 75). If it be Marcel's intention to insist on "*hypertrophy*" (i.e., *excessive* development), then the truth of his statement is patent: the hypertrophy of a partial value or a finite good is always the principle of sin; and if this hypertrophy begins to determine the shape of society, then it will indeed shape a "body of sin." This holds true for money, preferment, sex, etc., just as much as for technology. But Marcel's exposition tends to a depreciation of technology, as though technology had a special affinity with the body of sin. Marcel's basic principle is actually entirely in accord with Teilhard's: "Whatever is not done out of Love and for Love invariably ends by being done against Love" (*loc. cit.*, p. 58). (Cf. a public debate between Teilhard and Marcel, in Cuénot, p. 308 f.; Eng. trans., p. 251 ff.) A man with as much sound common sense as G. K. Chesterton committed the same sort of howler in coming out in favor of a reversion from modern industry to handicraft guilds and agriculture as a means of rehumanization and re-Christianization.

[35] *MD*, 201; Eng. trans., p. 138.

[36] *MD*, 117; Eng. trans., p. 78.

[37] *MD*, 108; Eng. trans., p. 71. We find this image of human effort as preparation of the sacrificial victim as early as the diary entry of December 29, 1919. Teilhard is addressing his friend A. Valensin and the remark is intended for M. Blondel: "First of all, I have no difficulty in agreeing that the universal effort of the World can be understood as being the preparation of a holocaust" (in *Archives de philosophie*, XXIV [1961], 151). This image may have been inspired by Blondel who had written in a diary entry of December 19, that he was not afraid of exaggerating human endeavor: "so that the matter of the holocaust

may appear more precious, and so that the value of the sacrifice may appear still more superabundant" (p. 149). But, whereas for Blondel the victim appears to be man's creative power, it becomes for Teilhard man himself and the world as man is building it up.

CHAPTER 11

[1] *MD*, 140–141; Eng. trans., pp. 94–95.

[2] *MD*, 24; Eng. trans., p. 14.

[3] "La messe sur le monde," *Hymne,* pp. 33 f.; Eng. trans., p. 36.

[4] "La messe sur le monde," p. 31; Eng. trans., p. 32.

[5] *MD*, 171; Eng. trans., p. 117.

[6] The discovery of this cosmic dimension of the person of Jesus was such a surprise for Teilhard and entailed such a drastic upheaval in his thinking that he allowed himself to be carried away into making one of the most dogmatically controversial of all his statements: "In the total Christ . . . there is not simply Man and God. There is also He who, in his 'theandric' being recapitulates and gathers together the whole of creation: '*in quo omnia constant*.' Hitherto, and despite the preeminent place accorded it by St. Paul in his vision of the World, this third aspect or function—or even in a true sense, this third 'nature' of Christ (a nature neither human nor divine but 'cosmic') has not been accorded much explicit attention" ("Le Christique," 1955).

We find the same idea, somewhat more cautiously expressed, in an earlier writing: "Between the Word on the one hand and the Man Jesus on the other, there can be distinguished a Christic 'third nature' (if I may presume to call it so . . .)—discernible everywhere in St. Paul's writings; it is that of the total and totalizing Christ, in whom, by the transformative effect of the Resurrection, the individual element born of Mary acquires the status, not only of cosmic Element (or Environment, or Curvature), but of ultimate psychic center of universal concourse" (*Comment je vois,* 1948 § 31).

But again there follows the typical exaggeration: the primacy of Christ over the whole of creation, hitherto thought of in an exclusively juridical and extrinsic fashion, can only become reality in an evolutionist notion of the world.

As if Paul and the Fathers of the Church, and indeed even the numerous contemporary theologians who highlight the cosmic role of Christ, had need of the evolutionist thesis! But Teilhard, trained as he was in a narrow and formalistic Scholastic theology, scarcely took the trouble to follow the current of present-day theological thinking.

Which explains but does not excuse the egregious blunder connected with the cosmic third nature of Christ. Patristic theology, like that of the last century, is at pains to show that the power over the whole of creation devolves upon Christ because he is really man, and man to a degree of fullness and perfection such as could only be realized in the God-Man. This universal function devolves upon Christ, not in virtue of a third (cosmic) nature, but in virtue of his absolutely perfect humanity. He holds the primacy over creation because in Him is fulfilled totally and transcendentally that domination, that dominion over the cosmos stemming from the nature of man; God "has . . . granted him power to execute judgment, since he is the Son of Man" (John 5: 27). Jesus is the Savior of mankind, because, as man, by the power of the hypostatic union and by his resurrection from the dead, he is the Lord of all creation, the Mighty One who vanquishes all the enemies of salvation.

Did Teilhard really intend to attribute to Christ a third (cosmic) nature, in some sense coterminal with the divine nature and the human nature as these have been admitted by Christendom since the Council of Chalcedon, a cosmic nature which would be really distinct from the other two? Then he would not only be introducing a novelty, unheard of and inadmissible, in this subject matter; he would be undermining the salvific meaning of the Incarnation, which consists precisely in the fact that the Man Jesus Christ is appointed Lord of creation. Furthermore, he would be sacrificing the main point in his own design, the cosmic universalist function of man.

Teilhard's way of putting this business of the "third (cosmic) nature" is pretty reckless. He probably allowed himself to be carried away to such an extent because of the failure of his years of theological training to really highlight the *cosmic* significance of the *human* nature of Christ. Doubtless the picture of the humanity of Christ which Teilhard retained from this training was quite narrow and restricted; he may have reacted by coming to consider the cosmic function of the Lord as a new magnitude not to be accommodated within the perfection of his humanity. Should the want of sufficient theological reflection on the sense of the mystery of the Incarnation be the psychological explanation of the inadmissible formula, it would be a confirmation of the fact that, for Teilhard, the discovery of the cosmic function of Christ was truly original and sensational.

[7] *MD*, 140; Eng. trans., pp. 94–95.

[8] "La vie cosmique" (1916); *Oeuvres*, V, 396 f.

[9] *Oeuvres*, V, 397.

[10] *MD*, 162; Eng. trans., p. 110.

[11] *MD*, 140; Eng. trans., p. 94.

[12] *Comment je vois*, 1948.

[13] *MD*, 186; Eng. trans., p. 126.

[14] *MD*, 183; Eng. trans., p. 125.

[15] *MD*, 58; Eng. trans., p. 37.

[16] Teilhard was using this expression, the "Christian presence," which has become so important a motif of the new Catholic spirituality, as early as 1918. To the priests who were at the front serving as simple privates or as stretcher-bearers, he wrote as follows: "You are the leaven sprinkled by God all along the 'front,' so that by the *mere fact of your presence*, your *simple act of being there*, the huge lump of our toil and our sufferings might be transformed and leavened" (*Le Prêtre*, 1918; italics ours, Author). There may be in this passage, as will soon appear, a certain amount of exaggeration of the hierarchical priesthood, the priesthood *ex officio speciali modo collato*, or rather a minimization of the universal priesthood of the baptized and confirmed members of the Church, an exaggeration and concomitant minimization which would not be astonishing, at that, in a text dating from 1918. But the perception of the power for sanctification of the Christian presence in the world here finds perhaps its first explicit expression in the modern period.

[17] January 25, 1955; cited in P. Grenet, *Teilhard de Chardin*, p. 49.

[18] *Le Prêtre*, 1918.

[19] Especially pp. 150–155, 171 f.

[20] *MD*, 154; Eng. trans., p. 102.

[21] L. Boros, "Evolutionismus und Spiritualität," in *Der grosse Entschluss*, XV (1959–1960), 349. Others see only a pious hyperbole in this reflection of Teilhard. Thus Rabut: "There is no cosmic host" (O. A. Rabut, *Dialogue avec Teilhard de Chardin* [Paris: Cerf, 1958], p. 160; Eng. trans., *Teilhard de Chardin: A Critical Study* [New York: Sheed & Ward, 1961], p. 190).

[22] St. Thomas, *Summa Theol.* III, q. 79, a. 1, ad 1: "*Hoc sacramentum ex seipso virtutem habet gratiam conferendi; nec aliquis habet gratiam ante susceptionem huius sacramenti, nisi ex aliquo voto ipsius.*" Cf. "De Eucharistie, berkoning en bron van de sacramenten," in *Bijdragen*, XIX (1958), 382–396.

[23] Cf. Rom. 8: 19–22.

[24] H. M. Féret seems to be alluding to such an idea in his fine study, "Messe et eschatologie," in *La Maison-Dieu* (1950), pp. 46–62: "The sacrament of bread and wine, when considered in all the dimensions thus imparted to it by the Lord, is unceasingly effecting the gathering together and the gathering up of creation into the mystery of love and unity which is in God. The whole of the material cosmos, from the distant physico-chemical transmutations (if I may so put it), which made possible the appearance of life upon our planet, to the slow germinations which culminate in our wheat and our grapes; the whole complex of human labor and industry, together with the multiple economic, social, even political relations they create between us, and culminating in the bread of the hosts and the wine for our chalices; all the religious import of the mystery of Christ and the Church . . . ; finally the whole transcendent mystery of a God . . . of love—all this is brought together and unified in the Eucharistic Mystery, whereby all things 'pass over' into God. The Passover into the Mystery of the God of Love: the whole of it is exhibited in the Eucharist . . ." (p. 56). The glorified humanity of Christ, thus assuming to Himself, out of his divine love, the whole Church and the whole creation" (p. 58).

[25] A thorough study and clarification of this problem is afforded in H. Hollander's monograph, *De gestalte van de Eucharistieviering* (Maastricht, 1959). Here is his conclusion: "The Mass is a sacramental sacrifice under the form of a commemorative repast" (p. 216).

[26] A. M. Roguet, "L'Unité du corps mystique dans la charité 'res sacramenti' de l'Eucharistie," in *La Maison-Dieu*, 24 (1950), 33: "In the matter of the Eucharist, there has been much insistence on the *res et sacramentum*, threatened by Berengarius and later by various Reformers; and there has been a concomitant almost total cessation of any discourse on the *res sacramenti*." Cf. p. 32: "The *res et signum* of the Eucharist (the immolated Christ) has as its proper aim and end the gathering and bringing together of Christians into one single Body of Christ."

[27] *Mystici Corporis* (AAS 35 [1943], 233).

[28] *Mediator Dei* (AAS 39 [1947], 556).

[29] *Mediator Dei* (AAS 39 [1947], 557).

[30] *Mediator Dei* (AAS 39 [1947], 558).

[31] Rom. 6.

[32] H. Hollander, *op. cit.*, p. 176.

[33] Council of Trent, Session XXIII, c. 1–2, *Dz.*, n. 938, 940.

[34] Cf. "Sacramenten en Kerk: kerkelijk recht-kultus-pneuma," in *Bijdragen*, XVIII (1956), 391–418; "Sacramenta et Ecclesia," in *Periodica* (1959), 3–53.

I was delighted to discover similar lines of thought in the writings of the pious Calvinist theologian D. M. Baillie: "When in the sacrament we plead the sacrifice of Christ and, in union with Him, offer ourselves to God, the whole of that process is a giving and receiving in one. It might indeed be urged that the receiving is *prior* to the giving, because the initiative is always with God and the response is ours. Yet it can hardly be said that there is a *temporal* sequence. The very giving of ourselves to God is a receiving of Him, and the very receiving of Him is already a giving of ourselves. There is no other way of receiving Him except by giving ourselves to Him. . . . Both of these are happening in every single process, in every moment when we are worshipping God; and the supreme instrument and medium of that double movement all in one is the sacrament which we call the Eucharist. . . ." (*The Theology of the Sacraments* [London: Faber and Faber, 1957], p. 122).

[35] E. Druwe, "Medebegraven en -verrezen met Christus," in *Bijdragen*, X (1949), 219.

[36] ". . . in the scriptures both of the Old and New Testament, *anamnesis* and the cognate verb have the sense of 're-calling' or 're-presenting' before God an event in the past, so that it becomes *here and now operative by its effects*" (Gregory Dix, *The Shape of the Liturgy* [2nd ed.: Westminster, Dacre, 1945], p. 161; cf. p. 245). [Italics in original; Smulders does not have the last phrase italicized and has himself italicized "re-calling" and "re-presenting."—Note to English translation.]

[37] P. Schoonenberg, "De tegenwoordigheid van Christus," in *Verbum*, XXVI (1959), 157: "The Christian commemoration consists in Christ acting so as to associate us with his mysteries, to cause us to consummate them with him, to cause us to enter into them, to render them present in our life (which, far from excluding, in fact includes our own active role)."

[37a] St. Augustine, *De civitate Dei*, X, 6; cf. X, 20.

[38] St. Augustine, *De civitate Dei*, X, 4.

[39] St. Thomas, *Summa Theol.*, II–II, q. 85, a. 2: "The soul offers itself to God as to the principle of its creation and the end of its felicity."

I–II, q. 102, a. 3: "By the sacrifices (of the Old Testament) was expressed the right ordering of the mind to God . . . to which right ordering it pertains that man should recognize that all he possesses comes from God as from his first principle and that he should direct all that he possesses to God as to his final end."

[40] *MD*, 145 f.; Eng. trans., p. 98.

[41] "True sacrifice, therefore, is every act contributing to weld us to God in a holy communion, every act directed to this consummation of all good, whereby we hope to become truly blessed" (St. Augustine, *De civitate Dei*, X, 6).

[42] St. Augustine, *Enarratio in ps. 65, 18* (PL 36: 798: "I will enter into Thy House with holocausts. . . . The Body of Christ is speaking, the unity of Christ is speaking: . . . let Thy zeal consume me utterly, let nothing remain of what is mine, let all become Thine. This is what will be realized in the resurrection of the just . . . The final victory is, so to speak, a divine fire."

[43] I Cor. 11: 26.

[44] Apoc. 5: 6.

[45] A. Cruiziat, "Quelques aspects sociaux du mystère eucharistique," in *La Maison-Dieu*, 24 (1950), 110 f.

[46] Cf. above, p. 151.

[47] John 16: 33.

[48] Luke 17: 20.

[49] Teilhard's reflection on the Eucharist leads him to thoughts on the cosmic consecration and communion. He exclaims: "This I know. We could not dictate, nor even anticipate, the least of all Thy works. Thou dost set all afoot, so chiefly this, my prayer!" ("La messe sur le monde," *Hymne*, p. 21). Earlier he had written: "More than a simple union, it is a *transformation* that is to be effected—and in its course all human enterprise can do is to make ready and to accept on bended knee." ("Le Milieu mystique," 1917, in *Hymne*, p. 166).

A NOTE ON THE TYPE

IN WHICH THIS BOOK IS SET

This book is set in Janson, a Linotype face, created from the early punches of Anton Janson, who settled in Leipzig around 1670. This type is not an historic revival, but rather a letter of fine ancestry, remodelled and brought up to date to satisfy present day taste. It carries a feeling of being quite compact and sturdy. It has good color and displays a pleasing proportion of ascenders and descenders as compared to the height of the lower case letters. The book was composed and printed by The York Composition Company, Inc., of York, Pa., and bound by William Marley Company of Philadelphia. The typography and design are by Howard N. King.